GLOBE FEARON'S

Skills for Independent Living

Globe Fearon Educational Publisher
A Division of Simon & Schuster
Upper Saddle River, New Jersey

We are grateful to the following educators. They served as reviewers during various stages of product development. Their valuable comments and suggestions served to enhance the quality of this book.

Carolyn Balsa-Hancock, Career Vocational Specialist
East Side Union H.S.D., San Jose, CA 95133

Sherié Campbell, TMH/SPMH Teacher
Coleman Middle School, Tampa, FL 33629

Debra A. Grunnet, Coordinator of Special Education
Rockdale County Public Schools, Conyers, GA 30207

Noel Livaudais, Ph.D., Special Education Coordinator
Hurst-Euless-Bedford I.S.D., Bedford, TX 76022

Kay D. Perryman, Special Education Coordinator
J.F. Ingram State Technical College, Deatsville, AL 36022

Adelaide Wicker-Huguley, M.A., Detroit Board of Education/Special Education Department Head
Denby High School and Northern High School, Detroit, MI 48224

Joann Crowder Wynn, Assistant Director of Student Services
Hattiesburg Public School District, Hattiesburg, MS 39403

Project Editors: Ann Clarkson and Keisha Carter
Senior Editor: Karen Bernhaut
Production Editor: Alan Dalgleish
Electronic Page Production: Mimi Raihl and Suzanne Keezer
Cover Design and Interior Illustrations: Armando Baez
Editorial Assistant: Ryan Jones
Photo Research: Jenifer Hixson

ISBN: 0-835-93479-9

Printed in the United States of America
4 5 6 7 8 9 10   01 00 99 98

Globe Fearon Educational Publisher
A Division of Simon & Schuster
Upper Saddle River, New Jersey

Contents

A Note to the Student

Getting ready to live on your own may sound frightening. You may not know how to find or get the things that you will need to live independently. You may not know how to prepare for the things that you will need to do. This book was made to help you develop the skills you will need to live independently.

The purpose of this book is to make your journey to living independently a success. Your journey will be comfortable and interesting. You will build new skills based on what you know already. You will make connections between the real world and the skills that are taught in this book. As you work through the exercises and practice sections in this book, you will build the skills you need to live on your own.

Each chapter presents concepts through a clear explanation of real world experiences. The chapters give you chances to try out your skills in the **Skills Practice** sections. Then you go on and use those skills in the **Decisions, Decisions!** features. Margin notes have also been included to give you helpful hints as you read.

There are many other study aids in the book. At the beginning of every chapter, you will find **Learning Objectives**. They will help you focus on the important points covered in the chapter. You will also find **Words to Know**. This is a look ahead at new vocabulary you may find difficult. At the end of each chapter, you will find a **Chapter Review**. This will give you a review of what you have just learned. A **Unit Review** also follows each unit.

Everyone who put this book together worked hard to make it useful, interesting, and enjoyable.

We wish you well on your journey to living independently. Our success comes from your success.

Focus on You

Chapter 1

Getting to Know Yourself

Chapter 2

Setting Goals

Chapter 1
Getting to Know Yourself

The way a person looks is only a small part of who that person really is. Think about the qualities and beliefs that make you who you are.

Chapter Learning Objectives

- Describe your appearance, interests, and skills.
- Describe beliefs that are important to you.
- Explain how people use their beliefs to make decisions.
- List the steps in wise decision making.
- Give examples of being responsible at school, at home, and at work.

Words to Know

honesty   the ability to be truthful and fair

responsible   dependable; able to make wise decisions and accept the results of your actions and decisions

courage   the strength to stand up for what is right

concern   an interest in other people

respect   the willingness to consider other people's needs, feelings, and opinions

health   mental and physical wellness

citizenship   membership in a community

excuse   an explanation for poor behavior

independent   able to take care of yourself

In the situations below, Maria and Tony each have to make a difficult decision. What they decide will tell a lot about who they are and what is important to them.

"Maria," Susan says, "do you want to come to my party on Saturday?" Susan asks only the most popular kids to her parties. Maria is excited that Susan asked her. Then Susan adds, "Don't say anything to Courtney, okay? I can't invite everyone, you know." Courtney is Maria's best friend. Now Maria isn't sure she should go to Susan's party.

Tony is trying to ignore Monica, who is sitting beside him in science class. "Please, Tony," Monica whispers. "Let me see your answers on the test. If I don't get at least a C, the coach won't let me play Friday." Monica is captain of the girls' basketball team. The team has a good chance of winning the city championship this Friday, but only if Monica plays.

Who Are You, Really?

If you asked Maria or Tony who they are, they might give you their names, ages, and addresses. They might also describe their families and say where they go to school. Maria might add that she has a friend named Courtney. Tony might say that he likes science. All of these are important descriptions. Yet, they don't describe who these teenagers *really* are.

Skills Practice

On a separate sheet of paper, describe yourself. Write down what you look like, where you live, and where you go to school. Include things you like to do. Add anything else you think is important about you. Save this paper so you can read it later.

How you look and what you like to do are only a small part of who you are as a person. A bigger part of who you are includes your beliefs about what is important. These beliefs guide your decisions and your actions each day. These beliefs guide your life.

Look back at the decisions Maria and Tony must make. Before they can make these decisions, they must think about what's important to them. Maria must decide if a party or her friend is more important. She must decide if it is more important to become part of the popular crowd.

Tony also has to decide what is more important to him. He must decide if he should help the school win the big game by letting Monica cheat or keep his promise to himself not to cheat on tests.

Six Important Qualities

After Maria and Tony think about what is important to them, they will be ready to make their decisions. Many people think the six following qualities are important. Having these qualities helps people gain the respect, trust, and admiration of others.

- **honesty** is the ability to be truthful and fair
- **responsibility** is the ability to be dependable, make wise decisions, and accept the results of your actions and decisions
- **courage** is the strength to stand up for what you know is right
- **concern** and **respect** for others is the willingness to care about others and consider their feelings, needs, and opinions
- good **health** is mental and physical wellness
- good **citizenship** is active, helpful membership in the community

Some schools have a "code of honor." Every student promises to tell the truth and be honest at all times. Honesty helps the students gain the trust and respect of others.

Skills Practice

Choose one of the six qualities above. On a separate sheet of paper, write how you could tell that someone has this quality.

Deciding What's Important to You

Our families and friends help us decide what is important in our lives. A teenager named Keith remembers how he learned that honesty is important. When Keith was only six, he took a candy bar from a store without paying for it.

When his mom found out, she made him take the candy bar back. She also made Keith tell the clerk he was sorry. Keith says he was embarrassed. Yet, this helped him learn that honesty is important. He also learned to be responsible for his mistakes.

You need to identify the qualities you admire. Knowing this will help to shape your beliefs and decisions. It will also help you become the kind of person you want to be. You might not want to be

People learn many of their values and beliefs from their families. Think about the values and beliefs you have learned from your family. ▶

friends with someone who had not thought about what was important in his or her life. It would be difficult to listen to or trust this person's advice.

Skills Practice

Choose a quality that is important in your life. On a separate sheet of paper, explain how your actions show that this quality is important to you.

Taking Steps to Make Wise Decisions

Thinking about what is important in your life can help you make decisions. However, making decisions can still be difficult. The steps below can help you make those difficult decisions. You don't need to follow these steps for easy decisions, such as what to eat for lunch. However, these steps can help you make difficult decisions.

Step 1: Identify the decision you need to make.

Step 2: List as many choices for your decision as possible. If you have many choices, you will have a better chance of making a wise decision.

Step 3: Cross out choices that are harmful or go against your beliefs.

If you cross out all of your choices, think of some more!

Step 4: Read each remaining choice. Think about what might happen if you select it.

Step 5: Select the choice that will probably have the best results for you and others.

Step 6: Carry out your choice.

Step 7: Think about the results of your decision. That way, you will know whether to select that choice the next time.

Using the Steps to Make Wise Decisions

Think back to Maria's situation. Susan had invited Maria to a party. However, Susan did not invite Maria's best friend, Courtney. Now Maria must make a difficult decision. Here is how the decision-making steps could help her make the decision:

Step 1: Identify the decision Maria must make:

Maria has to decide whether to go to Susan's party.

Step 2: List Maria's choices:

   a. Maria could tell Susan she can't come.

   b. Maria could go to the party and not tell Courtney about it.

   c. Maria could go to the party and tell Courtney about it.

Step 3: Cross out choices against Maria's beliefs:

If Maria went to the party without telling Courtney, she would not feel honest. Maria crosses out choice b. If Maria went to the party and did tell Courtney, she would hurt Courtney's feelings. Maria crosses out c.

Step 4: Think about what might happen for each remaining choice:

Only one choice is left: telling Susan she can't come. If Maria does this:

she might miss some fun and a chance to become part of the "in crowd."

Susan may not invite her to another party. However, if she doesn't go to the party, Courtney will not feel left out.

Step 5: Select the best choice:

Maria would like to go to Susan's party, but Courtney's feelings are more important to her. Maria decides to skip the party.

Step 6: Carry out the best choice:

Maria tells Susan that she cannot come to the party.

Step 7: Think about the possible results of the decision:

On the night of the party, Courtney and Maria go skating and have a great time. Maria is sure she made the best choice. Courtney's friendship is much more important to her than a party.

Ready for Responsibility?

Most young people want to make their own decisions. But not all teenagers are ready to make their own decisions as soon as others. They are ready when they show they are **responsible**. Responsible people make wise decisions that help themselves and others. Responsible people also do what they promised they would do.

Everyone makes mistakes. However, responsible people admit their mistakes. Then they do what they can to make up for their mistakes. For example, Lorna borrowed Jeannie's shirt. Then she accidentally dripped ketchup on it. Lorna did not try

Responsibility is one of the six qualities that most people think are important.

to hide the spots. Instead, she washed the shirt before she returned it. If the spots had not come out, she would have bought Jeannie a new shirt.

Responsible people accept the results of their decisions. A teenager named Lisa knew that taking orders over the phone might be a boring job. But she took the job because it paid well. After only two weeks, she hated going to work. She could have complained about being bored. She could have taken sick days when she felt fine.

Instead, Lisa reminded herself that she had chosen that job. Now she is looking for a more interesting job. But she always reports for work on time and does her best. Like other responsible people, Lisa does not blame others for her decisions or actions. Instead, she tries to learn from her decisions. That way, she can make a wiser decision the next time.

Responsible people do not expect others to solve the problems that they have caused. Mike, for example, often missed the bus because he slept late. Yet, he didn't expect his parents to drive him to school. Mike rode his bike to school, even in the rain. Each time he missed the bus, he made sure to get up earlier the next day.

No Excuses, Please

Responsible people don't make excuses to hide their mistakes. An **excuse** is an explanation for poor behavior. People who make excuses often blame someone else for their own mistakes. They are trying to make themselves look good. However, they are not being responsible.

When a boy named Pete was caught cutting class, he could have blamed his friends. After all, they had begged him to leave school with them. But Pete knew it was his own decision to go along with his friends. So Pete did not make excuses for cutting class. When

Making excuses is the opposite of being responsible.

his teacher made him stay after school, Pete did not complain. He knew his own decision had gotten him into this situation. Pete also understood that he had to make sure not to do it again. Pete made a bad decision to cut class, but he acted responsibly by not making excuses.

Responsible people are also honest. A teenager named Kay is honest, sometimes. For example, she would never steal a sweater from a store. But Kay steals pens at work. She thinks no one will miss the pens she takes. She is making excuses for stealing. Kay is not being honest or responsible. Her employer may soon stop trusting her.

Rodney believes it's okay to take extra-long breaks at his job. Rodney makes excuses by telling himself that he works hard. He needs time to relax. But if his boss catches him wasting time, she won't listen to his excuses. She will only see that Rodney is not doing his job.

No matter what excuses people give, they are judged by what they do. Their actions, not their words, show what they think is important.

Taking on Responsibility

Sometimes responsibilities are given to you. For example, you might be chosen as the leader of a team. Or you might be asked to wash the dinner dishes on Tuesdays and Thursdays.

Other times, you might volunteer for responsibilities. Maybe a friend is struggling with an oral report. You might offer to listen to it and help her improve it. Let's say your mom or dad comes home from work really tired. You might fix dinner without being asked.

Being responsible means doing your share—and a little more. When you do that "little more," you will feel good about yourself. Your parents and others will notice. They will see that you are becoming more responsible. Being responsible has many rewards. At home, you might be permitted to make more of your own decisions. At school, you might improve your grades. At work, you might get a raise.

Skills Practice

On a separate sheet of paper, write the headings below. Then fill in the information. You may be surprised at how responsible you are!

Responsibilities Assigned to Me:

At Home: At School: At Work:

Responsibilities I Have Accepted on My Own:

At Home: At School: At Work:

Getting Acquainted with You

Look back at the way you described yourself in the Skills Practice on page 4. Now you know there is more to you than what you first listed.

Now you might also list the qualities that are important to you and guide your life. These could include honesty and caring about others. You might also mention that you know the steps in making wise decisions. You could also list ways that you show you are responsible.

These qualities and skills are your personal strengths. In this book, you will explore more of your skills. You will also add to those skills. The skills you gain and strengthen will help you become more **independent.** Independent people are able to take care of themselves. This course will help prepare you to meet your own needs and handle challenges that come your way!

This book is called *Skills for Independent Living* because it teaches skills that will help you learn how to take care of yourself.

Chapter Review

Chapter Summary

1. Your beliefs about what is important are part of who you are. These beliefs guide the decisions you will make in your life.

2. Most people think these qualities are important in life: honesty, responsibility, courage, concern and respect for others, good health, and good citizenship.

3. Seven steps can help you make wise decisions. These steps help you think of possible choices and the results of each choice. Then you can select the choice that will probably have the best results for you and others.

4. Responsible people admit their mistakes and accept the results of their decisions. They do not make excuses for their poor decisions. Responsible people are willing to do their share and a little more.

5. Knowing what's important to you, being able to make wise decisions, and being responsible are valuable skills. These skills help you to become independent.

Chapter Quiz

Answer these questions on a separate sheet of paper.

1. What are some ways that people might describe themselves?

2. What are six qualities that many people think are important in life?

3. Honesty is important to Rosa. She just bought a sandwich that cost $1.50. However, the clerk asked her for only $1. What should Rosa do? Why?

4. Mike and Steven came to a party together. A friend offers Mike a ride home. However, there's no room in the car for Steven. What are Mike's choices? What would you do if you were Mike? Why?

5. Mike decides to take the ride. He tells Steven to find his own way home. Then Mike tells himself that he never promised to find Steven a ride home. What is Mike doing?

6. Does Mike think that concern and respect for others are important? How can you tell?

7. Why should you think about the results of your decisions?

8. What are two actions that show responsibility at school, at home, or at work?

9. Dana lost a library book. Her friends tell her to forget about it. What actions would be more responsible?

10. Why should young people act in responsible ways?

Putting Skills to Work

Imagine you agreed to baby-sit for a neighbor on Friday night. Then a friend invites you to a big party on the same night. Should you baby-sit or go to the party? With a partner, follow the steps on pages 6–7 to decide what to do. Afterward, share your decision with the class.

Skills Issues

In most states, 16-year-olds can drive cars. Do you think all 16-year-olds are responsible enough to drive cars? Why or why not? Explain your answer.

Chapter 2
Setting Goals

Knowing how to plan your time is a valuable life skill. It will help you reach your goals. Think about the ways you plan your time.

Chapter Learning Objectives

- Describe how our priorities affect our goals.
- Explain why having goals is important.
- Identify goals that are specific and realistic.
- Describe the difference between a short-term and a long-term goal.
- Write an action plan to meet a goal.
- Create a daily schedule to manage your time.
- Explain ways to avoid wasting time when studying.

Words to Know

goal   something you want to do

priority   a level of importance; a goal with a high priority is very important

obstacle   something that stands in the way of reaching a goal

specific   clearly explained; detailed

realistic   within your reach

long-term goal   a goal that can be met in several months or years

short-term goal   a goal that can be met in a few hours, days, or weeks

action plan   steps for reaching a goal

In the situation below, two teenagers have a goal. Find out which one reaches the goal and why.

One Saturday morning Eric and Dana wait at a city bus stop. They both want to go to the high school, but the bus is very late. Eric wants to pick up a CD he left in his locker. Dana is going to meet with the volleyball coach. They are going to talk about her chances of being on the volleyball team.

Finally, Dana's neighbor drives by and tells them that she had just seen the bus. It was parked up the street. There was smoke coming from its engine.

"There goes our ride," Eric says. "I guess I'll wait until Monday to get that CD. See you!"

Dana frowns. She has to get to the high school. It would take half an hour to walk there. She might make it if she hurries. When Dana gets to the school, she is just a little late for her meeting.

Goals and Priorities

A **goal** is something we want to do. As Eric and Dana waited for the bus, they both had the same goal.

They wanted to get to the high school. However, when the bus broke down, Eric gave up on his goal. He didn't care enough about getting his CD to walk to school.

Dana really wanted to get to the high school. Being on the team was very important to her. That's why she was so determined to meet with the coach. She was willing to walk several miles to school.

When a goal is important in our lives, we give it a high **priority**. A priority is a level of importance. Setting priorities means putting things in order of their importance. A goal may have a high priority for one person, but not for someone else.

Eric put a low priority on getting to the school. He gave up when he met an **obstacle**. An obstacle is something that stands in the way of reaching a goal. The obstacle in Eric's way was the bus breaking down.

Dana put a high priority on getting to the school. The higher priority we give a goal, the more important it is to us. When the bus broke down, Dana didn't give up. She overcame the obstacle by walking to the school.

Obstacles don't have to keep you from reaching your goals. When a goal is important to you, you can find ways to overcome most obstacles. For example, you might baby-sit to buy a gift for a friend.

Skills Practice

On a separate sheet of paper, list two goals that have a high priority for you. Write why each goal has a high priority in your life. Compare goals with a partner.

Who Needs Goals?

Goals give our lives purpose. People without goals tend to drift along without a clear direction. They might drop out of high school. If they don't have goals, graduating might not seem important to them.

When you know what is important to you, you can set goals.

However, five years from now, these dropouts might meet friends from high school. These friends did set goals. They graduated from high school, gained more training, and now have good jobs. The dropouts might call these friends "lucky." Yet, setting goals is not a matter of luck. Setting goals is a skill that can help you become independent.

Setting Specific Goals

Jill has set a goal of getting in shape. However, she doesn't know where to start. She also doesn't know how she will know when she has reached her goal. Jill's goal needs to be more **specific**. A specific goal is clearly described. It can be measured.

Let's say Jill gets out of breath when she climbs stairs. Her specific goal might be to walk up three flights of stairs without running out of breath. To work toward this goal, Jill might join an exercise class. She will know she has reached her goal when she gets up to the third floor without huffing and puffing!

Skills Practice

Decide which of the goals below are specific. List the specific goals on a separate sheet of paper.

1. I want to get better grades.
2. I want to get a B on my next math test.
3. I want to be popular.
4. I want to make one new friend each week.

Setting Realistic Goals

If you set a goal that is specific and important to you, you may or may not reach it. You need to choose a goal that is also **realistic**. To be realistic, a goal has to be within your reach. It has to be a goal you can meet with your own skills.

Do you have the skills you need to reach a goal? If not, find a way to learn them!

For example, a teenager named Kevin dreams about buying a new car in a year. He has already picked out the model he wants. This goal is important to Kevin. It is also specific. However, Kevin must decide if it is realistic.

Kevin earns $25 a week at his part-time job. He has $325 in the bank. Kevin writes down the price of the car he wants and adds gas, insurance, and other costs. He can see he doesn't have enough money for a new car. He understands his goal is not realistic. Instead, Kevin begins looking for a used car that he can afford.

Short-term and Long-term Goals

Getting an interesting, full-time job after high school is a **long-term goal**. A long-term goal is one you hope to meet in several months or years. Buying a car is another long-term goal for many people.

A **short-term goal** is one you expect to reach in a few hours, days, or weeks. Finishing an art project by Friday is a short-term goal.

Many long-term goals can be broken into smaller, short-term goals. For example, raising a grade from a C to a B is a long-term goal. You could meet this goal by setting smaller goals. One smaller short-term goal might be studying an hour longer for each test.

Skills Practice

On a separate sheet of paper, list three short-term goals and three long-term goals for yourself. Then show your lists to a partner. Explain why the goals you listed are specific, realistic, and important.

Taking Steps to Make an Action Plan

After you have set a goal, you need to make an **action plan**. An action plan is a list of steps that will help you reach your goal.

The following are steps for making an action plan:

Step 1:   **Write down your goal.**
Write your goal in your journal or diary. Or write your goal on a sheet of paper and tape it to the mirror in your bedroom.

Step 2:   **List steps to reach the goal.**
Break a long-term goal into several smaller goals. Break smaller or short-term goals into steps.

Step 3:   **Set up a time line.**
Decide how much time each step should take. Then write each step on a chart or calendar. Mark when you will start each step and when you will complete each step.

Step 4:   **Identify any obstacles.**
List things that might get in the way of meeting your goal. Let's say your goal is getting in shape. Your obstacles might be finding a time and a place to exercise. Beside each obstacle, write ways you might overcome it.

Step 5:   **Identify sources of help.**
Decide who or what could help you reach your goal. Maybe the community offers an exercise class for teenagers. You and a friend might also help each other work toward the same goal.

Step 6:   **Check your progress.**
As you work toward your goal, review your plan. Check if you are on schedule. If your plan is not realistic, make changes so you can still reach your goal.

Skills Practice

Look back at the short-term goals you set in the Skills Practice on page 18. Choose one of these short-term goals. On a separate sheet of paper, use the steps above to write an action plan to meet that goal.

Managing Your Time

Now you have set goals and made an action plan. But what if you don't have time to follow your plan? Knowing how to plan your time is a valuable skill because it helps you to reach your goals. You don't have to schedule every minute of the day. However, planning your time can help you reach important goals.

To make the best use of your time tomorrow, follow these steps:

1. On a separate sheet of paper, list all the things you *have* to do and *want* to do tomorrow. Things you *have* to do might include school assignments that are due and projects you should be working on. Don't forget lessons, meetings, tutoring, and sports practices. Then add things that you *want* to do or that your parents, friends, and others *want* you to do. All these tasks are possible goals for tomorrow.

2. Mark each item on your list *A, B,* or *C:*
   - A: very important tasks that have the highest priority and must be finished
   - B: important tasks that should be started or worked on
   - C: not-so-important tasks that can be put off for another time

Think about the goals ▼
that are important in your life. That will help you decide which tasks to mark A.

To do list

Finish book report — A
Take dog for a walk after school — A
Watch favorite soap opera on TV — C
Go to soccer practice — A
Check sale at CD store — C

Time schedule

3:00	go to soccer practice
3:30	(still at soccer practice)
4:00	get home and walk the dog
4:30	start book report

3. On a second sheet of paper, divide the day into 30-minute periods. Start with the time you get up. End with the time you go to sleep.

4. On your schedule, write in all the *A* activities from your list. Then fit in as many *B* activities as possible. If you have room, add some *C* tasks. Remember to allow enough time for each activity, including travel and clean-up. Set aside time for fun, and don't try to schedule every minute.

5. Follow your plan tomorrow. Notice whether you get more done. If you fall behind schedule, make a more realistic schedule for the following day. Allow more time for the activities that took more time. Planning your time may help you get so much more done that you decide to make a schedule for every day.

▲ *Planning your time each day helps you reach your goals.*

Wasting Time

Wasting time is often an obstacle to reaching a goal. Finishing homework is an important goal for all students. You might sometimes find that you work for a long time and do not finish an assignment. There are many reasons why that might happen. They are all time wasters.

Each time waster can be managed. Interruptions can keep you from getting your work done. To avoid them, don't answer the phone. Work in a quiet corner away from friends, family members, and the television. If necessary, explain to others that you are busy and will have time to talk later. Daydreaming is another way of interrupting yourself. Take five minutes to daydream. Then get back to work.

Prevent redoing projects and reports. Ask questions when your teachers give assignments. Make sure you understand what to do. Then you can do the assignments right the first time.

Forgetting necessary materials can also waste time. Make sure you have pens, paper, and other supplies at home. Keep a list in your school notebook of books and materials you need to take home. Then check your list before going home.

Skills Practice

Talk with a partner about ways that you waste time when you are studying. Which time waster is the biggest problem for you? How can you avoid wasting time in this way?

Choosing a Path

Setting a goal is like choosing a path to follow through a forest. Without a goal, you might wander into the trees and get lost. You could end up going in circles. Setting goals gives your life a clear direction. You know where you are going. You also know when you have gotten there. As you overcome obstacles, you can build self-confidence. Then you might start setting bigger goals—and reaching them!

Managing your time can help you meet the goals that are important to you. It takes practice and patience to learn how to set goals and manage your time.

Learning these skills is well worth the effort. These skills can help you be successful today, tomorrow, and years from now. They can also help you find the time to do all the activities you really enjoy.

Decisions, Decisions!

Read the following situation about Jan. Then follow the steps to help Jan decide the best use of her time.

It's 5:00 p.m. Jan needs to study at least two hours for tomorrow's geography test. However, the tryouts for the school play are also tonight. They will take place from 7:00 p.m. until 10:00 p.m. Jan thinks she wants to be an actress. Being in the play could help her decide on a career. At the same time, she wants to do well on the geography test. She must decide what to do.

On a separate sheet of paper, follow the steps below to help Jan decide the best use of her time tonight.

Step 1: Identify the decision Jan must make.

Step 2: List Jan's choices.

Step 3: Cross out any choices that might be harmful or against Jan's beliefs.

Step 4: Think about the possible results of the remaining choices.

Step 5: Select the best choice.

Step 6: Explain how Jan would carry out that choice.

Step 7: Describe the possible results of Jan's choice.

Chapter Review

Chapter Summary

1. The more important a goal is, the harder people are willing to work to reach it. People give important goals a high priority in their lives.

2. Goals can give your life direction. To be helpful, goals must be specific, realistic, and important to you.

3. A short-term goal might be met within hours, days, or weeks. A long-term goal might take months or years to reach.

4. An action plan breaks a goal into steps. It also sets a time line for each step.

5. To plan your time, start by listing all the tasks to be done. Then give each task a priority. Do the most important tasks first.

6. Time wasters include interruptions, daydreaming, having to redo projects, and forgetting needed materials.

Chapter Quiz

Answer these questions on a separate sheet of paper.

1. Jamal has set a high priority on getting a summer job. Akim has made it a low priority. Which person is more likely to get a job this summer? Why?

2. What do you call something that gets in your way when you are working toward a goal?

3. Kate set a goal of getting along better with her younger sister. Write a more specific goal for Kate.

4. What can happen if you set a goal that is not realistic?

5. Write an example of a short-term goal and a long-term goal.

6. What can you do if a goal seems too big?

7. How can making an action plan increase your chances of meeting a goal?

8. Some people get more done than other people. Why might that be so?

9. Imagine you have listed all the tasks you want to do today. How do you decide which ones you should do first?

10. Name one common time waster that can occur while you study. How can you avoid this time waster?

Putting Skills to Work

Manuel wants to help his older neighbors with their household tasks. That's a large, long-term goal. On a separate sheet of paper, write two or three smaller goals Manuel could set for himself to reach this large goal.

Skills Issues

Pretend that a friend wrote you the note below. On a separate sheet of paper, write back to the friend. Offer some advice about setting goals.

It's almost time for me to graduate from high school. I might not have enough money to go to college or a technical school. I'll probably just look for a job or something. What do you think I should do?

Unit One Review

Answer these questions on a separate sheet of paper.

1. Name three skills that can help young people be more independent.

2. John's friends want him to go to a movie. However, he hasn't finished his science project, which is due tomorrow. John thinks about his choices. He decides to go to the movie and turn his project in late. What is a possible result of his decision?

3. Andrea let a friend copy her answers on a test. The teacher caught them, and they both received failing grades. Which action below would be a responsible reaction? Why?

   a. Andrea tells the teacher it was all her friend's fault.

   b. Andrea promises herself to never cheat again.

4. Ben forgot to study for his math test. He didn't do very well on it. He told his parents that the teacher didn't explain the problems clearly. What is Ben doing?

5. How can setting goals help you live on your own and be independent?

6. If you set realistic goals, will you still face obstacles? Why or why not?

7. What kinds of decisions do you have to make when you plan your time?

8. Melissa wrote down the things she was supposed to do today. Then she did them in the order she listed them. Is she making the best use of her time? Why or why not?

9. What are some ways that you might waste time without realizing it?

10. Luis has set a goal of learning how to play the guitar. How might that affect the way he plans his time?

Unit Two

You and Others

Chapter 3
Dealing with Peer Pressure

Chapter 4
Communicating with Others

Chapter 5
Getting Along with Others

Chapter 6
Handling Change

Chapter 3
Dealing with Peer Pressure

Friends respect each other, learn from each other, and have fun together. True friends also stick together during difficult times.

Chapter Learning Objectives

- List questions to ask yourself when choosing friends.
- Give examples of positive and negative peer pressure.
- Explain ways to tell the difference between positive and negative peer pressure.
- Give examples of ways to resist negative peer pressure.

Words to Know

popular admired or sought after as a friend

pressure to encourage strongly or force

peer pressure influence from people your age to do or not do something

positive helpful, healthful

negative harmful, unsafe, against the law

resist to refuse; to say "No"

In the situation below, Gena's friend is forcing her to make a difficult decision.

"Gena, you're my best friend! I just need this one favor," Shana begs. "All you have to do is tell my parents I went to the movies with you last night."

"But you didn't!" says Gena. "I was home doing my book report. My mom knows that. What if your mom says something to my mom about us going to the movies? Then I'll be in trouble for lying to your parents!"

"Well, I can't tell my parents I was out with Jake last night, can I?" asks Shana. "Not after they told me not to go anywhere near him! If you won't help me, I'll never talk to you again!"

The Challenge of Having Friends

Like most teenagers, you may spend a lot of time with your friends. Friends can share fun and talk over problems. But friends can also force you to make hard decisions. Gena has to make a difficult decision. She must decide if she should lie for Shana or if she should tell the truth. If Gena doesn't lie for Shana, she may lose her as a friend. If the girls can't talk through the problem, Gena may need to find a new friend.

Gena needs to choose friends who won't force her to do something she doesn't want to do.

Looking for New Friends

When teenagers look for friends, they might consider the most **popular** students first. Popular students are those who are admired. They might include class leaders, star athletes, or cheerleaders. They might also be the teenagers who give the biggest parties or are the best looking.

Thus, teenagers might be popular because others like them as people or admire something about them. Being friends with popular people can be fun. However, popular people have to divide their time among many friends. That could rule out a close friendship with you.

Don't overlook people who are on the quiet side. To find a new friend, talk to people you see everyday but don't really know. Start by saying "Hi" to someone in your classes or neighborhood. Get to know the members of groups you belong to. They might share some of your interests. Interest in the same things will help you get to know each other.

Deciding if Someone is a Friend

You need to know when you have found a new friend. A friend respects and likes you for who you are. They would also help you when you need help. A friend listens to whatever is bothering you and is fun to be with. Most importantly, a true friend does not try to force you to do things you don't want to do.

A friend is someone you feel comfortable with, and you feel relaxed around them. They shouldn't try to make you act or dress in a certain way. A friend won't try to make all of your decisions or be upset if you have different opinions.

It is also important to respect a friend. You should choose friends that have qualities that you also feel are important. For example, a friend who believes honesty

The number of friends you have doesn't matter. Some people like to have many friends. Others are happy with one or two close friends and enjoy being friendly with other people.

is important will not ask you to lie. Choose friends who respect your values and beliefs.

If you share some the same interests with a friend, your relationship might last longer. Relationships sometimes last longer if you have activities that you both enjoy and can share. However, having friends who enjoy very different activities can also be enjoyable. You might be able to teach each other new ideas or share new experiences.

A friend is someone you will spend a lot of time with, so choose wisely. Don't make the mistake of choosing someone just because you think he or she will make you look cool. If you have nothing in common and can't rely on that person, the friendship won't last.

A new friendship can begin with a simple smile!

Skills Practice

On a separate sheet of paper, list three reasons why you would want to be friends with someone. Then list two ways you could be a good friend to that person. Discuss your lists with a partner.

Identifying Peer Pressure

Your friends may often ask you to do things. One friend may **pressure**, or strongly encourage, you to go to the basketball game on Friday. Another friend may want you to join a club that meets after school.

These demands are **peer pressure.** Someone your age is asking you to do or not do something. Peer pressure is **positive** when the activities suggested are helpful or healthful. For example, suggesting that you not cut class is positive peer pressure.

Some of your friends might pressure you in **negative** ways. Negative peer pressure is encouragement to do something harmful, unsafe, or against the law. For example, someone might pressure you to start smoking. Giving in to negative peer pressure often leads to problems.

Skills Practice

On a separate sheet of paper, list three examples of peer pressure. Trade lists with a partner. Talk about the examples in your lists. Decide which you think are positive peer pressure and which are negative.

Deciding If It Is Positive or Negative Peer Pressure

You must learn to recognize whether a friend's pressure is positive or negative.

When a friend suggests an activity, you need to decide if it goes against your beliefs. Ask yourself if the activity makes you feel uncomfortable. If it does, it is probably negative peer pressure.

Another way to decide if something is negative peer pressure is if the activity a friend is suggesting is unsafe. If the activity could be dangerous for you or someone else, it is a form of negative peer pressure.

Peer pressure is a part ▶ of life that everyone faces. Sometimes peer pressure can be positive. These girls feel positive peer pressure to be in the school band.

Ask yourself why you want to go along with an activity that someone is suggesting. If you just want to take part in the activity to be accepted or you are worried that you will lose a friend or be embarrassed, you are giving in to negative peer pressure.

Make your own decisions about what you want to do and what makes you comfortable. A true friend will respect your feelings.

If your answer to any of these questions is "Yes," the peer pressure is negative. You need to **resist** the pressure or tell your friend "No." You might be risking a friendship. However, giving in to negative pressure can cost you other people's trust.

It takes courage to say no to a friend. But it gets easier with practice.

A girl named Carla paid a high price for giving in to negative peer pressure. She let Greg copy a book report she had written. The language arts teacher recognized Carla's report. Carla and Greg were both called to the principal's office and given failing grades. Greg didn't care; he was used to being in trouble.

After being caught cheating, things changed for Carla. She soon realized that her teachers no longer trusted her. She had planned to ask them to help her get a scholarship for college. Now she could not ask them. She might not be accepted to a college without their help.

Skills Practice

Tamika's friends want her to go skating tonight. Most of the time, this would be positive peer pressure. But Tamika and her friends should be finishing a science project tonight. The invitation to go skating is negative peer pressure.

Imagine that another friend wants Tamika to go to a party. On a separate sheet of paper, explain how this could be positive peer pressure. Then explain how it could be negative peer pressure. Trade your answers with a partner and compare your answers.

Taking Control

It is important to learn how to work well with others. This skill is important in the workplace. Employees need to be able to work well with each other. You also need to practice making your own decisions. Employees who can make wise decisions often get raises and better jobs.

Last summer Terrence, Eduardo, and Gerald worked on a road construction crew. You may know someone like Terrence. Anything his friends do, he does.

Terrence almost never makes his own decisions. One hot afternoon, Gerald said to Terrence and Eduardo, "It's too hot. Let's get some ice water and take a break under that big tree over in the field." Without a word, Terrence followed Gerald. Eduardo knew it wasn't time for their break for another hour, so he kept working. The crew supervisor found Gerald and Terrence half an hour later relaxing against the tree. What was Terrence's excuse? "Gerald made me do it!"

Gerald was fired because he did not make a wise decision. Terrence was fired because he did not make his own decision. He went along with Gerald because he didn't know how to say "No."

There are many ways to say no to negative peer pressure. For instance don't agree to something before you know what's being suggested. Let's say a classmate asks for help with a test. Before you say "Okay," make sure she wants to study together, not copy your answers.

Say "No" calmly and confidently. Don't embarrass or anger the person asking. Simply look the other person in the eye. Use a firm voice to show that you have made up your mind. Then the person should stop pressuring you. Also, don't give a long explanation. Explaining your reasons may encourage the other person to argue.

If you don't know whether to say yes or no to a friend's request, talk it over with an adult. This adult might be a family member or teacher. It could also be a coach, counselor, religious leader, or neighbor.

If you want to spend more time with this person, suggest a positive activity instead. For example, you might say, "Cutting school to go to a movie could get us in trouble. Let's go to a movie tonight instead."

Skills Practice

On a separate sheet of paper, describe a time when you did not give in to negative peer pressure. What did someone want you to do? What did you say or do? What, if anything, would you do differently the next time?

Practice these responses:

"I don't want to do that."

"I've decided not to do that."

"I don't need to do that to have fun."

"I have to go now."

Providing Positive Pressure

Sometimes even good friends suggest negative activities. Many young people want to try things they have been told not to do. Gayla, for example, knows that stealing is wrong. Yet it seems exciting.

Gayla is in a store with Erica. "Erica," Gayla whispers, "let's both take a pair of earrings and hide them in our pockets. I bet no one will catch us."

Erica's mouth drops open. "Are you crazy?"

Gayla shrugs and smiles. "I was just kidding."

The truth is, Gayla really didn't want to steal the earrings. But she might have done it if Erica had agreed to steal. She really hoped Erica would say no. Gayla needed and wanted Erica's positive peer pressure to keep from making a bad decision.

When Negative Pressure Continues

Erica knew Gayla would still be her friend if she refused to steal the earrings. But sometimes people might not respect your feelings. If you say "No" to them, they might not want you in their group. If you say "Yes," you will probably be allowed in the group. A real friend will not pressure you to do things you don't feel comfortable doing. A real friend respects you and your decisions. Someone who tries to pressure you into activities that go against your beliefs is not a real friend.

Watching for Hidden Pressure

Sometimes the one applying negative pressure is you! For example, none of Jamie's new friends offered him a cigarette. Only one boy in the group was smoking. That boy, named Kevin, seemed to be the group's leader. Kevin must think smoking is cool, Jamie told himself. If I smoke, he'll want me in his group. Jamie asked Kevin for one of his cigarettes.

Kevin handed him one and said, "I'll give you one, but you really shouldn't smoke. I've been trying to stop smoking. I want to run on the track team again." Kevin looked at the other guys. "And I better never catch any of you smoking!"

Embarrassed, Jamie handed back the cigarette. "I don't really smoke," he admitted.

Jamie had given in to negative pressure from himself! The next time, he'll make sure that what he is telling himself is what he really wants!

Teenagers and Peer Pressure

It's natural for teenagers to want to have friends and be part of a group. Still, the need to be accepted can lead to problems. Some teenagers begin to ignore what they think is important. They let others guide their decisions and actions.

Some teenagers are so afraid of losing friends that they forget they have choices. They don't have to do what a friend or a group does. They can make their own decisions. They can even encourage others to get involved in fun, healthy activities. If you are sure of yourself and what's important, it will be harder for others to get you to do something you know is wrong.

If making your own decisions costs you a "friend" or two, you can replace them with better friends. Join a

Think about what you tell yourself. Don't tell yourself to do something you know is wrong!

club or team to meet new people. Go to an event you usually don't attend. You can find other people who share your interests. These new friends can help you feel accepted again.

Find friends who like you as you are. They will let you be yourself. They will let you make your own decisions.

Decisions, Decisions!

Read the situation below. Follow the steps to help Gabe decide what to do.

Anthony and Gabe have picked the movie they want to go to tonight. "Let's see if Victor wants to come with us," Gabe suggests.

"Nah!" says Anthony. "We'd probably have to pay for him to get in. Victor never has any money. Let him stay home." Gabe knows that Victor's father lost his job. Victor works part-time, but he gives all the money he earns to his family.

On a separate sheet of paper, follow the steps below to help Gabe decide what to do.

Step 1: Identify the decision Gabe must make.

Step 2: List Gabe's choices.

Step 3: Cross out any choices that are harmful or might be against Gabe's beliefs.

Step 4: Think about the possible results of the remaining choices.

Step 5: Select the best choice.

Step 6: Explain how Gabe would carry out that choice.

Step 7: Describe the possible results of Gabe's choice.

Chapter Review

Chapter Summary

1. Having friends is an important part of being a teenager.

2. A true friend respects and likes you for yourself. This friend also respects the things you feel are important. Friends usually share some of the same interests.

3. Positive peer pressure is encouragement to do something helpful and healthful.

4. Negative peer pressure is encouragement to do something that goes against your beliefs. This activity may be harmful or illegal.

5. Friends can apply positive or negative pressure.

6. If you give in to negative pressure, you let others make your decisions and control your actions.

7. If someone suggests a negative activity, say "No" calmly and confidently. Suggest a positive activity instead.

8. Sometimes when friends suggest a negative activity, they actually hope you will say "No."

9. People sometimes apply negative pressure on themselves. They need to be careful not to talk themselves into joining a negative activity.

Chapter Quiz

Answer these questions on a separate sheet of paper.

1. What are three questions to ask yourself when choosing friends?

2. Would a true friend insist that you wear a certain brand of jeans? Why or why not?

3. Sandy knows that Kisha lies to her friends sometimes. Sandy thinks that being honest is very important. Would Sandy and Kisha make good friends? Why or why not?

4. What are some ways to find new friends?

5. What are three questions you could ask yourself before agreeing to an activity?

6. Filipe wants Antony to go to the mall. How could this be positive peer pressure? How could it be negative peer pressure?

7. What might happen if a teenager gave in to negative peer pressure at a part-time job?

8. What should you do if a good and trusted friend suggests a harmful activity?

9. Gena and Kim were writing their names on a wall. They did not ask Jim to do it, but he joined in anyway. Jim knew writing on the wall was wrong. Why did he write his name beside theirs?

10. Should teenagers avoid having friends so they can avoid peer pressure? Why or why not?

Putting Skills to Work

On a separate sheet of paper, list three examples of positive peer pressure you have experienced at your school. Then list three examples of negative peer pressure on you or others. Tell the class which you think is stronger at your school: positive peer pressure or negative peer pressure.

Skills Issues

Do you think adults feel peer pressure? On a separate sheet of paper, answer one of the following:

1. If you think adults feel peer pressure, list some positive and negative examples.

2. If you think adults do not feel peer pressure, discuss why not.

Chapter 4
Communicating with Others

Communicating includes listening as well as speaking. Good listeners show that they understand the speaker's feelings and care about what the speaker is saying.

Chapter Learning Objectives

- Name actions that can discourage someone from speaking.
- Explain ways to be a good listener.
- Describe how people communicate with body language.
- Explain how some cultures communicate differently from others.
- Explain how being thoughtful helps people be better communicators.

Words to Know

communicate   to share thoughts, feelings, and ideas with others

advice   suggestions as to what should be done

express   to show or communicate thoughts, feelings, and ideas

summarize   to explain briefly what you heard, saw, or read

body language   showing feelings using your body and your face

In the situation below, Angelo needs someone to listen to him. Decide if you think Larry is a good listener.

Angelo and Larry are in the locker room after football tryouts. Angelo shakes his head. "I really messed up today," he tells Larry. "I slipped twice, and I nearly missed that long pass."

"Hey, did you see what happened to me?" Larry asks. "I dropped the ball! It slipped right through my fingers! But the coach knows that was an accident. I think he'll pick me to be a tight end."

"I don't think I'm going to make the team," Angelo says sadly.

"You should give up on football, Angelo," Larry tells him. "Try out for track instead."

"But my dad is going to be really disappointed if I don't play football," Angelo says. "He played for three years on his high school team."

"My dad was in the marching band," Larry says. "So was my mom. They talk about it all the time."

"My brother . . ." Angelo begins.

"Your brother played football?" Larry asks.

Angelo shakes his head. "No, but he . . . "

"Hey, didn't your brother graduate last year?"

Angelo sighs. "Yes, he graduated. But I'm trying to tell you that he's been helping me . . . "

Larry slams his locker shut. "I wish my brother would graduate. He thinks he's my boss, even at school. Hey, I'm ready. Let's go!"

Talking without Listening

When people **communicate**, one person explains a thought, feeling, or idea. Another person listens and understands the thought, feeling, or idea. Keep in mind that communicating is more than just one person talking. It also requires another person to listen.

Larry wasn't listening to Angelo. Larry had no idea how upset Angelo was about the tryouts. Larry could have listened to Angelo and encouraged him to talk about his feelings. Instead, Larry talked about himself and his own family.

Think of the people you like to talk to. They are probably good listeners. Think about what makes them good listeners.

Angelo needs a friend who not only talks, but listens. Listening is an important part of being a friend. A friend is willing and able to listen when you have uncomfortable or happy feelings to share.

Being a good listener takes some practice. You can be a better family member, friend, and employee by strengthening your listening skills. This chapter will help you get started.

Recognizing Poor Listening Skills

You can tell when someone is not listening to you. Maybe the person is looking around the room or watching television. Not listening can also be shown in other ways. Some "listeners" are not listening. They just wait for the speaker to finish talking. Then they jump in and tell their own story. They often talk about when the same thing happened to them, only it was worse.

Think back to when Angelo said he almost missed the pass. If Larry had been listening, he would have noticed how upset Angelo was. Instead, Larry pointed out that he did something worse: he dropped the ball!

Larry told Angelo he should have gone out for track instead of football. Angelo didn't ask for Larry's **advice**, or suggestions about what should be done. He was hoping that Larry would just listen to him.

Telling people what they should have done, or not done, is not good listening. Instead, unwanted advice can discourage speakers from talking. Good listeners wait until someone asks for their advice.

Like Larry, some people also have a habit of finishing other people's sentences. When Angelo said, "My brother," Larry thought he knew what Angelo would say next. Many speakers stop talking when others keep interrupting them.

Skills Practice

Talk with a small group about the ways that people show they are not listening. Write down the ways. Then share them with the class. Discuss how people feel when others do not listen to them. Remember not to mention the names of any people.

Guidelines for Good Listening

Now you know some ways people show poor listening skills. Poor listening discourages people from talking. Good listeners encourage people to **express** themselves. To express means to show or communicate thoughts, feelings, and ideas.

Good listeners look at the speaker. They ignore everything else. They also show they're listening by turning their bodies to face the speaker. Sometimes good listeners lean toward the person who is talking. Good listeners show that they care about what the speaker is saying.

Part of listening is letting the speaker talk. Good listeners do not interrupt the speaker. If the speaker stops to take a breath, they don't jump in and start talking.

Is looking at the speaker important? Think about how you feel when people turn away while you speak.

Instead, they wait until the speaker has finished what he or she wants to say. Even if a good listener has something important to say, he or she must wait for the right time to speak.

Asking questions is another way to practice listening skills. Good listeners don't just sit silently. When the speaker is finished talking, they ask questions. Asking questions shows they are interested in what the speaker has to say. For example, the listener might ask:

"What happened then?"

"What do you think she will say?"

"What will you do about that?"

Noticing the speaker's feelings shows you are listening to what they have to say. To be a good listener, try to understand the feelings behind a speaker's words. For example, a friend might say, "My sister is getting married." You can ask questions to find out how the friend feels. You might ask, "Are you looking forward to the wedding?" You could also ask, "Do you like who your sister is marrying?" "Will you miss her when she moves away?"

Listeners can also show that they understand the speaker's feelings. Some ways to do that are by saying, "That sounds exciting," or "That would bother me, too."

Summarizing what the speaker said is another good listening skill. Summarize means to explain briefly what you heard, saw, or read. Summarizing what people said is a way to see if you understood them. One example of summarizing is, "I see. You wanted to explain what happened, but he wouldn't let you." Another example of summarizing is, "So you think the experiment will work if you make that change?"

Good listeners also give the speaker a chance to clear up any misunderstandings. They might ask the speaker, "Is that right?" You don't always have to

When you summarize, try not to repeat exactly what the speaker said. Instead, try to briefly state the speaker's main idea.

summarize what a person says. In some conversations, it would be annoying. For example, if your friend is telling you about a movie she saw, you don't need to summarize what she says.

Skills Practice

Practice good listening skills with a partner. One of you can play the part of Angelo, and one can play Larry. Angelo will start by saying, "I really messed up today." Larry will be a good listener. He will follow the guidelines you just read. After the conversation, discuss what Larry did to show he was listening.

Body language often reveals a person's ▼ *true feelings.*

Talking without Words

The words people say can tell you a lot. However, **body language** can tell you even more. Body language includes tapping your toe and crossing your arms. It also includes the look on your face. For example, you might smile or raise your eyebrows.

We can tell right away how some of the students in the picture on page 45 feel. They don't have to say a word. They are showing their feelings with their bodies and their faces. This is called body language.

Sometimes body language is not clear. The same body language can have two or more meanings. For example, a tapping toe can mean someone is angry. It can also mean someone is in a hurry. Raised eyebrows can show surprise or disbelief.

Skills Practice

With a partner, make up a short scene. You will show how body language can communicate meaning. For example, one partner might pretend to read a letter. The partner could use body language to show whether the letter is happy, sad, or surprising. Or both partners could walk toward each other. Their body language could show whether they are friends, enemies, or strangers.

Show your skit to the other students. Afterward, ask them what you communicated using body language.

Confusing Messages

Imagine you are talking to a friend. You tell him you can't go to the movies with him tonight. He says, "That's okay. No problem." However, now he won't look at you. His body seems stiff. He is giving you a confusing message. However, his words say he isn't angry. His body language says he is very angry.

We confuse people when our words say one thing, but our body language says another.

Listeners may pay more attention to our body language than to our words. Our body language often shows our true feelings. When we talk, we may try to hide these feelings. However, our body language gives them away.

If you are angry, you need to express those feelings in words. Don't try to hide them. Your body language will tell others your feelings anyway. It is better to tell others you are angry without making the problem worse.

Skills Practice

Think of something to tell a partner, such as "I would be glad to come to your party." As you say the words, show a different feeling with your body language. For example, you might frown as you say you are glad. Talk about how these confusing messages make communication more difficult.

Communicating in Different Cultures

You learned to talk by listening to your family members talk. You learned to use body language the same way, by watching the people around you. You saw their faces when they were surprised. Then you made your face look like theirs.

If you had grown up in Japan, Saudi Arabia, Brazil, or the Congo, you would have learned different words. You might have also learned different body language.

It is important to remember that the way people from another country communicate may be very different from what you are used to. When you speak with someone from another country, try to understand and respect those differences. For example, Olga met Yoko, the Japanese exchange student at her school. Olga smiled and looked directly at Yoko. "How do you like our school so far?" Olga asked. Olga noticed that

Looking away from a person who is speaking is a way to show respect in some cultures.

when she talked to Yoko, Yoko didn't look at her. Yoko looked down at the floor. Olga thought Yoko was bored or wasn't interested in talking with her. Olga also noticed that Yoko seemed uncomfortable when she answered Olga's question. Then their teacher explained that in Japan, looking down was sometimes a sign of respect, while looking at the speaker's face was sometimes a sign of a lack of respect.

Roger was confused when he met Hakeem at a friend's house. Hakeem's family was visiting from Saudi Arabia. When Roger started talking to him, Hakeem moved very close to him. This made Roger feel uncomfortable. Roger stopped talking and took a few steps backward. When he started talking again, Hakeem moved closer to him. He wondered if Hakeem was being rude or trying to annoy him. He seemed friendly enough.

Later, Roger asked his friend about why Hakeem moved so close when they spoke. Roger's friend explained that in his culture, Hakeem was just acting in a polite way that showed interest.

Of course, different ways of communicating can lead to misunderstandings. Olga thought Yoko wasn't interested in talking with her. Roger thought Hakeem might be trying to annoy him.

Sometimes people do not communicate in the way we expect. If this happens, we should not judge them so quickly. Like Olga and Roger, we might find that these new friends express themselves in different ways than we do. In fact, like Yoko, they might wish we would stop looking at them while they talk. We might be making them uncomfortable!

The Golden Rule of Communicating

Good communicators listen to other people the same way they want others to listen to them. This is sometimes called the Golden Rule. Treat others the way that you want to be treated. This is a good rule not only for communicating, but for living. Work to understand what is being said and what people are feeling.

In the next chapter, you will learn more ways to be a better communicator. You will learn how good communication skills can help you get along with others and make yourself understood.

Decisions, Decisions!

Read the situation below. Then follow the steps to help Carrie decide what to do. Carrie is not sure she still wants to be friends with April. Here is one of their conversations:

CARRIE: "When I get home today, I need to call . . ."

APRIL: "You need to call your mom at work, right? Why are you telling me that, Carrie? I know you call her every day."

CARRIE: "No, I need to call the library and . . ."

APRIL: "And see if it has that new CD, right? If you get it, I want to hear it, too."

CARRIE: "April! Let me finish! I need to call the library and see when it closes today."

On a separate sheet of paper, follow the steps below to help Carrie decide what to do about April.

Step 1: Identify the decision Carrie must make.

Step 2: List Carrie's choices.

Step 3: Cross out any choices that are harmful or might be against Carrie's beliefs.

Step 4: Think about the possible results of the remaining choices.

Step 5: Select the best choice.

Step 6: Explain how Carrie would carry out that choice.

Step 7: Describe the possible results of Carrie's choice.

Chapter Review

Chapter Summary

1. Poor listeners can discourage speakers from talking. They do this by always telling their own stories, giving advice, interrupting, and not listening.

2. Good listeners encourage speakers to talk. They do this by paying attention, letting the speaker talk, and asking questions. They also listen for the feelings of the speaker and summarize what the speaker has said.

3. We also communicate with body language. Sometimes our body language says one thing, but our words say another. This can be confusing for listeners.

4. Our families teach us how to communicate. People from different cultures sometimes communicate in different ways.

5. Good communicators are thoughtful of others. They communicate with other people in the same way that they want others to communicate with them.

Chapter Quiz

Answer these questions on a separate sheet of paper.

1. What are three ways a listener might discourage a speaker from talking?

2. Every time Jason talks to Kurt, Kurt tries to tell him what to do. What is Kurt doing that makes him a poor listener?

3. What are five ways to encourage a speaker to talk?

4. When Sara talks to Brooke, she knows Brooke is listening. What are some specific things Brooke might be doing to show Sara that she is listening?

5. Kate just told Robert about her idea for a science project. Robert says, "My science project won first prize in the science fair last year." Is Kate likely to tell Robert more about her science project? Why or why not?

6. What are two kinds of body language?

7. You can tell a friend is sad by looking at her. What body language might tell you that she is sad?

8. How can different ways of communicating lead to misunderstandings?

9. Do good listeners just sit quietly and listen? Why or why not?

10. Can someone be a good friend without being a good listener? Why or why not?

Putting Skills to Work

Read the listening guidelines on pages 43-45. Then think of someone at home or at school who needs a good listener. Spend some time with this person. Practice being a good listener. Afterward, tell your class what you did to show good listening skills.

Skills Issues

On a separate sheet of paper, answer these questions:

1. Do you think people are poor listeners on purpose? Why or why not?

2. Why do you think a person might be a poor listener?

3. How do you feel when someone isn't listening to you?

4. Do you think someone can learn to be a good listener?

Chapter 5

Getting Along With Others

When people know how to work together, they can accomplish almost anything. Working with others can also be more fun than working alone.

Chapter Learning Objectives

- Explain how different needs and points of view can cause conflicts.
- Explain "I messages."
- Demonstrate how to show confidence and respect as you talk with others.
- Describe ways to cool off angry feelings.
- Explain how people's thoughts can lead to angry feelings.
- Name the steps in settling conflicts.

Words to Know

opinion   a belief

point of view   a way of thinking about something

conflict   strong disagreement caused by a difference in needs or points of view

respect   to show that something has value

In the situation below, Adam and Christa are having an argument. Read the situation and see if that means they have to stop being friends.

Adam and Christa are talking about an idea that might become a law. The law would stop lumber companies from cutting down the forests near their town. "So you think it's okay to cut down all those trees?" Adam asks Christa. "What about the birds and animals that live in the forest? Where are they supposed to live?"

"Most of them will move to another part of the forest," Christa tells him. "Anyway, the lumber companies always plant trees in place of the ones they cut."

"The trees they plant are tiny! It will take forever for them to grow into a forest," Adam says. "But the lumber companies don't care about that! All they care about is making money!"

Christa gives Adam an angry look and walks away. Adam doesn't know that Christa's parents work for a lumber company. If the law is passed, her mom and dad might lose their jobs. Christa doesn't know that Adam has a part-time job taking care of injured wild animals.

Seeing the Whole Picture

Christa does not share Adam's **opinion**, or belief, about the law that would stop lumber companies from cutting down the forests. Adam and Christa have a different **point of view**, or way of thinking, about the issue. Adam is concerned about the animals. He wants the companies to stop chopping down the forests. Christa also cares about the animals and forests. However, she is more worried about her parents' jobs. She wants to let the lumber companies cut the forests. She knows that the companies will replace the trees they cut.

It's okay for Adam and Christa to have different points of view. This is bound to happen because they have different interests and needs. However, their different points of view are keeping them from getting along. Christa is angry at Adam for putting down the lumber companies. Adam thinks Christa doesn't care about the animals.

Better communication may not make this problem go away. People will always disagree about certain issues. Christa and Adam may continue to disagree about cutting down the forests. Still, better communication could help them get along and stay friends.

Right now, Adam and Christa only see part of the picture. They both need to see the whole picture. They need to understand each other's point of view. Then they might not feel so angry with each other.

If Adam knew about Christa's parents, he might feel differently. Then he would understand why she defends the lumber companies. If Christa knew about Adam's part-time job, she might think differently. Then she would understand why he cares so much about saving the forests.

Knowing just your own point of view is like listening to someone having a telephone conversation. If you hear only one person speaking, you hear only part of the story.

Skills Practice

With a partner, role-play the conflict between two friends who disagree about whether they should go to a party where people will be drinking beer.

Causes of Conflicts

Like Adam and Christa, people often have **conflicts** with each other. A conflict is a strong disagreement that results when people have different needs or points of view.

Simon and Megan are brother and sister. Both of them have household jobs to do. They take turns setting and clearing the dinner table and washing the dishes. When Simon sets and clears the table, Megan washes the dishes. The next day, they switch jobs.

Yesterday, Simon wasn't home for dinner. He ate dinner at a friend's house. Megan had to set and clear the table and wash dishes. Tonight, Megan tells Simon she needs to work on her science project. That means Simon would have to do both jobs. Simon says he doesn't think that is fair. He won't have time to practice his lines for the school play.

This difference in needs is causing a conflict. Megan and Simon have to find a solution they can both agree on.

In some conflicts, people might never agree. Like Adam and Christa, they may look at a problem from different points of view. They need to try to understand each other's point of view. They might still have a conflict. However, they might be able to work out a solution. They could get along better with each other.

People often have conflicts because of different points of view. Let's say a school system has to cut back on its programs. Philip, who plays basketball, thinks the swim team should be cut. Juan is on the swim team. He thinks the basketball program should be cut. Neither is right or wrong. They just have different opinions. They need to try to understand each other's point of view. Then they could still be friends. They might even work together to think of other ways for the school to save money.

The next time you have a conflict with someone, think about the cause. Do you have different points of view?

Skills Practice

Teenagers and parents often have different points of view. With a partner, choose one of the topics below. One partner will explain a teenager's point of view. The other partner will explain a parent's point of view. Then talk about what you learned about how to get along. What if teenagers and parents always carefully explained their points of view to each other? How might that help them get along?

curfews	haircuts	using the car
homework	allowances	watching television
clothes	dating	using the telephone

"I Messages" and You

Sometimes conflicts lead to arguments and hard feelings. Think back to the conflict between Philip and Juan. Imagine that Philip and Juan are talking about which school program should be cut. Philip might remind Juan that the swim team lost the city championship. Philip defends his point of view by saying the swimmers are losers. They shouldn't get any school funds. Then Juan gets angry. He points out that Philip missed two shots at the last basketball game. Juan says the team lost the game because of Philip.

Juan and Philip are ready to fight. Yet they could explain their feelings about the school cuts in ways that will not lead to a fight. They could use "I messages." "I messages" can help people of all ages explain to others how they feel. "I messages" have three steps:

1. I feel . . . (describe how you feel, such as angry, embarrassed, or worried)

2. when you . . . (explain what is bothering you)

3. because . . . (tell why this bothers you)

In an "I message," you don't have to say, "I feel . . . when you . . . because . . ." You can use different words. Just explain how you feel and why.

Here are some examples of "I messages":

- "I feel angry when you put down the swim team because we work hard."
- "I feel embarrassed when you blame me for losing the game. I didn't mean to miss those shots."
- "It worries me that the school might cut the swimming program. Next year we have a good chance to win the championship."

Avoiding Attacking Messages

Be careful not to attack the other person when explaining your feelings. An attack can lead to hard feelings.

The two messages below show the difference between an "I message" and an attacking message. Jim and Chris share a locker at school. Which message do you think Jim would want to hear?

I message: "I feel frustrated when I try to find things in our locker. I was late for my math class again today because I couldn't find my book."

Attacking message: "You are such a pig! Why do you throw all your garbage in our locker? I can't find anything in this mess!"

If Chris gave Jim the first message, Jim might be willing to clean out the locker. This message explains the problem without blaming anyone. But if Chris gave Jim the second message, Jim might not be so willing to help. The attacking message blames Jim for

Use "I messages" to communicate your feelings with respect for the other person. This is especially important with adults. You don't want to seem to lack respect.

the problem. It even calls Jim names. Jim would be angry and hurt.

"I messages" take some practice. But they are worth the effort. They can prevent some conflicts and angry feelings. They can also help solve conflicts. They do this by allowing people to explain their point of view without insulting each other. You should use "I messages" to show that you **respect**, or value, someone's opinion even if you do not agree with it. In this way, "I messages" help us understand others and get along.

Skills Practice

Work with a partner to write the "I messages" below. Use a separate sheet of paper.

1. Your little brother lost your keys. Give him an "I message."

2. A friend told other people at school a secret about you. Give your friend an "I message."

3. Your mother never knocks on the door before coming into your bedroom. Give your mother an "I message."

Communicating with Confidence

Don't waste "I messages" by saying one thing with your words and another with your body language. For example, a girl named Hope was upset. Her friend Lisa kept interrupting her. "I feel angry when you keep interrupting me, Lisa. I have something important to tell you," Hope whispered as she looked at the floor.

"What did you say, Hope?" Lisa asked.

"Never mind," Hope said quickly.

◀ *Speaking with confidence shows that you respect yourself.*

Hope's body language made her "I message" weak. Hope should have looked Lisa in the eye. She could have said the same words, but in a clear, confident voice. Lisa would have heard her easily. Then Lisa might have stopped interrupting her.

Skills Practice

Have a partner listen as you say each sentence below. Say the sentence once as if you aren't sure of yourself. Then say the sentence with confidence. See if your partner can tell the difference.

1. Would you wait for me after school?

2. I feel left out because you went to the movies without me. I like to go to the movies with you.

3. I want to draw the pictures for our project.

Discuss the differences between the statements when they're said differently.

Communicating with Respect

Some people always say what they're thinking, even if they insult someone. Some people often use a loud voice. Some use attacking messages. This is not part of good communication.

Lisa's friend Hope didn't speak up when Lisa interrupted her. However, Lisa also has a friend named Molly. Once Lisa interrupted Molly. Molly frowned and put her hands on her hips. She said, "Lisa, you loudmouth, I was talking! You interrupted me! Wait until I'm finished!"

Molly does not care about other people's feelings. She often insists that everyone do things her way. It is also difficult to get this type of person to listen to your ideas.

Good communication comes from respect. Speaking with confidence shows that you respect yourself. Avoiding attacking messages shows that you respect other people.

Other ways to show that you respect yourself and others are to stand or sit up straight when you talk. Look the other person in the eye when communicating. It's also important to speak in a calm, clear voice. No whispering and no shouting!

Show that you respect others by using good listening skills. Do not put others down. Explain your own ideas without insulting theirs. Consider others' opinions, but make your own decisions.

Dealing with Angry Feelings

Imagine using an "I message" to ask someone not to interrupt you. Then he or she keeps doing it! When others do not treat us with respect, angry thoughts come into our heads. Then, we might say or do something that we will be sorry about later.

We need to watch for these angry feelings. Then we can deal with them before they get out of control.

Hope doesn't respect herself. Molly doesn't respect others. They both show their lack of respect in the way they communicate.

Use tricks to calm down. Count to ten—or even twenty. Counting gives you time to calm down. Another trick is to take two or three deep breaths. This will help you to relax.

If you're very angry, explain that you want to talk about this problem later. In the meantime, calm down by thinking calm thoughts. You could also discuss the problem with someone else. Find a good listener. A good listener might be able to help you sort out a way to solve the problem.

Sometimes by getting exercise, you calm down. You can overcome feelings of anger by being physically active. Take a walk, ride your bike, clean your room. It might get your mind off the problem or give you time to think it through.

Skills Practice

Talk with a small group about how you can tell that a person is getting angry. Does the person's face get red? Does the person frown? Make a list of the signs of anger. Then share it with the class.

Making Yourself Angry

Sometimes we make ourselves angry. We may make ourselves angry by the way we think about something we see.

Let's say you see a girl laughing in the hallway. You could think that she just heard a joke. You could also think that she's making fun of you. This second thought could make you angry, even though it might not be true!

Read over the sentences on page 62. The sentences on the left show how some thoughts can lead to angry feelings. The sentences on the right can lead to calm feelings.

Angry Thoughts	Calm Thoughts
I'll never learn this!	It will take time for me to learn this.
He'll be sorry he said that!	I won't let him bother me.
She's not my boss!	I can make my own decisions.
He lied to me!	I don't think that's what he said yesterday.
She broke it on purpose!	I'll ask her to buy me a new one.

If you start to feel angry, your thoughts might be the problem. If you change your thoughts, you might feel calmer. More importantly, you will be able to think more clearly. Feeling calm and thinking clearly will help you get along with other people.

Skills Practice

Think of calm thoughts to finish these sentences. Write an ending to each sentence on a separate sheet of paper. Then discuss them with a partner.

1. Lee lost my newest CD, but . . .
2. Dad won't let me get my driver's license, but . . .
3. Chris likes someone else better than he likes me, but . . .

Methods of Settling Conflicts

If you're having trouble settling a conflict, calm down before you speak. If you feel angry, you may say things you don't mean. Remember to listen carefully. Invite the other person to explain the conflict from his or her point of view.

Listening to the other person's point of view is always helpful. When you can look at a problem in new ways, you can often find a solution.

By explaining your point of view you might be able to think of ways to settle the conflict. Both of you should list as many possible solutions as you can think of. The more choices you have, the better chance you have of finding one you both like. Then discuss the choices. Cross out any that either person does not like.

Finally, choose the best solution for both of you. Try to choose a solution that helps both people. That way, neither one of you will feel angry or cheated.

Solving Conflicts

Doug just spent two hours helping JB study for a test. Doug works as a tutor and expected to be paid for his help. JB thought Doug was helping him as a friend. He doesn't have any money to pay Doug. Both are very upset about the misunderstanding.

Doug and JB used the methods mentioned above to settle their conflict. Doug took several deep breaths to let out his anger, while JB walked to the kitchen to get a drink of water. They both gave themselves time to cool off.

Then Doug asked why JB thought Doug's help would be free. Doug listened quietly as JB explained

An important step in settling any conflict is to explain your point of view. Use an "I message" to explain the conflict from your point of view.

◀ *Conflicts can be very upsetting. Taking time to calm down is the first step to solving a problem.*

that since they had been friends for a long time, he thought the tutoring was a simple favor. JB also admitted that he was broke.

Doug then explained his point of view. He calmly told JB, "I feel angry because you didn't plan to pay me. I am saving all the money I make for college. I need every cent."

Once Doug and JB explained their points of view, they began to think of ways to settle the conflict. Doug and JB list ways to solve their conflict:

1. JB pays Doug nothing.
2. JB pays Doug what he usually earns for two hours of tutoring.
3. JB pays part of Doug's fee now and the rest later.
4. JB repays Doug by baby-sitting Doug's little brother for two afternoons. That would give Doug more time to tutor other students.

After discussing their choices, Doug crosses out choice 1. JB won't have any money for a while, so he crosses out 2 and 3. To settle their conflict they must choose the best solution for both. Doug agreed to have JB baby-sit his little brother. In fact, the two friends decided to trade more tutoring for baby-sitting.

Coping with Conflict

Whenever people work or play together, they have conflicts. Yet conflicts don't have to lead to angry feelings. They also don't have to break up friendships. For example, Doug and JB found a way to settle their conflict in a way that helped both of them.

Solving conflicts begins with understanding the other person's needs and point of view. Knowing how to solve conflicts is a valuable skill at school, at home, and at work.

Decisions, Decisions!

Read the situation below. Then follow the steps to help Alice decide what to do.

Alice is angry at Pamela, but she can't decide what to do. Nearly every day at lunch time, Pamela asks for part of Alice's lunch. Sometimes Pamela wants half of Alice's sandwich. Other times, she reaches over and takes one of Alice's cookies.

Alice knows that some conflicts are not important enough to bring up. But conflicts can grow if you ignore them. On a separate sheet of paper, follow the steps below to help Alice decide what to do.

Step 1: Identify the decision Alice must make.

Step 2: List Alice's choices.

Step 3: Cross out any choices that are harmful or might go against Alice's beliefs.

Step 4: Think about the possible results of the remaining choices.

Step 5: Select the best choice.

Step 6: Explain how Alice would carry out that choice.

Step 7: Describe the possible results of Alice's choice.

Chapter Review

Chapter Summary

1. Conflicts often result when people have different needs or points of view. Understanding other's needs or points of view can often lead to solving a conflict.

2. "I messages" explain what is bothering you without attacking the other person. "I messages" can help settle conflicts.

3. Some conflicts are caused by not telling people when they are bothering you. Other conflicts are caused by attacking people when they bother you.

4. You avoid some conflicts by explaining your opinions with confidence. Look the other person in the eye and speak calmly and politely. Use good listening skills. Don't put down others.

5. Angry feelings can make a conflict worse. You can cool off by counting to ten, taking deep breaths, or asking for time to calm down. You can also discuss the problem with someone else or get some exercise.

6. What we tell ourselves about a situation makes a difference. If we tell ourselves something negative, we can make ourselves feel angry. If we tell ourselves something positive, we can help ourselves feel calm.

7. To settle a conflict, listen to each other's point of view. Then work together to think of ways to settle the problem. Choose a way you both agree to peacefully.

Chapter Quiz

Answer these questions on a separate sheet of paper.

1. What is your point of view about having a dress code at school? What is a different point of view about this?

2. What are the three parts of an "I message"?

3. How does using "I messages" help solve conflicts?

4. Jonathan yells at Karl, "You went to the game without me last night! Why didn't you call me? You never think of anyone but yourself!" Write an "I message" that explains Jonathan's feelings without attacking Karl.

5. Jenny looks at the floor and whispers, "I'm sorry, Carrie, but don't take my book without telling me." Explain how Jenny could make her point in a better manner.

6. Carrie stares at Jenny and yells, "I didn't take your stupid book, Jenny! Are you calling me a thief? You've got a lot of nerve!" Explain how Carrie could show Jenny more respect.

7. Name three ways to calm down if you're feeling angry.

8. Glen wasn't chosen for the soccer team. "The coach never did like me," he tells himself. How would this thought make Glen feel?

9. Write another thought that would help Glen feel better about not making the team.

10. What are the steps you should follow to settle a conflict?

Putting Skills to Work

Think of a conflict you had with someone. Describe it on a separate sheet of paper. If you settled the conflict, explain how you did it. If you didn't settle the conflict, explain why not. Then describe how you could find a solution to this problem that both of you would like.

Skills Issues

Some people think conflict is bad. They avoid conflict by letting others have their own way. They say nothing when someone or something is bothering them. On a separate sheet of paper, explain whether you think people should try to avoid conflict in this way.

Chapter 6

Handling Change and Stress

Teenagers go through many changes. Change can cause stress and confusion. Sharing your feelings with friends and family can ease the stress of change.

Chapter Learning Objectives

- Describe the changes that take place during the teenage years.
- Explain how changes can affect teenagers.
- Describe ways teenagers can deal with change.
- Explain how teenagers' relationships with their families can change.
- Describe how changes in the community can affect teenagers.
- Name some causes and ways to reduce stress.

Words to Know

stress   uncomfortable feelings caused when we have too much to deal with

mature   adult; fully developed physically and emotionally

hormones   chemicals in your body that are produced by glands

emotions   feelings

Julie feels confused. Here is what different people told her, all in the same day:

That morning, Julie's older brother told her—
"No, you can't ride to school with me and my friends. We don't want any little kids around."
Then her father reminded her—
"Don't forget to go to Grandpa's house and check on him after school, Julie. He might need your help. You know he depends on you."
At school, her best friend said—
"Your parents won't let you go out with Jerome? They really treat you like a baby, Julie. They should start letting you make your own decisions!"

Change and Stress

Julie is getting confusing messages from her friends and family. She is expected to act like an adult but is often treated like a child. Julie wants to make more of her own decisions. Yet she has no idea what to do with the rest of her life.

Nothing seems to stay the same during the teenage years. Young people suddenly have to deal with all kinds of changes within themselves, their families, and their communities.

This chapter will explore some of the changes you are experiencing and how they may affect you.

Stress affects you physically. Your heart beats faster and you breathe faster. Your muscles become tense, and you may start to sweat. Too much stress can cause headaches, upset stomachs, shortness of breath, trouble sleeping, and even blurred vision.

Change can cause **stress**. Stress is the uncomfortable feelings you get when you have too much to deal with. This chapter includes suggestions that can help you deal with stress.

Skills Practice

Start thinking about the changes going on in your life. On a separate sheet of paper, list:

- ways you are changing
- ways your family is changing
- ways your community is changing

Save this list for yourself. Read it again after you finish the chapter. You might want to add to it.

Types of Changes within Yourself

Physical changes are some of the major changes we face in our lives. As children become teenagers, they get taller, wider, rounder, and stronger. They even get hairier. Their bodies are becoming **mature**, more adult. **Hormones** are the chemicals in the body that cause and help control these changes.

Everybody develops at a different speed. Some teenagers develop a little more quickly than others; some develop a little more slowly.

This means that some teenagers end up looking different from their friends for a while. Looking different can feel uncomfortable. It can be harder to deal with than the changes themselves. Still, by the age of 16 or 17, the slow developers have often caught up with the quick ones. By then, most teenagers have their adult bodies. Most of the physical changes are over.

Nevertheless, teenagers need time to get used to their new bodies. Growing four to six inches in a year does take some getting used to.

Why do many teenagers seem clumsy? Their bones grow more quickly than their muscles. This makes it harder for them to control their arms and legs. Sooner or later their muscles catch up with their bones.

The same hormones that help your body become adult also affect your **emotions**, or feelings. Sometimes they send your emotions on a roller coaster ride. Julie says she feels like smiling one minute and crying the next. Her emotional ups and downs confuse her family. At times they even confuse Julie.

Her friend Jerome is having trouble controlling his temper. He gets mad about things that never used to bother him. Other times he feels like crying or says things he doesn't mean.

All these emotional changes can make it harder to get along with others. It helps to understand that these changes are just part of growing up. Remember, the hormones that cause physical changes can also affect moods and feelings. In time, emotions do become easier to manage.

With all these physical and emotional changes, many teenagers worry about being "normal." If other young people like them, they think they must be normal. If other teenagers ignore or tease them they may feel "different" and unlovable. It's important not to let others judge you or affect how you feel.

The fact that people look and act differently adds to the variety of the world. If we were all exactly the same, we wouldn't be able to tell each other apart! Our differences make each of us special.

Skills Practice

Discuss these two questions with a small group. Then share your answers with the class.

1. In what ways do teenagers try to look and act like other teenagers?

2. What problems can be caused by the emotional changes teenagers go through?

Having friends is important, especially when you are a teenager. Doing things with friends helps you learn how to get along with people. Friends listen

As people grow and change, their friendships often change as well. Accepting changes in your friends and in yourself can be difficult.

when you want to talk about problems. They can help you feel good about yourself.

Some teenagers are scared of looking or acting different from their friends. They want to be just like everyone else. They think that this way they will be accepted by other young people and have many friends.

These young people may be willing to do almost anything to be part of a group. They may let a group tell them what to do. They should be learning to make their own decisions. Teenagers may find that making a decision that goes against their group causes them to lose friends.

But friends may come and go. When some teenagers lose a friend, they think it means no one likes them. It usually just means that they or their friends have changed.

For example, Rick, James, and Tony were best friends when they were younger. They spent hours together making and launching model rockets. Now Rick has band practice after school. He often goes away on band trips. James runs track and hangs around with guys on the track team. Tony has a new girlfriend. She takes up lots of his time. Rick, James, and Tony don't spend much time with one another anymore. They are no longer best friends because their interests have changed.

Teenagers often grow closer to some friends as their interests change. Rick was always friends with Greg. But now Greg is his best friend. They both enjoy playing in the band. They discovered they also share other interests.

Change is a normal part of being a teenager. No one becomes an adult without experiencing change.

Skills Practice

On a separate sheet of paper, list things you liked to do when you were much younger. Then list the things you like to do now. As your interests have changed, your friends have probably also changed.

As teenagers get older, their thinking patterns change in ways that help them plan for the future and solve problems. This allows them to consider their choices. They can make wiser decisions.

Teenagers tend to become more aware of other people's feelings. They try not to do or say things that may hurt others' feelings. These changes in thinking patterns are just another part of becoming an adult.

Handling Changes within Yourself

Being faced with so many changes at once can cause stress. Talk with friends or family members about anything that is bothering you. You will learn that many of your friends are worried about the same things.

Types of Changes within a Family

Families are important in helping children grow and become independent. But families often change. Parents may have another child or adopt one. Older children may move out of the home. Married brothers or sisters may have children of their own. Grandparents and other relatives may move in—or out.

Divorce is also a big change that affects many families. As a result, many children and teenagers live with just one parent. Some live with one parent part of the time and the other parent the rest of the time. When the parents remain friends, living in two homes can work out fairly well. When the parents feel angry with each other, living in two homes can be difficult. Then their children are more likely to feel angry, too. Their children may also worry about their future.

When two divorced adults marry each other, their children may live together as one family. Sometimes these parents have another child together. The relationships among the members of these families can be warm and loving. But sometimes those relationships are tense. Talking about your feelings and problems with family members can help.

Families face many kinds of changes when a member has a serious illness or accident. Sometimes disease or injury may cause the death of a family member. This is upsetting for children and teenagers in the family.

Having less money can also cause stress in a family. A family may have less income if a parent becomes too ill to work. Many parents lose their jobs through no fault of their own. Their companies close or decide they don't need as many employees. Divorce can also change a family's income level. When parents have to pay for two separate homes, there is less money for other things.

Of course, a family's income can also increase. A parent may get a raise, or an older child may begin working. Gaining more income, however, usually does not cause as much stress as losing income.

A divorce, new job, or job transfer may cause a family to move. Some families decide to move closer to a sick relative. Or a family member's health problems may require a warmer climate. Whatever the reason, a move can affect nearly every part of a teenager's life.

Family Changes and Teenagers

When a family changes, routines change. For example, if a parent takes on a second job, the family's daily schedule may be upset. Family members may no longer be able to eat dinner together.

Teenagers may be expected to take on more responsibilities. For example, they might be asked to care for younger children or cook the meals. They might become the family taxi. One afternoon, they might have to take a brother to soccer practice. The next afternoon, they might be asked to drive Grandma to her doctor.

With so much going on, young family members might not be able to find a good listener when they need one. An older brother or sister may move out and not be there to listen. Or a parent or grandparent may not be there.

In the meantime, teenagers must still go to school, do homework, go to their own sports practices, and so on. They must also deal with all the normal changes that are happening within themselves.

Family changes can cause uncomfortable feelings for teenagers. It is normal for teenagers to feel angry, scared, or upset by family changes. Some young people become angry with a grandparent for getting so sick. They might be scared about whether a parent will find another job. They may be upset about having to help out so much at home. They need help themselves! Learning to cope with these feelings can help ease the stress during times of change.

Handling Family Changes

There are ways to help you deal with the stress of family changes. Accept changes that you cannot do anything about. You cannot stop your parents from getting a divorce. However, you can work to keep a good relationship with both parents. Remember that it's not your fault. If a family member has a serious illness,

Here's an old piece of advice:

Accept the things you cannot change.

Change the things you can.

Think carefully so you will know the difference.

try to cheer up the person or offer comfort. You can't cure them, but you can try to help. Fighting change is a normal part of life. Try to fight unwanted change positively.

A family may have many needs during a change. However, teenagers cannot meet all of their family's needs. If someone asks you to do more than you can do, try using I messages to explain how you feel. Or ask another family member to help you talk with your parent or parents. Accepting too much responsibility can cause too much stress. It might even hurt your health. That won't help anyone.

Nearly every change has its good points. For example, if your grandfather moves in, you will be able to learn more about your family history. If you write down his stories, you can share the stories with the rest of the family.

If someone in your family is ill, learn about the disease. Find out what kinds of help are available. Gaining knowledge about a problem can teach you how to handle other problems in the future.

Skills Practice

Work with a partner. On a separate sheet of paper, list three family changes that a teenager might face. Next to each change, write how the teenager could best handle the change. Share your answers with the class.

Other Kinds of Family Changes

All families change, even if no one moves into the home or gets sick. As teenagers get older, their relationships with their parents change. Young people want to make more of their own decisions. They want their parents to give them more freedom and set fewer rules.

Yet some young people are not ready to make wise decisions. For example, Joanna asked her parents to give her money every Monday to buy her lunches at school.

But Joanna decided to spend her lunch money on CDs. Since she did not eat lunch, she had no energy in the afternoons. Joanna began falling asleep in her classes. By the time she got home from school, she was starving and grouchy. Her grades fell, as well.

Joanna's parents may still need to help make her decisions. However, other parents may make too many decisions for their children. They may not realize that their children are maturing.

For example, Pete's mother still picks out his shirts. She buys styles that no one at school wears. When Pete does not wear these shirts, his mother becomes angry. Talking calmly with his mother about the problem and asking her to talk to other parents might help. If Pete is respectful, his mother might realize that it's time to give Pete more responsibility.

Changing relationships between teenagers and parents can cause stress. To handle these changes, everyone needs patience and good listening skills.

Types of Changes within the Community

Some communities have not changed much over the past 50 or 60 years. Others change every month. In these changing communities, houses might be built, or apartment buildings might be torn down. People might move into or out of an area. New factories might be set up, or companies might go out of business.

When a business moves into a community, it usually hires new employees. More people may move into the community to take those jobs. With more customers available, new stores may open.

However, when a business closes, its employees lose their jobs. They may have to move to another city or state to find work. There will be fewer people in the community. Stores, shops, and movie theaters will have fewer customers. They may have to close, too.

It can be difficult for parents to know when to give children more freedom to make their own decisions. It can be even harder for teenagers to wait for this freedom.

If you live in a changing community, you might see changes at your school. A community that is losing families is also losing students. It might have to close a nearly empty school and send those students to another school. The students will have to get used to new teachers, new friends, and new rules. This can be very stressful for the students.

Schools in a growing community may have too many students. Some classes might have to be held in the gym or library. Noise and confusion could make it hard to concentrate.

Handling Changes within Your Community

Many of the tips for dealing with the stress of family changes can also help you deal with changes in your community. For example, if your school is closed, look on the bright side of going to a new school. You will have the chance to meet new people and make new friends. Some of these friendships may last a lifetime.

Handling Stress

Everyone experiences some stress. A little stress is good for you. It gives you energy and helps you do your best. Still, too much stress can make you sick. Below are some signs of too much stress:

- Frequent illnesses
- Teeth grinding
- Nail biting
- Lack of patience
- Problems in getting along with others
- Sleeping problems
- Tight muscles
- Tiredness
- Headaches and other pains

If you have these signs of stress, you might be dealing with some kind of change. But change is not the only cause of stress.

Expecting too much of yourself also causes stress. People who always expect to win are under a great deal of stress. They need to find other ways to feel good about themselves. For example, they might learn how to play the piano. Or they might help out at the hospital. Then winning will be less important. Losing will cause less stress.

Some people are always hurrying. Managing their time will cut down on this stress. With some planning, they will be able to get important tasks done. They will also have more time to enjoy life.

Different things cause stress for different people.

◀ Teenage years can be very stressful. It is important to find ways to lower the stress in your life before it causes health problems.

Wanting to fit in causes some teenagers to worry all the time about whether others like them. To avoid this stress, they should find friends who accept them as they are. They will feel comfortable with these friends. Then they can relax and be themselves.

Conflicts with parents, teachers, friends, and others can cause stress. Teenagers may feel angry, guilty, or just uncomfortable about these conflicts. They need to learn how to settle arguments peacefully. Then they can cut down on this source of stress.

A balanced diet can help your body deal with stress. Instead of junk food and sugar, eat more fresh fruits and vegetables. They give your body what it needs to repair body parts that get worn out by stress.

Exercise strengthens your muscles, especially your heart. Exercise also works off that extra energy that builds up when you are angry and stressed. A strong, relaxed body is more ready to deal with stress.

Exercise helps to ease the effects of stress. At the same time, it builds up your body so you can deal with more stress.

Here are good ways to deal with stress. Be realistic about what you can and cannot do, and don't expect to win all the time. Try to plan your time so you don't need to hurry. Also, find friends who make you feel comfortable. Another way to fight stress is to learn how to deal with conflicts. Remember to eat a balanced diet and get lots of exercise.

Skills Practice

Look back at the list you made from the Skills Practice on page 70. Add any more changes that you can think of. Then write a sentence about how you could deal with each of these changes going on in your life.

No one can escape change or stress. They are part of life. However, being able to handle change and stress is a sign that you are ready to live independently.

Decisions, Decisions!

Read the situation below. Then follow the steps to wise decision making to help Tom decide what to do.

Tom's relatives always eat dinner together on Thanksgiving. However, this Thanksgiving, Tom's ski club will have its first trip. The group will leave Thanksgiving morning and return on Sunday. Tom's best friends are going on the trip. This would also be his chance to learn to ski. At the same time, Tom's Aunt Ellen will be driving 300 miles to be with the family at Thanksgiving. He has not seen her for a year.

On a separate sheet of paper, follow the steps below to help Tom decide what to do.

Step 1: Identify the decision Tom must make.

Step 2: List Tom's choices.

Step 3: Cross out any choices that are harmful or might be against Tom's beliefs.

Step 4: Think about the possible results of the remaining choices.

Step 5: Select the best choice.

Step 6: Explain how Tom would carry out that choice.

Step 7: Describe the possible results of Tom's choice.

Chapter Review

Chapter Summary

1. Teenagers face physical, emotional, social, and mental changes. These changes can be confusing. Still, they are normal and natural.

2. Families also face changes. They may gain or lose members. Family members may have health problems or lose their jobs.

3. Teenagers can deal with family changes by accepting them. They should set limits on how much they can help their families.

4. Many teenagers want to make their own decisions. However, they need to be responsible first. Parents need to realize when young people are ready to make decisions.

5. A community might change by gaining or losing residents. These changes may affect local jobs and school conditions.

6. Causes of stress include dealing with change, expecting too much of yourself, and hurrying. Other causes are wanting to fit in and arguing with others. Eating the wrong foods and not getting enough exercise can make stress worse.

7. To handle stress, teenagers should be realistic about what they can do. They should plan their time and find friends with whom they feel comfortable. Good communication skills can help them deal with conflicts. Eating right and exercising can also help.

Chapter Quiz

Answer these questions on a separate sheet of paper.

1. What are three physical changes teenagers face?

2. What is the term for the chemicals in our bodies that can cause changes in our feelings?

3. Why does belonging to a group keep some young people from learning how to make wise decisions?

4. Why is a 15-year-old usually better at solving problems than a 5-year-old?

5. Carly's parents have adopted a 6-year-old boy. How might this change in her family affect Carly?

6. Bob's parents have just gotten a divorce. Bob and his brother live with his dad. His dad expects Bob to watch his brother every day after school. Bob has missed many soccer practices. The coach may kick him off the team. What should Bob do?

7. Bernard keeps cutting classes. Still, he can't understand why his parents won't let him stay out later on weekends. Why do you think Bernard's parents are so strict about when he should be home?

8. A big company is building a factory in your town. How might this factory affect you, even if you don't work there?

9. What are three causes of stress?

10. What are three ways to cut down on the stress in your life?

Putting Skills to Work

Your cousin Jenny has written to you. Her grandmother is moving in with the family. Her grandmother will take Jenny's room. Jenny will have to share a room with her little sister. Jenny is very upset about this change in her family. On a separate sheet of paper, write to your cousin. Give her some advice about what she should or should not do.

Skills Issues

Kathleen is 16 years old now and wants to get her driver's license. However, her parents want her to wait another year. Kathleen wants to show her parents she is responsible enough to get her license. On a separate sheet of paper, list some things Kathleen could do.

Unit Two Review

Answer these questions on a separate sheet of paper.

1. How can peer pressure be helpful?

2. Some young people do what their friends do, even when they know it is wrong. Why does this happen?

3. What are three ways to show that you are listening to someone?

4. A new friend does not look at you when you are speaking. Is this friend not interested in what you have to say? Explain your answer.

5. Shelly got a new sweater for her birthday. Nanci thinks Shelly should lend the sweater to her. However, Shelly has a different point of view. Explain what that might be.

6. Carlos told everyone that Mark failed the math test. Mark is embarrassed. Write an "I message" that he could give to Carlos.

7. Jody laughed when Lisa missed a serve during volleyball. Write a thought that would cause Lisa to feel angry. Then write a thought that would help Lisa feel calm.

8. Teenagers face changes in their bodies, emotions, relationships, and thinking patterns. Which type of change do you think bothers teenagers most? Why?

9. Frank's parents plan to move the family to another state. Frank has been trying to talk them out of moving. How could Frank cut down on the stress in his life?

10. Meg tries to get top grades but had trouble with a math test this morning. She is worried that her friend Tanya got a better grade on the test. How can Meg cut down on the stress in her life?

Your Health and Safety

Chapter 7
Staying Healthy on Your Own

Getting regular exercise is an important part of staying healthy. Physical activities, such as sports and dancing, are great ways to stay in shape and have fun.

Chapter Learning Objectives

- Describe a healthful diet.
- Identify the type of exercise that keeps you fit.
- Explain how alcohol, tobacco, and other drugs can be harmful.
- List ways to keep the body clean.
- Describe how to avoid dangerous situations.

Words to Know

diet   everything that a person eats or drinks regularly

balanced diet   foods that provide your body with what it needs to stay healthy

serving   the amount of a certain food usually eaten at one time

prepared food   food that is treated in some way so it will last longer

ingredients   the parts of a mixture; what things are in a packaged food

nutrition   the process of taking food into your body and using it for energy and growth

nutrients   what is in food that the body needs to grow and stay healthy

calories   units that measure the amount of energy your body gets from food

vitamins   types of nutrients your body needs to stay healthy; examples include Vitamins A, E, and D

aerobic exercise   an activity of 20 minutes or more that makes the heart work harder

addiction   physical dependence on a drug

germs   tiny life forms that can cause disease

risk   a chance that something harmful might happen

Read this story about a busy teen. Sometimes he just grabs whatever is handy to eat and rushes off.

Mark came home and dropped his backpack on the kitchen floor. His parents were still at work. He was hungry, and he was running late. It was 5:45. Shirley and her mom would pick him up in five minutes for their Community Youth Group meeting. Mark wrote a quick note.

"Mom–Soccer practice ran late. See you around 8:00 tonight. Mark." He grabbed a cookie, some potato chips, and a can of soda. Then he went to watch for his ride.

Mark had a busy day. Because he was so busy, he had a snack instead of dinner. The snack he had did not give his body enough of the things it needs to work properly. He may feel tired later.

Healthful Food

Think about the snacks that Mark chose when he was in a hurry. He might have chosen a cup of yogurt, a handful of wheat crackers, and some orange juice. Instead he chose a cookie, potato chips, and soda.

Your **diet** is everything that you eat and drink regularly. A **balanced diet** provides all the foods that

Use the food pyramid to ▼ help you choose a balanced diet

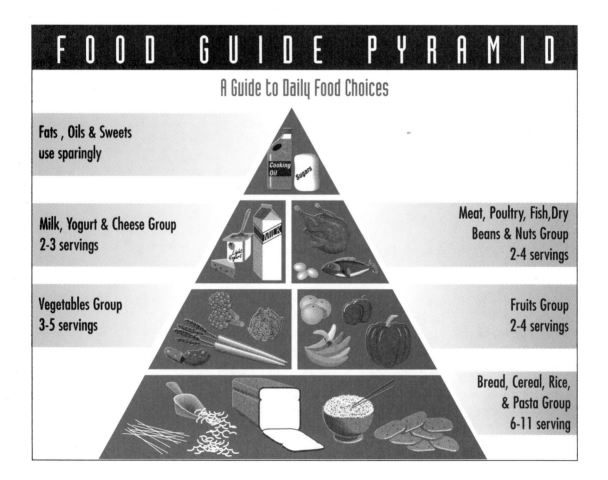

FOOD GUIDE PYRAMID

A Guide to Daily Food Choices

Fats, Oils & Sweets use sparingly

Milk, Yogurt & Cheese Group
2-3 servings

Meat, Poultry, Fish, Dry Beans & Nuts Group
2-4 servings

Vegetables Group
3-5 servings

Fruits Group
2-4 servings

Bread, Cereal, Rice, & Pasta Group
6-11 serving

the body needs to stay healthy. Everyone needs a balanced diet.

Look at the Food Guide Pyramid on page 88. It divides foods into food groups. It explains how many servings you should eat from each food group every day to have a balanced diet. A **serving** is the amount of a food usually eaten at one time. Notice that you should eat more of the foods at the bottom of the pyramid each day. You should eat less of the food group at the top.

Mark's cookie, potato chips, and soda all fit in the Fats, Oils, and Sweets group. Yogurt would have been a better choice for Mark. It fits into the Milk, Yogurt, and Cheese group. Crackers would fit into the Bread, Cereal, Rice, and Pasta group. Orange juice would fit into the Vegetables and Fruits group. Those choices would have helped Mark eat a balanced diet for that day.

Skills Practice

Name the food group that each of these foods belongs to: carrots, rice, chicken, cornflakes, grapes, frozen yogurt. Name three food groups found in a turkey breast sandwich with lettuce, tomato and mayonnaise on whole wheat bread.

Food Shopping

When you shop, you can choose foods that are fresh or ones that are prepared. Fresh fruits and vegetables are usually the most healthful. These foods only stay fresh for a few days.

A **prepared food** is treated in some way so that it will last longer. Prepared foods may be dried, smoked, cooked or have chemicals added to them.

Prepared foods have package labels. The package label lists what is in the food, or the **ingredients**. The ingredients are listed in order of the amounts present.

Read the labels of ▶
packaged food to
find out the ingredients
they contain.

INGREDIENTS: WATER, LENTILS, CELERY, SPINACH, TOMATO PASTE, DEHYDRATED ONIONS, SALT, OLIVE OIL, SPICE.

READY TO SERVE

Let's say the items listed on a package of trail mix are raisins, bananas, coconut, almonds, and apricots. That means the trail mix contains more raisins than anything else and more bananas than coconut.

Most prepared foods are mixtures, so the ingredients are parts of the mixture. Ingredients added to foods can be things such as sugar, salt, and spices. Some foods also might have chemicals added that will make the food spoil less quickly.

Skills Practice

Read the label on the can of soup shown above. What three ingredients make up the largest amounts in the soup?

Nutrition Facts Labels

Prepared foods also have Nutrition Facts labels on their packages. **Nutrition** is the process of taking food into your body and using it for energy and growth. A Nutrition Facts label lists some nutrients in the food.

Nutrients are the parts of food that the body needs to grow and stay healthy. Some nutrients you might find on a food label are:

- Fats (solid fats or oils) which are needed in small amounts for growth and to repair body cells
- Carbohydrates (sugars and starch) which are needed to give your body energy
- Proteins which are needed for growth and to repair cells
- Calcium which is needed for strong bones and teeth
- Iron which is needed to keep your red blood cells working
- Sodium (part of table salt) that controls water balance in your body
- Vitamin A which is needed for good vision at night
- Vitamin C which is needed for healthy gums, teeth, and bones
- Water (all foods contain some water) which is needed to keep your whole body working properly

The Nutrition Facts label tells you the amount of each serving, or serving size. It also tells you how many servings are in the package. Some of the things on the label are:

- *Calories* tells how many calories are in each serving. **Calories** are units that measure the amount of energy your body gets from food.

- *Calories from Fat* tells how many calories in a serving are from fat. A healthful diet is low in fat.

- *Total Fat* tells how many grams of fat are in a serving. One gram of fat is about 9 calories. If the label says the Total Fat is 4g, that means you get 9 x 4 or 36 calories per serving from fat. For a balanced diet, you need only a little fat. The lower the number of grams of fat, the better.

Nutrition Facts	
Serving Size 1 cup (239G)	
Servings Per Container 2	
Amount Per Serving	
Calories 90 Calories from Fat 20	
% Daily Value*	
Total Fat 2g	**3%**
Saturated Fat 1g	**3%**
Polyunsaturated 0g	
Monounsaturated 1g	
Cholesterol 20mg	**7%**
Sodium 870mg	**36%**
Total Carbohydrate 13g	**4%**
Dietary Fiber 2g	**8%**
Sugars 0g	
Protein 6g	
Vitamin A 30% · Vitamin C 0g%	
Calcium 2% · Iron 4%	
* Percent Daily Values are based on a 2,000 calorie per day diet	

HOME

CHICKEN &

WILD RI

MADE WITH 100% CHIC

Check the nutrition facts ▲ on prepared foods before you buy them. Try to avoid foods that are high in fat and sodium.

Skills Practice

Answer these questions about the Nutrition Facts label above. Use a separate piece of paper.

1. What is the serving size of the soup?
2. How many calories are in one serving of soup?
3. How many calories are from fat in one serving?

Preparing Fresh Foods

The way you prepare food can change how healthful it is for you. Frying takes away some vitamins and adds fat. If you boil vegetables in a pan full of water, you may destroy some **vitamins**, or they may come out of the vegetable and into the water. Vitamins are types of nutrients your body needs to stay healthy. The most healthful way to cook any vegetable is to steam them.

To steam vegetables, add about half an inch of water to a pan. Bring the water to a boil. Then add the vegetables. Cover the pan and cook for a few minutes. You can buy a special basket called a steamer that will keep food out of the water while it cooks.

Exercising to Stay Fit

Exercise is important for staying healthy. You have more energy when you get regular exercise. Energy lets you think clearly and act quickly.

Exercise also helps people control their weight. People who take in more calories than they burn will

◀ Fresh vegetables are an essential part of a balanced diet. You can find a wide variety of fresh vegetables in the supermarket and some smaller grocery stores.

gain weight. Exercise burns calories, so it can prevent weight gain or help a person lose weight.

The best kind of exercise that makes you fit is **aerobic exercise**. It is an activity that makes the heart work harder. Aerobic exercise helps strengthen the heart and blood system. In order for an exercise to be aerobic, it should be done for at least 20 minutes at a time. You should do aerobic exercises at least three times a week. Running, bicycling, jumping rope, and dancing are good aerobic activities.

You can turn a daily activity into an aerobic exercise. For example, when you need to go somewhere, walk or ride a bike instead of riding in a car. If you walk a dog, walk fast, run, or jog part of the way.

For your aerobic workouts, choose activities that you enjoy doing. That way you won't get bored.

Skills Practice

Work with a partner. Replace each snack listed below with one that would be more healthful. Then replace each activity with one that would make you more fit. Write your ideas on a separate piece of paper.

Snacks: potato chips, candy bar, cookies, and soda.

Activities: reading a magazine, watching TV, playing computer games.

Alcohol, Tobacco, and Other Drugs

Now that you know how to choose healthful foods to put into your body, you also need to know what to keep out of your body. Alcohol, tobacco, and other drugs can harm your body. It is important to avoid them.

Certain drugs can help treat or cure diseases if the drugs are used correctly. However, all drugs can be dangerous if they are used incorrectly. You must follow the directions that come with the medicine. You should never take someone else's medicine. A drug that helps one person could harm someone else.

Any drug changes the way your brain and body work. Always follow the directions on a label of a drug you buy at a store or any one that is given to you by a doctor.

You should never take illegal drugs. Drugs can harm your body's organs very quickly. You may become very ill. Drugs also damage the body in ways that will not show up until later in life.

Driving a car after drinking or using other drugs is also very dangerous. You could have a serious accident. You could hurt yourself or someone else. Remember that alcohol is also a drug.

Using illegal drugs or misusing drugs you've bought at a store can become a habit. After a while, that habit can become an **addiction**. Addiction is a physical dependence on a drug. The drug can be alcohol, tobacco, or another drug. Drug abuse can lead to crime, serious illness, and even death.

One harmful habit that leads to addiction is smoking. Smoking cigarettes is the most common way people use tobacco. Smoking can cause lung cancer. Smoking can also cause heart disease and a lung disease called emphysema. Both of these diseases cause a slow death. Non-smokers can get the same diseases by breathing smoke in the air.

Some people use smokeless tobacco. Two kinds of smokeless tobacco are chewing tobacco and snuff. People can get cancer of the mouth from smokeless tobacco.

Saying "No"

You know that using drugs can lead to addiction. Think about why people begin using drugs. Many teens try cigarettes, alcohol, or other drugs because people tell them they should. Some people might pressure you and make you feel that you are not cool or part of their group if you don't try what they suggest.

Learning to resist peer pressure helps you carry out your decision not to use drugs. Making your own decision ahead of time will make resisting peer pressure easier. If people are your friends, they will want you to make your own decisions. They will also respect your decisions.

Some teens try different drugs because they think it will make them feel good. They make think smoking, drinking, or using other drugs will make them look or feel more grown up. Or they may use drugs to try to escape from problems. But using drugs usually makes problems worse. Drug use also causes new problems.

It is important to learn to say "No" each time you are offered cigarettes, alcohol, or drugs. It doesn't have to be hard to refuse drugs. It just takes confidence.

When someone offers you a drug, it may help to remember a few facts. Alcohol kills more teens every year than any other drug. Use of illegal drugs can kill the user at any time.

Practicing saying "No" can be helpful. Say it over and over in your mind. Practice with a friend or family member. Here are some other ways teens say "No":

- No, I don't drink (or do drugs, or smoke).
- No, I'm allergic to smoke.
- NO WAY!
- No, I work hard to stay healthy.
- I promised my (father, friend, sister, self) I would stay away from drugs.

Think of other ways to say "No" to drugs, alcohol, or cigarettes.

Skills Practice

Imagine that you have to write a warning for teens about the problems of alcohol. Write your warning on another sheet of paper.

Keeping Your Body Clean

Good health means avoiding drugs that can harm your body. Good health means choosing foods that your body needs to grow and stay healthy. Good health also means taking care of your body. One way to take care of your body is to keep it clean. Being clean helps you look and feel your best. It also helps prevent diseases. Some **germs** carry disease. Germs are tiny life forms that are always in the air.

Hands may look clean but still carry germs. The main way that germs get into your body is from your hands. When you put your hands near your mouth, nose, or eyes, germs that you can't see can get into the body. For example, you can get a cold by shaking hands with someone who has a cold and then rubbing your eyes or nose.

You can get germs on your hands from touching things handled by other people.

Washing your hands with soap and water gets rid of most germs. Washing your hair keeps your hair and scalp clean. Baths or showers also wash away most germs. When germs and sweat combine, they cause odor. Deodorant helps to stop that body odor.

Teen bodies change. Extra oil may cause skin or scalp problems, such as acne or dandruff. You can choose a soap, shampoo, and deodorant that work best to handle those changes.

Your teeth and gums also need daily cleaning. Brushing after meals and at bedtime will help keep your teeth clean. Brushing is important to remove germs that cause tooth decay. Brushing will also help prevent bad breath.

Dental floss reaches places between teeth and gums that a toothbrush can't reach. Tooth decay often starts between teeth near the gums. Keeping teeth clean is the best way to keep teeth and gums healthy.

Skills Practice

On a separate sheet of paper, write a sentence describing how each of these items can help you keep your body clean and why it is important: soap, shampoo, deodorant, toothpaste, dental floss.

Protecting Yourself

Even when you take good care of your body, you need to protect yourself from other risks to your health. A **risk** is a chance that something harmful might happen. The best way to avoid risks is to be aware of what is around you. Get in the habit of taking a few seconds to think before you act. Ask yourself if you are in a dangerous situation. Decide if the situation could become dangerous. If your answer is yes to either situation, remove yourself from that situation.

Know what to do when you feel you are in danger. Know how to avoid danger or at least how to get away from a dangerous situation. Stay away from dark or empty places. For example, avoid walking in a dark parking lot late at night. When walking, stay on public roads. If you see someone you think might be dangerous, act on your feelings and avoid the person. Remember to trust your judgment. Listen to your feelings.

If you think someone is following you home, don't go to your home. Go to a police station, fire station, nearby business, or other public place filled with people. If you are driving and someone starts following you, drive into a public place where there are many people. Remember to keep your car doors locked.

It is important to protect yourself from people who could hurt you. Never ride with a driver who has been drinking or taking drugs. Never get into a car with a stranger. Make sure to never let a stranger into your home. You don't have to answer your door if you don't want to. If someone is at your door and will not leave, call the police.

Another way to keep safe is to avoid giving any personal information to someone who calls on the phone. Do not let a caller know if you are alone. If you plan to go away overnight and no one will be at home, ask your neighbors or friends to help watch your home. Have them take in your mail or pick up your newspaper. Don't let it look as if your apartment or house is empty.

By following the hints above, you can help keep yourself safe and reduce the risks of becoming a victim of crime.

Decisions, Decisions!

Read the story below about a teen named Jake.

It was late one evening and Jake was home alone. Jake heard a loud knock at his door.

"Please let me use the phone," a woman's voice called through the door. "My car broke down." She sounded scared.

Jake had a problem. He didn't want to refuse help to someone in need. But he knew he should never open his door to a stranger. He had to think carefully. How could he help the woman and protect himself from danger?

On a separate sheet of paper, follow the steps below to help Jake make a wise decision.

Step 1: Identify the decision Jake must make.

Step 2: List Jake's choices.

Step 3: Cross out any choices that are harmful or might be against Jake's beliefs.

Step 4: Think about the possible results of the remaining choices.

Step 5: Select the best choice.

Step 6: Explain how Jake would carry out his choice.

Step 7: Describe the possible results of Jake's choice.

Chapter Review

Chapter Summary

1. For good health, eat a balanced diet. The Food Guide Pyramid and the Nutrition Facts labels on food packages can help you choose healthful foods.

2. Aerobic exercise is very helpful for staying fit. It makes the heart work more so that more blood and oxygen reach the different parts of the body.

3. Part of being healthy is to avoid using alcohol, tobacco, and other drugs. The use of a drug can become a harmful addiction, which can ruin or end your life.

4. Keeping your body clean can help remove germs that cause disease. Being clean also makes people look good and feel good.

5. Taking care of your health includes staying away from danger. It is important to know how to avoid dangerous situations.

Chapter Quiz

Write your answers on a separate piece of paper.

1. Describe a balanced diet.

2. What part of a food package should you read to find out if the food is healthful?

3. What is one difference between fresh foods and prepared foods?

4. What is the most healthful way to cook vegetables?

5. Describe one of the best types of exercises for staying fit.

6. Name two reasons to exercise.

7. What should you do when another person offers you tobacco, alcohol, or other drugs?

8. How can alcohol, tobacco, and other drugs cause harm?

9. Why is keeping clean important?

10. List three ways to avoid dangerous situations.

Putting Skills to Work

Make a list of all of the foods you eat during a day. Then look over your list to check for healthfulness. Turn to the Food Guide Pyramid on page 88. Compare what you ate to the suggestions there. Ask yourself these questions:

1. How did the number of servings I ate from each food group compare to the suggestions on the Food Guide Pyramid?

2. Did I make sensible choices each time I picked something to eat?

3. What could I have chosen that would have been healthier?

Skills Issues

In most states, the use of alcohol by persons under the age of 21 is against the law. What do you think of this law? Discuss your opinion with a partner. Then share your ideas with the class.

Chapter 8

Getting Help with Your Health

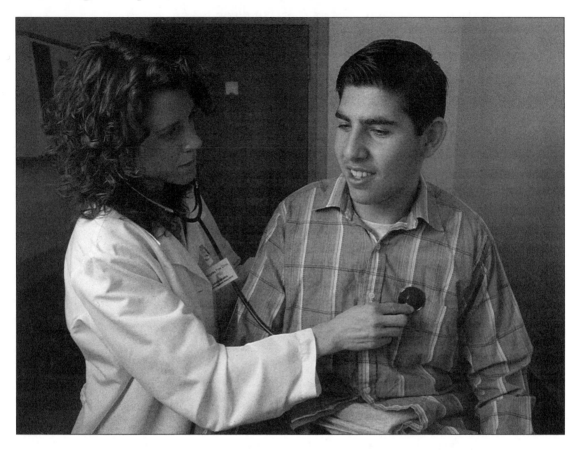

Getting regular checkups by your doctor and dentist can help prevent health problems later.

Chapter Learning Objectives

- Define doctors, patients, and specialists.
- Describe how to choose a doctor.
- Explain the advantages of checkups.
- Describe what happens during a checkup.
- Tell what to do before taking any medicine.
- Explain why health insurance is important.

Words to Know

doctors   people trained and licensed to treat diseases and disorders

patient   person under the care of a doctor

specialists   doctors who treat only certain diseases or disorders

cavity   a hole in a tooth caused by decay

medical license   a document that gives a person the right to give health care

appointment   a set time to meet someone or do something

symptom   a sign of illness or disorder

blood pressure   the push of the blood as it moves through the body

prescription   medicine ordered by a doctor

pharmacist   a person who prepares and gives out medicines according to a doctor's orders

health insurance   a plan that helps you pay for health costs

over-the-counter medicines   medicines people can buy without a doctor's order; nonprescription drugs

ambulance   a special van driven by people trained to help anyone who is sick or hurt; transports sick or hurt people to hospitals

emergency   a situation that needs to be taken care of quickly

treat   work to cure or relieve a disease or disorder

Sometimes you might feel that something isn't quite right with a part of your body. Perhaps, like Arlene in the story below, you have a problem with your teeth.

Arlene and Meghan were walking home from the library one day. "Let's stop at the store and get some frozen yogurt," said Meghan. "We can eat it on the way home." Arlene shook her head. "No," she said. "I don't want any."

Meghan was surprised. "I thought you loved frozen yogurt," she said.

"I do," said Arlene. "But it makes my teeth hurt."

"What does your dentist say?" asked Meghan.

"I don't know," Arlene answered. "I haven't been to the dentist in a long time.

"You should. Your teeth shouldn't hurt like that. Maybe you have a cavity or something. You don't want to end up having to get a tooth pulled, do you?"

"No, you're right. I should see my dentist."

Doctors

Doctors are people trained and licensed to treat diseases and disorders. There are many kinds of doctors. Some are called general practitioners or family doctors. They can take care of most of your basic health needs. Doctors who treat only certain diseases or disorders are called **specialists**. For example, an orthopedist treats the bones, joints, and muscles. An optometrist checks eyesight and fits glasses on patients who need them.

A dentist cares for the health of teeth and gums. Think back to Arlene's tooth problem. She said frozen yogurt made her teeth hurt. Meghan thought she might have a cavity. A **cavity** is a hole in a tooth caused by decay. If you have a cavity, you need to see a dentist to get a filling. This can prevent the loss of a tooth.

Choosing a Doctor

To find a family doctor, ask family and friends who their doctor is. Another way to find a doctor is to call a local hospital or medical society. Someone there can give you names of doctors near you. If you move, your old doctors may be able to help you find a new one. If you need a specialist, ask your doctor to recommend someone.

Before you choose a new doctor, find out if he or she has a medical license. A **medical license** gives a person the right to give health care. Never go to a doctor or other health care worker who doesn't have a license.

Your doctor and any people who work in that doctor's office should be friendly and helpful. It's important to get complete and helpful answers to your questions.

Another important point to think about when choosing a doctor is how easy it is to visit the office. If the office is far away, it might be difficult for you to travel there.

You also want it to be easy to make an **appointment** with the doctor. An appointment is a set time to meet someone or do something. If you are sick, you want an appointment soon.

Finally, when shopping for a doctor, think about how that doctor wants to be paid. Some doctors want to be paid right away. Others will send you a bill or send a bill to your medical insurer.

Skills Practice

Imagine you are moving to a new town. You will need a new family doctor. Write a list of questions to ask when you first call the new doctor.

Checkups

Most people go to a doctor when they are sick or hurt. However, people should also go to the doctor when they are well. Regular physical examinations, or checkups, help people stay healthy. Checkups can catch illness early. Many times, doctors find illness before a person sees or feels any symptoms. A **symptom** is a sign of illness or disorder. For example, a sore throat is a symptom of a cold, the flu, or strep throat.

Finding an illness early can mean it will take less time to get well, or cured. Some diseases can be cured only if they are found before the **patient**, or person under the care of the doctor, has any symptoms. For example, many kinds of cancer can be cured if they are found early.

Getting a Checkup

When you go for a physical exam, or checkup, the doctor may start by asking you questions. You might be asked if you are eating right or if you get enough exercise and rest. The doctor will ask if you have any symptoms or if there is anything you want to ask or discuss.

The doctor will examine your eyes, ears, throat, heart, lungs, and reflexes. The doctor may also check to see if the other parts of your body look and feel okay.

During a checkup, your doctor also checks your **blood pressure**. Blood pressure is the push of the blood as it moves through your body.

The doctor uses a machine to check your blood pressure. A blood pressure machine looks like a band around your arm that is attached to a plastic tube and ball.

If your pressure is too high, it can be harmful to your body. A person cannot feel if they have high blood pressure. The only way to tell if blood pressure is normal is to check it. Doctors can **treat**, or work to cure or relieve, high blood pressure before the patient has any problems.

During your checkup the doctor will also take a little of your blood. You will be asked to give a sample of your urine in a cup to a nurse. The office sends the blood and urine to a lab for tests. Your doctor can tell a lot about your health from lab tests.

At the end of your checkup, the doctor will talk to you about it. This is a good time to ask the doctor any questions you have about the checkup or your health. Usually, you need to call the office later to get your lab test results. If all goes well, you do not have to return to the office for another year.

A symptom is a sign of an illness. It is not the illness itself. Remember to carefully explain all of your symptoms to your doctor during a visit.

If you have any symptoms of an illness, the doctor may order more tests. Suppose the tests show you have an illness. The doctor will explain to you what kind of treatment you need.

Medicines

If you are sick or hurt, your doctor may write a **prescription**, which is an order for medicine on a special slip of paper. You take the prescription to a drugstore. At the drugstore a **pharmacist** prepares and gives out the medicine that the doctor ordered for you. Medicines that a doctor orders are called prescription medicines.

All medicines come with directions on how to take them. The directions explain how much medicine to take and when to take it. Directions will be on the bottle or on a piece of paper that comes with the medicine.

Some medicine directions may say "Take with food." That means you should take the medicine when you eat. Always follow the directions from the doctor or on the medicine package. If you don't, the medicine will not work the way it should and you may be harmed.

People can buy some types of medicines without a doctor's order. These medicines include aspirin and cough medicine. They are called **over-the-counter medicines**. Treat these medicines the same as prescription medicines.

▼ *The bottle on the left is an over-the-counter medicine. The box on the right is a prescription medicine. Be sure to read all the directions on any medicine package.*

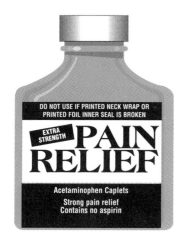

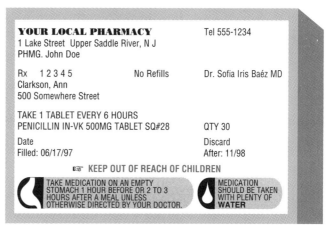

YOUR LOCAL PHARMACY
1 Lake Street Upper Saddle River, N J
PHMG. John Doe

Tel 555-1234

Rx   1 2 3 4 5   No Refills   Dr. Sofia Iris Baéz MD
Clarkson, Ann
500 Somewhere Street

TAKE 1 TABLET EVERY 6 HOURS
PENICILLIN IN-VK 500MG TABLET SQ#28   QTY 30

Date   Discard
Filled: 06/17/97   After: 11/98

☞ KEEP OUT OF REACH OF CHILDREN

TAKE MEDICATION ON AN EMPTY STOMACH 1 HOUR BEFORE OR 2 TO 3 HOURS AFTER A MEAL UNLESS OTHERWISE DIRECTED BY YOUR DOCTOR.

MEDICATION SHOULD BE TAKEN WITH PLENTY OF **WATER**

DO NOT USE IF PRINTED NECK WRAP OR PRINTED FOIL INNER SEAL IS BROKEN

EXTRA STRENGTH **PAIN RELIEF**

Acetaminophen Caplets
Strong pain relief
Contains no aspirin

Read everything on any medicine package. Notice if it says "EXP." followed by a date. EXP is short for *expires*. After a medicine has expired, it should not be used. If the seal is broken or is not there when you buy it, don't take the medicine.

Both prescription medicines and over-the-counter medicines may have WARNING labels. They explain important facts you need to know. Be sure to read and follow the warnings. It is also important that you never take two different medicines at the same time unless your doctor tells you to. If you have questions about a medicine, call your doctor or pharmacist. They can answer your questions.

Skills Practice

The directions below came from medicine packages. Use a separate sheet of paper to write each one again in your own words. Make a check mark by each one that you think is a warning.

- Keep out of reach of children.
- May cause drowsiness.
- Keep refrigerated.

Getting Care When Sick or Hurt

If you are sick or hurt, you should call a doctor. If possible, call the doctor that you see for your checkups. The doctor will tell you what to do over the telephone.

If you are very sick or badly hurt, the doctor may tell you to go to a hospital. If you can't reach your doctor, don't wait. Go to a hospital. If you are very hurt and can't get to a hospital on your own, telephone for an **ambulance**. An ambulance is a special van driven by people trained to help anyone who is sick or hurt. They can take you to a hospital.

Hospitals are always open. Hospitals have doctors, nurses, and equipment to handle emergencies. An

emergency is a situation that needs to be taken care of quickly. Emergency rooms are where hospitals handle emergencies.

Be prepared when you call or go to a hospital emergency room. Give as much information as you can. You will need to give a doctor or nurse your name, birthdate, and reason for coming to the hospital. You will also need to explain your symptoms and any medicines you might be taking. You will be asked many questions. You need to work with the doctors and nurses so that they know how to help you.

Understanding Health Insurance

Imagine you've cut your hand badly on broken glass. You go to the emergency room at the hospital. A doctor says you need stitches to close the cut and it will cost $250. Like many people, you probably are not prepared to pay $250 on your own. But if you have **health insurance**, it will probably pay for all or most of the cost. Health insurance is a plan that helps you pay for health costs. Having insurance is called being covered.

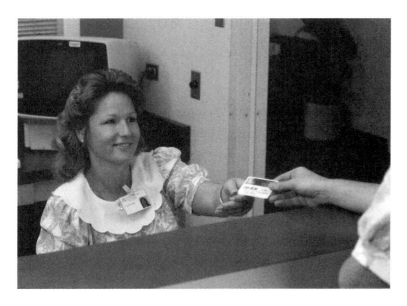

◀ *Your health insurance company may send you an insurance card as proof of membership. Take this card with you when you go to the doctor or dentist.*

When you work full time, you may have insurance through your employer. Your employer pays a set amount to an insurance company for you and other workers each month. This is called group insurance. You and your employer might share the cost of your health insurance.

If you do not have group insurance, you need an individual policy. Then you would pay the set amount of money each month to the insurance company yourself. You need to know what you are covered for if you have health insurance. Health care is very expensive. That is why it is important to have health insurance.

Shopping for Health Insurance

Health insurance plans can differ. Shop around for a plan that works best for you. Talk to your employer or an insurance agent. You can also call the insurance company and ask questions. Find out the total cost of each insurance plan for a year. Find out how you can pay it. Sometimes you pay every month or every two months. You might also have to pay something for each doctor's visit and your prescriptions.

If you need to stay in a hospital, find out if you have to pay part of the cost of your care. The insurance company will probably pay for most of it. Another important point to ask is if you can choose your own doctor. Some insurance groups have a list of doctors. Those insurance companies will only pay when you see doctors on their list. You might be more comfortable with another doctor.

If you buy an individual insurance policy, you may have an insurance agent. Make sure your insurance agent is helpful. You are paying for a service with your policy. You should be satisfied with the service.

When you are insured, you get an insurance card to carry with you at all times. Doctors and hospitals will ask to see your insurance card if you need health care. You might also have a separate card to use to buy your prescriptions.

If you do not have insurance, the doctor's office or hospital will explain the costs. You may have to pay before they will help you. Some doctors or hospitals won't accept you if you do not have health insurance.

The best thing about health insurance is that you are covered for emergencies and expensive health costs. Being able to choose health insurance is another skill that will help you live independently.

Decisions, Decisions!

Leonard just moved to a new town. One night, he fell down the stairs in his new house. His leg hurt a lot! He thought it might be broken. Leonard had no doctor. He did not know anyone in his new town. He tried to stand, but he fell again. Leonard was in pain.

What should Leonard do?

On a separate sheet of paper, follow the steps below to help Leonard make a wise decision.

Step 1: Identify the decision Leonard must make.

Step 2: List Leonard's choices.

Step 3: Cross out any choices that are harmful or might be against Leonard's beliefs.

Step 4: Think about the possible results of the remaining choices.

Step 5: Select the best choice.

Step 6: Explain how Leonard would carry out this choice.

Step 7: Describe the possible results of Leonard's choice.

Chapter Review

Chapter Summary

1. Doctors take care of people's health needs. Specialists take care of patients with certain problems.

2. One way to find a doctor is to ask someone you trust to suggest a doctor.

3. Physical examinations or checkups help people to stay healthy. Doctors may find diseases early with checkups.

4. In a checkup, the doctor examines the patient. Different tests may be carried out.

5. Only doctors can order prescription medicines to treat illnesses. People buy over-the-counter medicines without prescriptions. Always follow directions for using any medicine.

6. Health insurance helps people pay their doctor and hospital bills. Insurance buyers can shop for the insurance plan that meets their needs.

Chapter Quiz

Answer the following questions on a separate piece of paper.

1. Name three kinds of doctors.

2. What are some ways to find a doctor?

3. List four things to find out about a new doctor.

4. What is a checkup? What is one advantage of having checkups?

5. What are some of the things a doctor might do during a checkup?

6. Define symptom; then name two symptoms.

7. Explain what prescription medicines and over-the-counter medicines are.

8. What should you do before taking any medicine?

9. What is a pharmacist?

10. What is health insurance?

11. How does health insurance help you?

12. What are four questions to ask when shopping for health insurance?

Putting Skills to Work

Look under "Insurance" in the Yellow Pages. List words and phrases used to advertise insurance. How do the ads help you think about what to consider when choosing insurance? Share your ideas with the rest of the class.

Skills Issues

One night two friends named Deanna and Charlotte ate dinner in a small restaurant. An hour later, they both became sick. They had food poisoning. They were on vacation so they were far from home. The friends decided to go to the emergency room at a local hospital. Deanna had health insurance. Charlotte did not have health insurance.

Finish the story by describing what might have happened to each of these friends. Write your story endings on a separate piece of paper. Then read your story endings to the class.

Chapter 9

Staying Safe

Smoke detectors give off a warning sound when they sense smoke. Each room of a house or apartment should have a smoke detector that works.

Chapter Learning Objectives

- Identify ways to make your home a safer place.
- Identify ways to be safer outside the home.
- Name things you can do that can help avoid accidents.
- Explain ways to prepare for emergencies.
- Describe how to find help in an emergency.

Words to Know

smoke detector a device that gives off a warning sound when it senses smoke

risk a chance that something harmful might happen

fumes gases given off by chemicals

emergency a situation that needs to be taken care of quickly

prepared ready

fire extinguisher a device used to spray special chemicals on a fire to put it out

Your home should be comfortable. It should also be safe. There are many ways to make a home safe. Read the story below about Joe and his friends' search for an apartment.

Joe is preparing to move. For two years, he has saved the money he earned working part-time jobs. Now he is going to move to an apartment. His three best friends will be his roommates.

Joe's telephone rang. It was Mike. "I found a great apartment! It has plenty of room. And it's the right price. Tell Carlo and Shawn and meet us there at 6:00 tonight." Mike gave Joe the address.

At 6:00 P.M., they all met at the apartment. The friends were all excited. This might be their new home. Joe, Mike, Shawn, and Carlo entered the apartment together.

As they looked around, they all began to smile. Mike had been right. The apartment met all of their needs.

"This place is great!" said Carlo. "Let's rent it before someone else does."

"I love it too, but I see one problem," Joe said. "There are no smoke detectors." A **smoke detector** is a device that gives off a warning sound when it senses smoke. If there is a fire at night, the sound is loud enough to wake people in time to escape.

"So what?" Shawn said. "We don't smoke."

"Yeah, we'll just be extra careful in the kitchen," said Carlo.

"Fires can start for lots of reasons and in a lot of places," said Joe. "There really should be smoke detectors here."

Mike turned to Joe. "Don't worry. We can go buy smoke detectors. We can install them ourselves."

Joe, Mike, Shawn, and Carlo are taking on new responsibilities. They are planning to live on their own. All four are learning to see **risks** around them for the first time. A risk is a chance that something harmful might happen. The friends saw that there was a risk of fire in their new home.

By agreeing to install the smoke detectors, Mike and Joe were proving that they were being responsible. Mike and Joe recognized the danger of fire. However, Shawn and Carlo were not thinking in a responsible manner.

Safety inside the Home

Most accidents happen in the home. The possibility of fire is just one kind of risk in an apartment or any home. Poison, electrical shock, cuts, and falls are other risks that could happen in the home. However, there are steps you can take to avoid each of those risks.

Be careful when cooking. Stay in the kitchen while you cook. Handle pots and pans carefully to avoid burning yourself. Grease from cooking can burn, so keep stoves clean. Always remember to turn off stoves, ovens, and heaters after use. Outdoor barbecues and indoor fireplaces should feel cool before you leave them or go to sleep.

Keep things that can burn away from space heaters and heating vents. Also be careful with matches. Don't throw away anything that is burning or very hot. Don't let anyone smoke in bed. And always use electrical products safely. All these things could start a fire in your home. Finally, be sure to install smoke detectors.

Poison is another danger around the home. Medicines can be poisons when misused. Soaps and other cleaning supplies can be poisons if you swallow them or breathe in the **fumes**. Fumes are gases given off by chemicals. Chemicals used for painting can also be poisons.

Make sure all medicines, cleaning supplies, and chemicals are out of the reach of children. Put them where they can't fall. Remember to keep poisons out of the reach of your pets.

Old or poorly made electric wiring can cause electrical shock or a fire. You can get shocked if electrical current flows through your body. Have worn or broken wires replaced. Check all wiring in the home. Check all of the electrical plugs. Plugs should fit tightly. There should not be too many plugs in one socket. To unplug an electrical cord, pull on the plug, not on the wire. Keep electrical products such as radios or hair dryers away from water. Don't touch them with wet hands. If you do, you could get shocked.

Many areas of the home are also risky spots for falls. For example, slippery floors and stairs are places where people might fall and get hurt. To prevent falls, keep objects off the floors and stairs. When you need to reach up high, stand on a stable ladder or step stool. Don't stand on a chair. Chairs can break or fall over. Wipe up water spills. Put away toys, sports equipment, and tools. Make sure all paths are clear. Don't wait until an accident happens in your home. Prevent falls now.

Broken glass, knives, and other sharp objects can cause cuts. To avoid cuts, clean up broken glass. Fix broken objects, and use knives carefully. Keep all sharp things away from children. Handle tools carefully. Follow all directions for the safe use of power tools.

Safety outside the Home

Accidents, injuries, and illness can also occur outside the home. Whether you are working or playing outdoors, you need to reduce the risks of being outdoors.

One rule of outdoor safety is to be aware of the weather. Tornadoes, thunderstorms, heatwaves, and snowstorms can't be prevented. But you can protect yourself by being prepared.

Don't stay outdoors during thunderstorms. Go indoors or get in a car if you see lightning. If you must be outside in very hot weather, cover your head and drink lots of water. In very cold weather, dress warmly and stay dry.

The snow and cold ▶
of winter allow for fun activities, such as skating and sledding. In very cold weather, be sure to dress warmly and stay dry.

You also need to stay safe when you walk, jog, skate, drive or ride your bicycle. One rule for all these forms of travel is to obey traffic lights and rules.

Walkers or joggers should always look both ways for traffic when crossing a street. Don't cross in the middle of a block. If you're out at night, wear reflectors on your clothing. Drivers need to see you to avoid hitting you.

Bicycle riders and skaters should wear safety equipment. Remember to ride or skate with the traffic, not facing it. Keep equipment in good working order. Have a bell or whistle to warn others on the road and look out for people on foot.

To be safe in a car, everyone must wear seatbelts. Never drink and drive. Don't ride with a driver who has been drinking. Also, try to talk someone out of drinking and driving. You could be saving a life.

Swimming and other water sports can also be dangerous. To enjoy the water safely, you need to know how to prevent drowning and other water accidents.

The first rule of water safety is to know how to swim. If you can't swim, then learn how at school or at a pool in your community. Always have a buddy with you when you swim.

Don't dive unless a swimming teacher has taught you how. At a pool, only dive in areas that are marked for diving. Be sure other swimmers are out of the way. Never dive into water at a lake or pond. The water could be too shallow. There might be rocks or tree stumps in the water. By following these rules, you can avoid head and neck injuries.

Boating is another water sport that you may enjoy. Even if you know how to swim, always wear a life jacket when in a boat. If the boat tips, you might have to stay afloat for a long time before help arrives. Don't stand up or move about in a small boat. It could tip over. Proper training before you steer or sail a boat is important.

Know and follow water traffic rules for the area where you are boating. Don't go boating with an operator who has been drinking alcohol. Remember, driving a car or a boat is a serious matter. A drunk driver could cause an accident.

Skills Practice

Think about everything you did yesterday. How many times did you see a risk? Make a list of the risky areas or things that you saw on a separate piece of paper. Then compare your list with a classmate's. What things are the same on both lists? What are some differences?

Being Prepared

You have learned about ways to lower the risks of some accidents inside and outside the home. Of course, no one can be ready for everything that will happen in life. But you can try to be **prepared** for what might happen. To be prepared is to be ready.

One way to prepare for any **emergency** is to make a list of important telephone numbers you may need to call. An emergency is a situation that needs to be taken care of quickly. The numbers are of places you can call for help. Place the list near all telephones. Include phone numbers for the police and fire departments.

Also include phone numbers for your doctor, police, fire department, a hospital, and a neighbor or relative who lives near you. Some other numbers you might include are: the local poison control center, a pharmacy, and an ambulance service.

One emergency you should prepare for is fire. Put smoke detectors in your home, as Mike and Joe did in their apartment at the beginning of this chapter. Smoke detectors should be placed in hallways and over stairs. When a smoke detector senses smoke, it sounds a loud

◀ *Be sure to plan for emergencies in your home. Map out escape routes for each room in case of a fire.*

alarm. It warns everyone in the home of danger. Many people don't notice a fire until it's too late to get out, especially if they are sleeping.

Keep **fire extinguishers** in your home. A fire extinguisher is a hand-held device that can put out a small fire. It works by spraying special chemicals on the fire. Fire extinguishers should be placed in the kitchen, garage, and on each floor of the house.

Plan a way for everyone to get out of the house safely in case of an emergency, especially a fire. Practice using it many times. Practice it in the dark. In an emergency, you may need to leave your home at night. The power might be off so that the lights are out. Stay low if there is smoke in the air. If possible, cover your nose and mouth with a wet towel. Crawl to safety, trying to avoid breathing the smoke.

Another important thing to plan for in case of an emergency is a meeting place. Plan a place to meet family or roommates outside the home. By meeting in one spot outside of the home, everyone can see if everyone else is safe. Someone in your home might need help getting out quickly. Make a plan to help that person.

The word *detect* means "to discover." What does a smoke detector do? The word *extinguish* means "to put out." What does a fire extinguisher do?

You might also have an emergency caused by a poison. There are many poisons in the home. They include cleaning materials and other household chemicals. These items should be kept in a locked cabinet. Poisons also include medicines that are misused. In case someone, many times a small child, swallows or inhales poison, call the poison control center. Get the number of the poison control center from your list of telephone numbers. You can also usually find the number in the front pages of the telephone book.

Call the center and explain what happened. Follow the directions given to you by the person at the center. Save the container of the poison that was swallowed or inhaled. You will need to give it to a medical worker when you go for help.

Sometimes water and gas pipes break or leak. It can happen in your home or in your neighborhood. A broken water pipe can cause flooding. Know how to turn off the water. Then call a plumber for help. Gas pipes can also break or leak. If you think you smell gas, leave the building quickly. Then call the gas company for help from a neighbor's phone.

Finding Help in an Emergency

If you are home in an emergency, use your telephone to get help. You can use a number from your prepared list.

If you need to make an emergency call and cannot see the numbers of your phone, dial 0 for the telephone operator. Give your name and explain the problem. The operator will help you.

In most areas, when you need help fast, you can dial 911. You can dial 911 from a pay phone without using coins. The person who answers your call will ask many questions. He or she will then tell you what to do. You may be told to stay on the line until help arrives. Even if you move away from the phone, leave the receiver by the phone. Don't hang up unless the operator says it's okay.

Practice dialing 0 (zero) or 911 on the telephone without looking. If there is smoke in the air, you might not be able to see the numbers.

In some emergencies, you may have to leave home quickly. Sometimes it is safer to get out of danger first. Then you can phone for help at a neighbor's or a pay phone.

Skills Practice

Look back at your list of risky areas or things from the Skills Practice on page 120. For each item on your list, describe what you could do to lower that risk.

You have learned that risks are a part of life. Thinking about risks and knowing what you can do about them are skills you need to live independently.

Decisions, Decisions!

Imagine that you are baby-sitting a two-year-old child named Mara. The phone rings and you talk to the caller for only a minute. When you hang up, you see Mara playing with bottles under the kitchen sink. Some of the bottles are open. You realize Mara has something smeared around her mouth.

On a separate sheet of paper, follow the steps below to help you make a wise decision.

Step 1: Identify the decision you must make.

Step 2: List your choices.

Step 3: Cross out any choices that are harmful or might be against your beliefs.

Step 4: Think about the possible results of the remaining choices.

Step 5: Select the best choice.

Step 6: Explain how you would carry out this choice.

Step 7: Describe the possible results of your choice.

Chapter Review

Chapter Summary

1. Risks are chances that something harmful might happen. Avoid as many risks as you can inside and outside the home.

2. You can take actions to avoid accidents before they happen. Take actions to avoid fires, accidents with poison, electric shock, and other accidents in the home. Outside the home, follow safety rules at work and play.

3. Be prepared for accidents. Have smoke detectors and fire extinguishers around the home in case of fire.

4. Plan and practice a way for everyone to get out in an emergency.

5. Know how to turn off the water and what to do if you smell gas.

6. Know how to get help in an emergency. Keep emergency telephone numbers near each phone. In a public place, ask for help from someone nearby. Give as much information as possible when asking for help.

Chapter Quiz

1. Define risk. Give one example of a risk.

2. Name two ways to try to prevent fire in the home.

3. What steps can you take to prevent accidental electric shock?

4. List three kinds of telephone numbers that should be near each telephone.

5. What two things should you have in case of a fire? What do they do?

6. Explain why it is important to plan a way for everyone to get out of the house and meet in an emergency.

7. Why should people practice leaving the house in the dark?

8. Name two numbers to dial for help in an emergency.

9. What two things should you do if a water pipe breaks?

10. Are you lowering the number of risky areas in or outside your home as part of living independently? Why or why not?

Putting Skills to Work

Make an emergency telephone list for your home. Include the types of phone numbers that are suggested in this chapter. Then add any important numbers of your own. Leave space to add or change numbers. Make a copy for every telephone in your home. Show your list to a classmate to share ideas.

Skills Issues

Your eight-year-old brother, Tim, broke his leg. He will be in a cast for six weeks. What changes could you make in your home to make it safer for Tim while he is in a cast? Discuss your ideas with a small group of students.

Unit Three Review

Answer the following questions on a separate sheet of paper.

1. Describe a well-balanced diet. Give an example of a healthy snack.

2. What information should you find on a Nutrition Facts label of a prepared food?

3. What is one advantage of a prepared food over a fresh food?

4. Tell what exercise does for the body.

5. What is aerobic exercise? Give an example.

6. Explain how alcohol, cigarettes, and other drugs can be harmful to your health.

7. Explain the difference between prescription medicine and over-the-counter medicine.

8. Define health insurance. What can happen to people who do not have health insurance?

9. List three ways to stay safe inside the home. List three ways to stay safe outside the home.

10. Why is it important to be aware of the weather when you are outdoors?

Getting and Keeping a Job

Chapter 10

Looking for a Job

Chapter 11

Getting a Job

Chapter 12

Keeping a Job

Chapter 13

Making the Most of Your Job

Chapter 10

Looking for a Job

Big cities offer a wide variety of job opportunities. Think about what kind of job you would like to have after you finish school.

Chapter Learning Objectives

- Name skills, interests, and personal qualities that you have and would help you in certain jobs.
- Name several needs that a job can meet.
- Decide which job needs are most important to you now.
- Describe ways to learn about a job.
- Name other sources of information about jobs, including newspaper ads.

Words to Know

personal qualities   ways you relate to other people and to the world around you; your personality

skill   something you do well

interest   something you care about or like to do

income   the money you earn

flexible   able to change

career   the type of work a person does throughout his or her life to earn a living

informational interview   a discussion with someone who has a job that interests you

---

Read the story in the paragraphs below to find out what is bothering Floyd. Maybe you have faced the same problem. If not, you might face it soon.

Floyd often watched the people who rode the city bus with him in the mornings. He was on his way to school, but he wondered where they were going. Most of all, he wondered what kinds of jobs they had. Floyd was graduating from high school in a month. He knew he had to start looking for a job–and soon!

He noticed that some people riding the bus wore uniforms. Floyd could usually tell what their jobs were. Some were security guards or mail carriers. Maybe I'll be a security guard, he thought. Or maybe I'll work for a cleaning company. I could even be a bus driver.

But Floyd couldn't tell what kinds of jobs the other people had. Some were dressed in suits or dresses; some weren't. Some looked bored while others looked happy to be going to work. Floyd wanted to be one of the happy people. Floyd shook his head. How in the world could he pick a job that he would like?

As you think about jobs, look for ones that sound interesting.

Before Floyd can choose a job, he has to think about the kinds of work he can do. He also needs to consider the kinds of work he wants to do. He needs to know what jobs are out there. Floyd must also think about his reasons for getting a job. He has to decide if he just wants to earn money or learn skills that may lead to a better job.

Finding the right job takes time and planning. This chapter will help you get started. First, you need to take a close look at yourself. You also have to figure out your strengths, interests, and needs. Later you will learn how to gather information about jobs.

Identifying Your Strengths

Your strengths include the **personal qualities** and skills that can help you do a job. Personal qualities are the ways you relate to other people and to the world around you.

People have many different personal qualities. Some people are comfortable talking with just about

Salespeople have to talk to customers all day long. An outgoing personality is an important quality for a salesperson to have.

anyone. Some people are willing to listen and consider different points of view. Some people are eager to help. Others are more concerned about their own needs.

Some jobs require certain personal qualities. For example, someone in sales should be outgoing and full of energy. A child care worker needs to be calm and gentle and should love children. A security guard should be firm and careful. Being dependable is a good personal quality for any job.

The combination of all of your personal qualities is what makes up your personality.

Skills Practice

On a separate sheet of paper, list any of the personal qualities below that describe you. Add any other words you think describe your qualities. Then write down two or three jobs that might need your personal qualities. Show your work to a partner. Talk about whether the jobs you listed need the qualities you listed.

forceful	organized	friendly
calm	artistic	dependable
careful	outgoing	fair
full of energy	cheerful	independent
cooperative	helpful	creative
firm	thoughtful	patient

Your strengths also include your **skills**. A skill is something you do well. For example, you might be good at solving math problems or fixing motors. You might know how to help people settle arguments. You might know the best way to roast a turkey. You also have to think about your skills when choosing a job.

Identifying Your Interests

Just because you are good at something doesn't mean you like to do it. For example, you might be good at cleaning, but hate to clean. It might really bore you.

Consider your interests ▶
when you look for a job.
Doing work that you
enjoy can be fun and
satisfying.

If you know this, you may not want to apply for a job
on a cleaning crew. You could do that job well.
However, you might not be happy doing it.

It's important to think about what you like to do.
Consider your **interests** when thinking about jobs.
An interest is something you care about or like to do.
Some people are interested in working with computers.
Others want to help clean up the environment. Still
others are interested in exercising or in growing
plants.

Identifying Your Needs

You must decide what you need from a job before
choosing one. Nearly everyone works to earn money
to pay for basic needs. Basic needs include housing,
food, and clothing. But you might have other needs
in a job.

Income is the money you earn. You might be
looking for a job that pays well. Maybe you want to
buy a car or get an apartment. Your goal is to earn
as much money as possible.

While you're in school, you might want a part-time job. Working in the evenings or on weekends might fit in with your classes and study routine. You might also think about looking for a job that could become full-time after you graduate.

You might need a job with **flexible** hours. Flexible means "able to change." Let's say you have an important test in a week. You need to study. If you have flexible hours, you might be able to work fewer hours before your test and more the next week.

You also need a job you can get to easily. If you have a car, you need to think about how long you want to spend going to and from work. If you don't have a car, you need to be able to take a bus or train. Remember to consider the cost of getting to that job. Think about how much you would spend on gas or bus fare to get to your job.

Sometimes people take jobs just so they can learn skills for better jobs. For example, working in a daycare center might help someone get a job as a teacher's aide in an elementary school later on.

Jobs take place under many different working conditions. You may like working indoors better than working outdoors. You may work well with other people, or alone. Using your muscles might also sound good. Or you might prefer a job in which you discuss ideas or solve problems.

Working conditions are important to think about when deciding on a job. If you are happy with your working conditions you will be happier with your job. For example, if you do not like being outdoors, you would not be happy being a trail guide.

Jobs can also meet emotional needs. Some people work in hospitals because they feel good when they help others. Some people enjoy the quiet setting of a library. Others work in an auto repair shop because they like cars. It is important to choose a job that fits your needs, skills, and interests.

A job with flexible hours is easier to fit into a busy schedule.

Different jobs have ▲ different working conditions.

Skills Practice

Think about your skills and interests. On a separate sheet of paper, list eight or more of your skills and interests. Ask a partner to help you think of jobs that might use your skills and interests. For example, you may be good at working in a group, and you may be interested in cooking. The job of a chef might be your dream job. Share with the class each job you thought of and how it matches your skills and interests.

You have now taken two steps in choosing a job that suits you. You have identified some of your personal qualities, skills, and interests. You have also named some jobs that use your qualities, skills, and interests. These are all important steps in choosing a job.

Jobs and Careers

Your job needs now might be different from your job needs a year from now. Your job needs will change in five or ten years. You will need to think about what you want for your future. You will need to plan for a **career**. A career is the type of work a person will do throughout his or her life to earn a living.

Very few jobs will meet all your needs perfectly. You often have to give up some things in order to get other things. For example, you might find a job that pays well and could lead to an even better job. However, that job might be 45 minutes away. You have to decide whether the pay and opportunities are worth the long trip. Remember, you will need to take that trip ten times each week.

Or maybe you are looking for a full-time job in a restaurant. The only job you can find is at a nearby restaurant, but it's only part-time. You decide to take it. It's possible that the job could change. It could become a full time job. By working part-time now, you might get the job you really want later on.

Deciding which job to take can be difficult. It requires balancing the things you like about a job with the things you may not be happy about. You must also think about your job needs now and your career needs for the future. You might change your mind many times before you find the career you want.

Skills Practice

On a separate sheet of paper, make a list of six needs that a job can meet. Then put the needs in order of importance for you right now. Write your most important need at the top. Then show your list to a partner. Explain why you put the needs in that order.

Gathering Information about Jobs

You have identified your personal qualities, skills, and interests. You have thought about which job needs are most important to you. Now it's time to find out more about jobs that might suit you.

Your guidance counselor might have information about types of jobs. Your library may have these books, which describe thousands of jobs:

- *Occupational Outlook Handbook*
- *Dictionary of Occupational Titles*
- *Occupations Digest*

These books explain what kinds of training jobs require and about how much they pay. They also explain which job fields are growing and need more workers.

One of the best ways to find out about a job is to talk with someone who has that job. This is called an **informational interview**. During an informational interview, you are not asking for a job. You are just asking for more information about the job and the company. Your school guidance counselor, parents, or friends might know people who have jobs that interest you. They might help you set up meetings with these people. Then you could find out more about these jobs. You can see if they still interest you.

Before your informational interview, list questions to ask. Here are some examples:

- What kinds of things do you do on your job?
- What skills do you need to do this job?
- What special training did you have that helped you get this job?
- What do you like best about your job?
- What do you like least about it?

Do not ask the person how much money he or she makes. However, you can ask about the average pay for someone in that job.

To set up an interview, call and ask if the person is willing to meet with you. Set a time to meet. Then arrive on time, looking your best. After the interview,

write a thank-you note to the person or people you met. Remember, you might ask the same person to hire you some day!

Finding Out What's Available

Now you know more about jobs you think you'd like and could do well. The next step is finding out what jobs are available. Be sure to tell friends and family members you are looking for a job. They might know of openings that would suit you.

Your school or local library may have a bulletin board of job openings in the area. You might also see "Help Wanted" signs in store windows. State agencies may have phone numbers you could call to learn about available jobs.

Your newspaper can also help you learn about the job openings in your community. Look for the "Want

Ads" or "Employment Guide" section in the paper. Jobs are usually grouped under headings such as "Secretarial/Clerical" or "Sales." The job openings under each heading are listed in alphabetical order.

Want ads can also tell you what kind of jobs have the most openings. For example, you may find ten want ads under "Restaurants/Hotels" for cooks. However, you might find nearly 100 ads under "Computers." These jobs are for people who know how to use computers. If you are interested in computers, you might take some courses on word processing or programming. Then you would have a much wider choice of jobs.

Want ads shorten some words to save space. Here are some common examples:

F/T	full time (usually 40 hours a week)
P/T	part time (less than 40 hours a week)
Exper. req'd	experience required
c/o	in care of (the address to write to)
Attn.	attention (the person to write to)
E.O.E.	Equal Opportunity Employer (This employer does not hire or reject people because of their age, race, sex, or disability.)

A Learning Experience

Many people today have a number of different jobs and different types of jobs during their lifetime. If you think about your strengths, interests, and needs, you should have a better chance of finding jobs you enjoy. If your first job disappoints you, consider it a learning experience. Figure out why that job was wrong for you. Then try to avoid the problem in your next job.

Decisions, Decisions!

Dolores has just graduated from high school. She wants to work full-time and share an apartment with a girlfriend. Dolores will need $550 a month for rent and other expenses. She does not have a car.

Dolores loves people and would like to learn more about art. After many interviews, she has been offered the three full-time jobs listed below.

Job #1. Ticket-seller at a theater only one mile from her home. She would work alone in the ticket booth. She would be paid $800 a month.

Job #2. Assistant to a newspaper cartoonist. Delores would help the cartoonist and learn what he does. The bus ride to his office is an hour each way. She would be paid $800 a month.

Job #3. Telephone sales. Delores would call possible customers for a company. She would work from her apartment. Delores would be paid $740 month.

On a separate sheet of paper, follow the steps below to help Delores decide which job to take.

Step 1: Identify the decision Delores must make.

Step 2: List her choices.

Step 3: Cross out any choices that might be harmful or against Delores's beliefs.

Step 4: Think about how each choice fits Delores's personal qualities, skills, interests, and needs.

Step 5: Select the best choice for her right now.

Step 6: Delores would accept the job you chose.

Step 7: Describe how this job might affect Delores, now and in the future.

Chapter Review

Chapter Summary

1. Before you look for a job, think about your personal qualities, skills, and interests. Try to choose a job that matches these things. Then you will have a better chance of enjoying your job and doing well at it.

2. A job can fill a need for income, scheduling, location, training and education, working conditions, and personal satisfaction. You must decide which needs are most important to you.

3. People's job needs change over the years. They have to decide how well a job meets their needs at a particular time in their life. They also have to think about the future and their career goals.

4. Learn more about certain jobs. Go to the library. Several books describe different kinds of jobs. You can set up informational interviews to talk with people who have jobs that interest you.

5. Libraries and some state agencies may have information about what jobs are available in the community. Newspaper want ads list available jobs. They also show which job fields have more openings.

Chapter Quiz

Answer these questions on a separate sheet of paper.

1. Before you look for a job, what are three things you should consider about yourself?

2. What are some examples of personal qualities?

3. What are some examples of skills?

4. How can your interests help you make a job choice?

5. What needs could a job meet?

6. Does everyone have the same job needs? Why or why not?

7. Why is it important to find out how far away a job is from your home?

8. What are some questions you could ask during an informational interview?

9. What can newspaper ads tell you?

10. When one teenager accepted her first job, she couldn't wait to start. A month later, she wishes she had a different job. What could be wrong?

Putting Skills to Work

Find a job in the want ads that you think you would like. Show the ad to a small group. Tell the group how that job fits your personal qualities, skills, and interests. Name some needs that job might meet for you.

Skills Issues

Parents often suggest that their teenager apply for certain jobs. In a small group, discuss whether a parent should try to influence a teenager's choice of jobs. Should this decision be left completely up to the teenager? Why or why not? Explain your group's opinion to the class.

Chapter 11
Getting a Job

To get the job you want, you must show that you are the best person to hire. Think about how you might convince an employer to hire you.

Chapter Learning Objectives

- Name the kinds of information that a résumé and a cover letter should include.
- Explain how to fill out a job application.
- Explain how to prepare for a job interview.
- Give examples of common questions asked at interviews and ways to answer them.
- Explain how to decide between two job offers.
- Identify examples of job benefits.

Words to Know

résumé   a summary of your education and work experience

references   people who know you well and will tell others you are a good worker

cover letter   a letter to introduce you to an employer; sent with a résumé

job application   a form you fill out when applying for a job

Social Security number   a number assigned to each person by the government; a form of identification

interview   a meeting in which one person answers another person's questions

job benefits   insurance, vacation time, and other things you receive in addition to your pay

---

Tyler has decided to apply for a job as a salesperson at an athletic shoe store. Tyler figures that his outgoing personal qualities will help him be a good salesperson. His interest in sports won't hurt, either. However, Tyler does have a problem. Read about it in the paragraphs below.

Tyler read the tall woman's name tag. It said she was Barbara Cole, store manager. Just the person I should talk to, Tyler thought.

"Excuse me, Ms. Cole," Tyler said in his most confident and friendly voice. "I understand you are hiring salespeople. I'd like to apply for that job."

Ms. Cole nodded and pointed at a pile of papers behind the counter. "Just leave your résumé here," she said. "I'm going to read them this afternoon. Then I'll choose some people to call for interviews."

Tyler swallowed hard. He didn't have a résumé, so he couldn't leave one. Ms. Cole wouldn't call him. Tyler would not get the job without a résumé.

Getting a job isn't easy. You have to prove you are the best person to hire. Knowing how to write a strong résumé and how to fill out job application forms will help. Preparing for the job interview is also important. This chapter will help you increase your chances of getting the job you want.

Writing a Résumé

A **résumé** is a summary of your education and work experience. It's best to limit it to one page. The purpose of a résumé is to convince an employer to call you for an interview. Your résumé should introduce your work experience to the employer.

Not all résumés have an objective. You can include an objective in a letter that goes with the résumé.

Miriam Ashaad
222 Yearling Avenue
Durham, North Carolina 27701
(919) 555-4199

OBJECTIVE Assistant food manager in a supermarket or restaurant

EDUCATION Graduated from Williams High School, June 1997
Durham Adult Education courses completed:
"Cooking for Families," July 1996
"Basic French Cooking," July 1995
"Kids Can Cook, Too!" July-August 1994

WORK EXPERIENCE

1/97-present **BOYLE'S RESTAURANT**
Chef's Assistant Ordered supplies; planned special event menus; supervised kitchen staff

7/96-1/97 **JUDY, JUDY, JUDY CATERERS**
Server Supervised two servers

3/96-6/96 **LET'S EAT CATERING COMPANY**
Server Served 1,000 people for a Feed-the-Homeless event.

SKILLS Can manage and serve meals for large groups
Good business and "people" skills

Look at Miriam's résumé as an example. It will help you see how to write the information needed in a résumé.

Your full name, address, and phone number should go at the top of the page. Use large letters or bold type. Make it easy for the employer to know how to contact you. Then describe your objective or the kind of job you would like to have. However, many people choose to describe their job objective in a letter. The letter would go with the résumé.

A list of when and where you went to school and graduated should also be included on a résumé. Include any classes or courses you've taken that would help you on the job you want. This education section should come first if you are still in school or just graduated. The section can also be at the end of the résumé if you've been out of school for a long time.

The most important section of your résumé is the list of your experience. Start with the job you have or the last job you had. Write the date each job started and ended. Include the company name and your job title. If you don't have any experience working for an employer, list your volunteer work. You can also list jobs such as baby-sitting, lawn mowing, or other things you have done to earn money.

Include any information on the job that an employer would want to know. For example, Miriam was a server. However, she doesn't say that she served customers. The reader already knows that. That's what a server does. Instead, Miriam says that she also supervised people. This information is something an employer would want to know because it shows she is responsible.

Include a section on skills at the bottom of your résumé. Describe things you do well that will help you on this job. List any of your interests that relate to this job. Name any honors or awards you've won.

Keep your résumé up to date. Add or change information as you gain experience and skills.

Résumé Do's and Don'ts

Always tell the truth when preparing your résumé. If an employer finds out you lied on your résumé, you will not get the job.

Remember that your résumé introduces you. If it is messy or has spelling mistakes, you will look bad. Make sure your résumé is neat, complete, clear, and well organized. Then the employer will be more likely to call you for an interview.

Another rule to follow when making a résumé is to start each description with a strong verb. Don't use *I, me,* and *my.* For example, don't write "I took orders from customers." Instead, start with a strong verb, "Handled customer orders."

Add details and numbers to show that you did your job well. For example, don't just write, "Answered the phones." Instead, write "Answered phones and took messages for four attorneys."

Skills Practice

On a separate sheet of paper, rewrite each sentence below. Change it so it could be included in a résumé. The first one is done for you.

1. I cut the grass for my neighbors.

   Rewrite: Mowed 12 neighbors' lawns.

2. I took the customers' money for the job.

3. Sometimes I made lunch for the children.

4. The boss asked me to order supplies.

There are also some things you should not do when preparing your résumé. Don't explain why you left a job. You can do that during your interview. You don't have to list your age, race, ethnic background, religion, or sex.

Using References

References are people who know you well and can tell employers that you have good work habits. You list references on a job application or in a letter to an employer. Choose people who you can depend on to give an employer a good description of you and your work.

A reference might be a person you have worked with or worked for in the past. You might list a teacher who knows your work. Don't use family members. Give a list of your references to employers when they ask for it. Include each person's name, job title such as Guidance Counselor, address, and phone number.

Some forms you fill out for jobs will ask you to list references. Before you list any references, be sure to call these people yourself. Ask if they are willing to speak to employers about you. Then your references will not be surprised when an employer calls them.

Keep your references on a sheet of paper. Then give the paper to the employer during the job interview if he or she asks for references.

Skills Practice

On a separate sheet of paper, list three people you might use as references. Be sure to include the phone numbers an employer can use to contact them during the day. Save this list in case you need to give references to an employer. Be sure to call these people before you give their names out.

Writing a Cover Letter

To make a good impression, send a **cover letter** along with your résumé. A cover letter helps to introduce you to an employer. You might send the same résumé to different companies. However, you should write a different cover letter for each job.

Your cover letter should describe why you want to work for that company. You might stress that you have certain skills or experience that would help in that job. Here is the cover letter that Miriam wrote to Mitchell's Food Mart:

Miriam Ashaad
222 Yearling Avenue
Durham, North Carolina 27701
(919) 555-4199

June 9, 1997

Manager
Mitchell's Food Mart
100 Main Street
Durham, North Carolina 27701

Dear Manager:

I would like to apply for the position of assistant food manager. I saw your ad in Sunday's *Durham Times*. I shop at Mitchell's often and would really like to work there.

My résumé is enclosed. As you will see, I just graduated from Williams High School. For the past three summers I have taken business courses. I love to work with others, and I want to begin working on my career.

I hope to pursue a career in food management. A position with your company would fit perfectly with my career plans. Please call me at 555-4199 if you have any questions or would like further information. I hope to hear from you soon.

Sincerely,

Miriam Ashaad

Miriam Ashaad

Filling Out a Job Application

When you apply for a job, you might be asked to fill out a form called a **job application**. Job applications often ask for the same information that is on a résumé. However, some companies want to have the information on their forms instead of a résumé.

The form will ask for your **Social Security number**. This is a number assigned to each person by the government. Each U.S. citizen has a Social Security number. It's a form of identification employers use.

If you were not born in the United States, you have to fill out a special form to get a Social Security number and a card.

In addition to asking for the same information that is on a résumé, a job application may also ask these questions:

- How long have you lived at your current address?
- Are you a citizen of the United States?
- How did you learn about this job?
- Do you have any health problems that would affect your ability to do this job?
- Have you ever been convicted of a crime?
- Whom should we contact in case of emergency?
- When could you start work?

Read the whole application before you start filling it out. Be neat; sloppy writing makes you look bad. Ask for two copies of the application. If you make a mistake, you can start over. Check your spelling. Make sure your dates are correct.

Do not write in the sections marked "for employer only." Fill in the other sections. Some questions may

▼ *Below is one section of a job application.*

APPLICATION FOR EMPLOYMENT

Name _____
(Please print)   Last   First   Middle

Address _____
            Street and Number   City   State   Zip Code

                                    School or
Home Phone (   ) _____   Business Phone _____   Social Sec. No. _____

Are you at least 18 years of age?   ☐ Yes   ☐ No

Are you legally eligible to work in the U.S.?   ☐ Yes   ☐ No

Do you have relatives working in this company or any of its operations?   ☐ Yes   ☐ No

If so, name _____   Company / Department _____

Position Objective

Type of Employment _____   Total number of hours per week desired _____

☐ Full-Time   ☐ Temporary

☐ Part-Time   ☐ Seasonal

Please describe the type of position you are seeking _____

Salary required $ _____ per _____ What day would you be available to begin work? _____

not apply to you. Just leave these sections blank or write "N/A" which means "Not Applicable."

Job Screening

Some companies ask you to take a test as part of your job application. For example, a company might ask you to take a typing test. If the job is putting small parts together, you might have to show that you can do it. A few companies may ask you to complete a drug screening test. You can always refuse to take these tests. However, if you refuse, you may not get the job.

The Job Interview

The next step in getting a job is doing well during the job **interview**. During a job interview, someone from the company will ask you questions about yourself. Your answers will help the employer decide whether to hire you. You might meet with the store manager for the interview. At a large company, you might talk with someone in the human resources or personnel department. These departments interview and hire people for large companies.

An interview is your chance to show that you are the best person for the job.

Be prepared for an interview when you drop off your résumé or fill out an application. You might be asked to talk to someone then. Usually, you will have to go home and wait for a call from someone at the company to schedule an interview.

If someone calls to arrange an interview, set it up as soon as possible. The day of the interview, be sure to arrive on time. The day before, travel to the store or company office. Then you will know for sure how to get there and how long it takes. Make sure you look your best. Always dress up for the interview.

Preparing for the Interview

Prepare before you go to an interview. Find out as much as you can about the company. Talk to anyone you know who works there. Try to learn as much as possible about the job.

Think of questions you might be asked during the interview. Plan how you will answer each question. Be prepared to explain why you want to work at their company and why they should hire you. You could describe what you like about the company. Explain how working for the company could help you meet your career goals. Stress that you know you can do a good job and that you are also eager to learn new things.

You might be asked to point out your strengths and weaknesses. For your strengths, name some things that would help you do the job well. Working on a team or solving problems could help on a job where you might work closely with others. For your weaknesses, think of a positive way to describe a weakness. You might say that you don't know much about word processing. However, you are taking a course so you can learn. Avoid giving a weakness that will make you look bad.

Handling the Interview

You will probably feel nervous during your interview. The interviewer will expect that. Try to relax. Remember that this is not your only chance to get a job. You will have many more interviews. You will learn from each one. You will get better at answering questions and staying calm. Each interview is a learning experience.

During the interview, look the other person in the eye. Sit up straight to show you are sure of yourself. Speak clearly and avoid using slang.

You should also try to ask questions during the interview. You want to know if the job is right for you. It also shows an employer that you are serious about wanting the job. One question you might ask the interviewer is to describe the type of person the company wants for this job. Then you can explain why

Usually, the more interviews you have, the more relaxed you will feel.

During an interview, the ▶ way you dress may be as important as what you say. Always dress neatly and appropriately for an interview.

you are the one to hire. If you cannot work certain hours, ask what days and hours you would have to work. You might find that you could not work the hours the job requires.

Skills Practice

Work in groups of three to practice a job interview. One person will be the interviewer. One person will be applying for a job. The third person will watch and listen. Together, make up details about the company and the job. Then start the interview. Remember to ask the questions listed earlier. Afterward, the third person will help the other two decide what went well. Try to think of even better answers to the interviewer's questions.

During the interview, the interviewer probably won't tell you whether you got the job. The company has to compare you with other people applying for the job. They will decide who will get the job later. It sometimes takes several days or weeks for a company to decide.

After the interview, always send a thank-you letter as soon as possible. Thank the interviewer for talking with you. Include a sentence or two on why you would be perfect for the job. If you have decided you don't want the job, politely explain why.

Choosing between Jobs

You might not get the job you want. Very few people get every job they apply for. However, you might get job offers from different places. Then you will have to choose between them. You will have to decide which job best meets your needs.

To do this, think about which job pays enough to cover all your expenses. Maybe one has better hours or a flexible schedule. Also think about travel time and transportation costs.

You will want a job that is interesting and important to you. You might also look for a job that offers training or courses that will prepare you for a better job in the future.

Working conditions should also be considered. If you like to work with people, you may want to be part of a team. If you like to work outside, an office job might be the wrong choice for you. Finally, think about which one has the better job benefits.

Understanding Job Benefits

Job benefits may include health insurance, vacation time, and other things you receive in addition to your salary. Part-time employees often do not receive the same benefits as full-time workers.

Having health insurance is very important. Many companies pay part of the cost of health insurance. Then each employee pays his or her share. This can range from a small cost to a few hundred dollars a month. Before you accept a job, find out how much this cost will be. If you need health insurance and the job doesn't offer it, you might want another job.

Vacation days and sick days may also be job benefits. A number of companies also pay for courses so their employees can learn new skills. Other companies offer excellent savings plans for employees. Learning about these benefits can help you decide whether to take a job.

Skills Practice

Talk about vacation days and sick days with a parent, family member, or friend who is working full time. Find out how many vacation days and how many sick days this person gets each year. Share what you learn with the class.

Getting the Job

Getting a job can be complicated, but you can do it. Now you know how to write your résumé and a cover letter. You can fill out a job application. You have learned what to do before and during a job interview. You even know how to choose between two jobs. Now you're ready to search for a job!

Decisions, Decisions!

Read the paragraphs below and help Alexis make a decision.

Alexis left her apartment at 10:20 A.M. for her job interview. The interview was at 11:00 A.M. with Mr. Blake. Alexis knew where the office building was located. It would take her 15 or 20 minutes to drive there. Then she could park and get to Mr. Blake's office in plenty of time.

BAM! Was it a flat tire? Alexis pulled over to the side of the road. Sure enough, her right back tire was flat. Alexis knew how to change a tire. She also knew that changing it would make her late for her interview. And it would make her dirty.

On a separate sheet of paper, follow the steps below to help Alexis decide what to do.

Step 1: Identify the decision Alexis must make.

Step 2: List her choices.

Step 3: Cross out any choices that are harmful or might be against Alexis's beliefs.

Step 4: Think about the possible results of each remaining choice.

Step 5: Select the best choice for Alexis.

Step 6: Tell how Alexis would carry out that choice.

Step 7: Describe how this decision might affect Alexis's job interview.

Chapter Review

Chapter Summary

1. A résumé is a summary of your education and work experience.

2. When applying for a job, you may be asked to list references.

3. Write a cover letter to send with every résumé. A cover letter introduces you and explains why you want the job.

4. A job application form asks for some of the same information that is in a résumé. Fill it out accurately, completely, and neatly.

5. During a job interview, a company employee asks you questions. Your answers help the company decide whether to hire you.

6. Prepare for a job interview by learning all you can about the job and the company. Plan your answers to questions that the interviewer might ask.

7. On the day of the interview, you should look your best and be on time. Try to relax and answer the interviewer's questions with confidence.

8. If you need to choose between two jobs, decide which one better meets your needs.

9. Job benefits can include health insurance, vacation days, and sick days.

Chapter Quiz

Answer these questions on a separate sheet of paper.

1. What should be included on a résumé?

2. One teenager described his work experience this way: "I worked at Yarnell's Farm Market from about 1994 to 1996. I was the cashier. Sometimes I helped customers with their problems." What is a better way to describe this job on a résumé?

3. Why should you write a cover letter?

4. Why is neatness important on a résumé, cover letter, and job application?

5. What is the purpose of a job interview?

6. What should you do before a job interview?

7. What should you do during a job interview?

8. What would you say if an interviewer asked you to name your strengths? A weakness?

9. Pretend you have been offered a job. What should you think about before you take that job?

10. What are some examples of job benefits?

Putting Skills to Work

Imagine you're applying for a job delivering pizza. The employees who deliver pizza for this restaurant wear jeans on the job. Should you dress up for your job interview? If so, what should you wear? Talk it over with a partner. Share your opinion with the class.

Skills Issues

Some parents arrange for their children to be hired by the company where the parents work. Do you think it should it be against company rules to hire the children of employees? Why or why not? Work with a small group to discuss your answer. Share your group's thoughts with the class.

Chapter 12

Keeping a Job

The first day on the job is a new beginning. It is natural to feel a bit nervous. Just remember that you were chosen for the job. You can do it.

Chapter Learning Objectives

- Explain ways to do well on the first day at work.
- Describe the kinds of information in an employee handbook.
- Describe actions that will help you keep your job.
- Explain how problem solving can help you get along at work.
- Explain why it's important to learn new skills on a job.

Words to Know

coworkers   people who work for the same company

employee handbook   a book that describes company rules and job benefits

fired   to be dismissed from a job

schedule   a list of times to do things

shift   a period of time for work

deadline   the latest time something can be done

layoff   a period of time when a company has no work for employees

---

The first day on any job can make new employees feel a little unsure of themselves. Read the paragraphs below and see how Juanita felt on her first day.

"I'm very nervous," Juanita said to her cousin Carl. "It's my first day and I'm afraid I'll make a big mistake."

Juanita was getting ready for her new job at a radio station. She knew she had the skills for this job. She also knew the job had many responsibilities.

"You'll do fine!" Carl said.

"But what if I forget something?" Juanita was getting more and more worried. "What if I forget that the red light means 'on the air'? What if I talk when the microphone is on?"

Carl tried to calm her. "Your supervisor doesn't expect you to remember everything on your first day. She just expects you to do your best."

Carl was right. Juanita just had to try to do her best. Like Juanita, many people are nervous on their first day at a new job. Employers expect new people to be nervous. However, it is important to make a good impression. Employers are more concerned about what employees will do after their first day. They are more concerned with new employees getting along with their supervisors, other employees, and customers. Employees have to learn new skills and follow a schedule. They may have to work on a team. This chapter will help prepare you for your first day at work and for the days after that.

The First Day

On your first day at a new job, remember that you were chosen for this job. Your employer is confident that you can do it. That's why you were hired.

Your first day will go more smoothly if you follow certain tips. First, be on time and dress nicely and correctly for your job. If you aren't sure what to wear, call the person who offered you the job. Ask what you should wear.

Next, try to relax and be yourself. Stay calm. Remember that most problems will work themselves out after a while. No mistakes are permanent. Just do your best.

On your first day, you will probably meet many new people, including **coworkers**. Your coworkers are the people who work for your company. No one expects you to remember all their names. You will slowly learn their names over the next weeks and months. However, you should remember your supervisor's name. Write it down so you won't forget. Find out how it is spelled in case you have to write him or her a note.

Someone will show you where you will work. You probably will be given some work to do. If you aren't sure what you are supposed to do, ask questions. It's much better to ask lots of questions than to do the work incorrectly.

You may also be asked to fill out several forms. These forms might include tax forms for the state and U.S. government. You might not have some of the

New employees have many different feelings on their first day at work. Some feel excited or scared or both on that day.

information with you. If so, ask to take the forms home. Bring the completed forms to work the next day.

In any case, don't fill out the forms incorrectly just to get them done.

The Employee Handbook

You will probably be given an **employee handbook**. This book describes the company rules and job benefits. It might also explain what each department does. You don't have to remember all of this information, but you should look through the handbook. Notice the kinds of information in it. Then when you have a question, you will know where to look for the answer in your handbook. Keep it on your desk or where you do your work so you can find it easily.

Some rules in employee handbooks tell what to do if you are sick and cannot come to work. A rule might tell you to call your supervisor as soon as possible. Rules might also tell you to call if you will be late for work.

Rules may also include a smoking policy. For example, a rule might say that you cannot smoke anywhere in the building.

▼ *Pay attention to the safety rules posted at every job you have.*

☞ **SAFETY RULES** ☜

✓ Keep your work area clean.
✓ Wear safety goggles at all times.
✓ Don't wear any loose clothing or jewelry.
✓ Stay alert.

Thank you.

Most companies have phone policies. Your handbook should explain when you are allowed to make personal calls. For example, you can make personal phone calls during your breaks or lunchtime. You cannot make them during work hours.

Company rules can also explain what not to wear to work. For example, you may not be allowed to wear jeans, shorts, halter tops, or sandals to work.

Breaking or not following company rules could result in losing your job. You could be **fired**, or dismissed from your job. Then you might have a hard time getting another job. Because of this, it is important to know and follow all the rules in the company handbook.

If you cannot follow a rule for some reason, talk to your supervisor about it.

Skills Practice

Imagine that a restaurant wants to make an employee handbook. Work with a small group to write four or five rules for the company handbook. You might list the working hours and vacation days. You might tell when to take breaks or whether employees can have snacks at their work areas. Share your group's list of rules with the class. Discuss why it's important to read an employee handbook.

Keeping Your Job

It's usually not difficult to keep a job. All you have to do is be responsible, follow rules and instructions, and have a good attitude. Those three things will make you a valuable employee at any company.

Responsible employees come to work on time every day. They work hard, and they always try to find better ways to do their jobs. They do not take long breaks, make personal phone calls, or waste company time in other ways.

When something needs to be done, responsible employees do it, even if it's not their job. They do make mistakes, but they don't make excuses for them. Instead, they find ways to fix whatever they did wrong.

Most employees have supervisors who guide their work. Listen to your supervisor and follow his or her instructions. As you learn your job, you might think of better ways to do it. Some supervisors welcome new ideas. They may want to hear yours.

Other supervisors think their own ideas are best. Think carefully before you suggest changes to this kind of supervisor. Make sure you show a great deal of respect for his or her ideas.

Good employees also have good attitudes. They do not put down the company, its products, or other employees. They do not gossip. They know that people get into disagreements when they work together. However, they find peaceful ways to settle these disagreements. That way, no one ends up angry.

Employees with good attitudes are willing to learn new skills. They know these skills will help them do a better job. When they are asked to do something a different way, they don't insist that the old way is better. They try the new way.

Getting Along at Work

You may like some supervisors and some employees better than others. Still, you must try to get along with everyone. Good communication skills can help. Good communicators are able to share their ideas and opinions without annoying others. They are also good listeners. Good listening helps them understand other people's points of view. When you know what others think and care about, it's easier to get along with them.

Even with good communication skills, getting along with the people at work can be difficult. Sometimes

Good listening skills can help settle conflicts. Being able to settle conflicts peacefully will help you get along at work.

you may wonder what you should say. You may even wonder to whom you should say it. Just remember to show respect to everyone. Treat others as you would like to be treated.

Solving Problems at Work

Even if you respect your coworkers and treat them fairly, you will still face some difficult decisions. Below are some problems that you may face someday. Keep reading to find out how you can solve them by making wise decisions and communicating well.

Suppose something a coworker is doing is causing a problem for you. For example, suppose a coworker mixes paint in large cans. Then you stack the cans on shelves. You notice that some lids are not closed tightly. Paint is leaking out of these cans.

Coworkers is another name for the employees who work for the same company.

You must decide what to do about the problem. You could try to solve the problem yourself. You could try to tighten the paint-can lids. Another option you have is to tell your coworker about the problem and ask him or her to fix it. You could also discuss the problem with your supervisor.

If you aren't sure how to tighten the lids, that's out. If you're busy, you might not have time to fix the lids. You might also be worried that if you go straight to your supervisor, your coworker may be angry with you.

The only other choice is to point the problem out to your coworker. It's important to fix the problem. Be careful not to accuse your coworker of causing the problem on purpose. Instead, you could say, "Did you notice that some of these lids are not on tight?"

Your coworker should be glad you pointed out the problem. Now he or she can fix it. However, the coworker may do nothing. Then you should discuss the problem with your supervisor.

Tell your supervisor that the lids have not been put on correctly. Your supervisor will tell you what to do.

Do not mention that your coworker ignored you when you pointed out the problem. "Tattling" can get you in deep trouble with your coworkers.

Another common problem you might face at work is avoiding gossip. Suppose a coworker mentions that another worker is always late for work. Or a coworker says that another worker's new haircut looks awful.

You want to avoid gossiping. Bad feelings can grow between coworkers because of gossip. Try to avoid conversations that might turn into gossip sessions. You could say, "I didn't notice." You could walk away or get very busy with your work. Any of these responses might discourage the coworker from more gossiping.

Skills Practice

With a partner, read what each coworker says below. Then think of a good way you could respond. Share your responses with the class.

1. "I don't care if the paint is leaking out of the cans. It's not my problem."

2. "Come outside with me. I'm going to take a nice long break. It's against company rules, but we can hide behind the building."

3. "We have the worst supervisor! Nothing is ever good enough for him!"

If your job involves dealing with customers, you may face many other problems. Part of your job is to keep customers happy. Customers who are not happy will not come back. They may also complain to your supervisor about you.

Suppose you deliver flowers for a florist. What should you do if a customer says, "I don't want these flowers." This is a challenge for your communication skills. You need to find out politely why the customer isn't happy. You might say, "I'd be glad to take them back. Is there a reason you don't want them?" Then the customer might say, "These aren't the kind of flowers I ordered." Taking the time to communicate allows you to learn more about the problem. Getting more information helps you solve any problem.

Skills Practice

With a small group, think of times when you have shopped at a store or eaten in a restaurant. List the things that you like clerks and waiters to do to keep you happy. Then list things that you don't like them to do. Share your lists with the class. Discuss what these lists tell you about how someone can do a good job.

Learning New Skills

The more skills you have, the better you can do at your job. Suppose your job involves working with a computer. Classes or courses on new computer programs may help you do your job better. Watch for

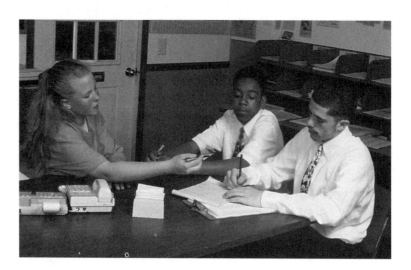

Every job offers new ▶ learning opportunities.

flyers and newspaper articles describing these courses. Choose courses that will help you at work.

You also can learn new skills outside the classroom. Imagine you have a new job sorting mail. You work from 9:00 A.M. until 3:00 P.M. After one week, you are able to sort all the mail by 1:00 P.M. You have two hours with nothing to do. Ask your supervisor or coworkers to show you how to do other tasks. Maybe you could learn how to prepare packages that the company is mailing out. Your supervisor will be impressed that you want to gain more skills. Over time, you could earn a promotion.

Skills Practice

With a partner, choose one of the jobs below. Then think of new skills someone with that job could learn from a coworker. Share your ideas with the class. One skill is given for you. Try to think of two or three more.

1. Shelving books at the community library.
    Skill: checking out books for customers borrowing books.
2. Mowing lawns for a landscaping company.
    Skill: learning how to plant flowers and trees.
3. Cleaning cages at a pet shop.
    Skill: learning what and how to feed the pets.
4. Washing dishes at a restaurant.
    Skill: learning how to prepare some small dishes.

Following a Schedule

Keeping to a schedule is a very important part of any job. A **schedule** is a list of times to do things. For example, you will have a time to start working and a time to stop.

A time clock records the ▶
time each person starts
and stops working.

Many companies just expect you to arrive and leave work at certain times. At some companies, you might be asked to keep track of the hours you work by writing them down on a time sheet.

Other companies use a time clock. Each employee has a time card next to the time clock. The card is slipped into a slot in the time clock. The clock prints the time on your card. When you leave work, you do the same thing. This way, the company has a record of the time you started working and the time you stopped.

Some work places have scheduled meal times and break times. Supervisors set up the schedules so some employees are working while others take a break or eat. Remember to punch your time clock when taking breaks and eating meals if it is the company's policy.

If you work at a place that stays open 24 hours a day, you might work a certain **shift**. A shift is a period of time for work. The morning shift might be 7:00 A.M. to 3:00 P.M. The night shift might be 11:00 P.M. to 7:00 A.M. People work shifts at hospitals, some stores, police stations, nursing homes, and other places.

Think about how your life would change before you decide to take the night shift at work.

Meeting Deadlines

You might have **deadlines** at work. A deadline is the latest time when something must be done. Let's say you work in a mail room. You might have to deliver all the mail by 1:00 P.M. If you work in a restaurant, you might have to set all the tables for dinner by 4:30 P.M.

Employees who are able to follow a schedule and meet deadlines are valuable. Employees who are often late and miss deadlines might get fired. People who are fired because they couldn't follow a schedule or meet deadlines may have a hard time getting another job.

If your company has shifts, you will need to be flexible. Most people would rather work during the day. Yet, some businesses are open around the clock. So, someone has to work at night. Sooner or later, it may be your turn to work nights.

Working on a Team

If you work with one person or twenty people, you are part of a team. Certain qualities will make you a valuable member of that team.

Team members need to listen to each other and respect each others' opinions. In fact, teams can get more done when their members have different ideas and skills. Think about each team member's skills and how they can be used. Some team members may be good at planning while others might be better at solving problems. If you know this, it will be easy to respect what each person brings to the team.

Sharing tasks is an important part of working together. All team members need to do their share of the work. Although each person may have different tasks, each should do what he or she does best.

Take pride in your work. This pride will show in your finished product, whatever it is.

The Facts of Life

Sometimes, through no fault of your own, you lose your job. You might be working hard and doing everything right. But you and many of your coworkers could be victims of a **layoff**. A layoff is when a company has no work for certain employees for a period of time.

Sometimes a layoff will last only a few months. Sometimes it is permanent; you may lose a job forever to a layoff.

Layoffs occur for many different reasons. Suppose a company decides to move from Chicago to Atlanta. They lay off all the workers in Chicago. Then they hire new workers in Atlanta. Imagine that a product you are working on isn't selling very well. The company might decide to stop making the product and close down your department. They might decide to sell the part of the company that makes that product to a different company. In either case, you would lose your job. It wouldn't matter how hard you had worked.

If you lose your job because of a layoff, you may feel upset or even angry. But there are several things you can do. First, don't feel guilty. Losing your job wasn't your fault. Second, think of your job as a learning experience. Now you have more experience to add to your résumé. Update your résumé and practice your job interviewing skills. If possible, take some classes to improve your job skills.

Finally, while looking for a new job, you might do temporary work. Temporary workers, or temps, fill in when regular workers are sick, on vacation, or have quit suddenly. Temporary work is a good way to get more work experience. A company you work for as a "temp" might see that you are a good worker. Then it might offer you a full-time job with the company.

Being a Good Employee

Once you have a job, you need to be a good employee. You need to be responsible, follow instructions, and do your best. Doing your best includes getting along with others and learning new skills. It might also mean learning how to follow a schedule and work on a team. If you can do this, you're one step closer to living on your own!

Decisions, Decisions!

Read the problem below. Then follow the steps to decide which choice is the best solution.

Your coworker takes letters from a printer, checks them, and hands them to you. Then you fold each letter and put it in an envelope. One day you notice a big ink blot on a letter. You tell your coworker, "Be careful! I just found a letter with an ink blot."

Your coworker says, "Then don't look at the letters. That's not your job."

On a separate sheet of paper, follow the steps below to decide what to do.

Step 1: Identify the decision you must make.

Step 2: List your choices.

Step 3: Cross out any choices that are harmful or might be against your beliefs.

Step 4: Think about the possible results of each remaining choice.

Step 5: Select the best choice.

Step 6: Tell how you would carry out that choice.

Step 7: Describe how this decision might affect your job.

Chapter Review

Chapter Summary

1. Many new employees are nervous on their first day of work. They just need to try to do their best.

2. On the first day of work, employees are introduced to coworkers and shown where they will work. They may also fill out forms and receive an employee handbook. Handbooks list company rules, benefits, and other important information.

3. To keep your job and avoid being fired, you need to be responsible, follow rules and instructions, and have a good attitude.

4. Good communication and problem-solving skills can help you get along with others on the job.

5. Learning new skills at work helps you do a better job. It also shows your supervisor that you are a good worker.

6. Good employees know how to follow schedules and meet deadlines.

7. Good employees are good team members. They respect their coworkers, cooperate with them, and take pride in their work.

Chapter Quiz

Answer these questions on a separate sheet of paper.

1. What can you do to make your first day at work go smoothly?

2. You want to know how many vacation days you will have after you work for a year. How could you find out?

3. Explain why companies make rules.

4. Name three ways to make yourself a valuable employee.

5. What are some ways to be responsible at work?

6. Why are good problem-solving skills important at work?

7. Your coworker asks you to tell the supervisor she is working in another part of the building. Actually, she is leaving to meet her boyfriend. You don't want to lie for her. What could you say to your coworker?

8. James's supervisor asked him to learn how to take inventory. James said no because he was too busy with the work he already had. Was this a mistake? Why or why not?

9. What is the difference between a schedule and a deadline?

10. What are some qualities of good team members?

Putting Skills to Work

Work with a partner to think of a difficult situation that could happen at work. Then plan a short skit that shows a good way to handle this situation. Show your skit to the class.

Skills Issues

Sometimes a business does not make enough money to pay its help. When this happens, it may try to save money by laying off some employees. Deciding which people to lay off is difficult. Some businesses fire the last people they hired. This means the employees who worked there the shortest time are the first ones to go. In a small group, think of other ways to choose the employees who must lose their jobs. Then share your ideas with the class.

Chapter 13

Making the Most of Your Job

Your first job will probably not be your lifetime job. Still, it is a good place to start thinking about your career goals.

Chapter Learning Objectives

- Explain things to consider in setting a specific, realistic, long-term career goal.
- Describe how to set up a career plan to meet that goal.
- Name some ways to gain an employer's trust.
- Explain how to handle a job review.
- Explain how to ask for a raise or promotion.

Words to Know

career the type of work a person does throughout his or her life to earn a living

career goal the type of work you would like to be doing several years from now

career plan a step-by-step way to meet a career goal

job review a rating of how well you do your job

promotion a new job with more responsibility and more pay

Getting a job and keeping it are important achievements. Kaylee was starting to wonder about the job she had. Read the paragraphs below to find out what was bothering Kaylee.

Kaylee liked her job serving customers at a fast-food restaurant. The work was okay, and her friends often stopped by. The manager didn't mind if she talked to them, as long as she got her work done.

Lately, Kaylee had begun to wonder what she would be doing when she got older. She wondered if she would still be working at that restaurant. She didn't think so. She thought about how boring her job got when there weren't many customers.

Kaylee worked hard. Her job kept her on her feet all day. She didn't think she would want to stand up all day when she got older. Even now, Kaylee's legs ached by the end of the day.

Maybe, Kaylee thought, I should be thinking about my future and a different job.

Once you've learned how to get and keep a job, it's time to look ahead. It's time to think about a **career**. A career is the type of work you do throughout life to earn a living. This chapter will help you think about where you want to be several years from now. It will also help you learn how to get there.

Setting Career Goals

It's best to think about your personal qualities, skills, and interests before you look for a job. That way, you will be more likely to find a job that suits you.

However, it is also important to consider your job needs right now. For example, you need to think about whether you need a job that pays you enough money to buy a car. You might want a job that will fit into your schedule.

At some point, you will need a job that pays you enough money to meet all your basic needs. So, like Kaylee, you must also plan farther ahead. You need to think about what you'll need five or ten years from now.

You should think about setting a **career goal**. A career goal is the work you would like to be doing several years from now. Setting a career goal gives you something to aim for in your future. It helps you make the most of your life.

Deciding what you want to do with your life takes some thought. You still need to consider your personal qualities, skills, interests, and needs. You should choose a job that suits you. However, your career goal might require skills that you don't have right now. You can start learning those skills, once you've chosen your goal.

To set a career goal, think of what you want from a job. Don't limit yourself to what you want right now. Think about what you might want in the future. For example, maybe you want to help others. Your career goal might be to become a nurse. Maybe you want to have your own business, and you like working with cars. Your career goal might be to open a car repair shop.

Being Realistic and Specific

A career goal needs to be realistic. Many people would like to be famous actors, athletes, or models. However, only a few people can reach those goals.

Setting a career goal is a big decision. You can start working on it now.

They are not realistic goals for most of us. You can still try to be an actor, professional athlete, or model, but you also need another more realistic goal. It's important to work on a realistic goal at all times. You can always set bigger goals later on.

Evan had been thinking about being a physical therapist. He learned he would need some special training. The training would include several science courses. Science had not been one of his favorite subjects. He would have to work very hard to improve his science grades. Evan also wanted to make sure he wanted to be a physical therapist. He decided to take a related job first. He decided to try a job as an assistant trainer. He could work in a gym or health club. He already had the skills to be an assistant trainer. That job would help him decide if he really wanted to be a physical therapist.

A career goal should be specific. Candace set a goal of working in Florida within two years. This goal would be easy to reach. But it is not specific enough. Her goal doesn't describe the kind of work she can do.

Skills Practice

The goals below were written by teenagers who had just graduated from high school. Work with a partner to decide which goals are realistic and specific. Discuss your answers with another set of partners.

1. In three years, I want to be the star of a television comedy show.

2. In two years, I want to be a home health aide and set my own work hours.

3. By the end of this year, I want to get a job where I supervise at least ten people.

4. In five years, I want to be a carpenter and have my own tools.

A Career Plan

After you choose a specific and realistic career goal, you need a **career plan**. A career plan is a step-by-step way to reach a career goal.

Write down your career goal. Choose a job that fits your personal qualities, skills, interests, and needs. Make sure the goal is specific and realistic.

List the steps to reach your goal. For example, Kaylee decided to work toward a goal of owning her own flower shop. She thought the best way to start working toward her goal was to learn about plants and flowers. Her next step was to get a job in a flower shop. Once she began working at the shop, she could learn from her coworkers. She could learn more about flower arranging. She could learn how to order plants and supplies and how to keep on a budget. Most importantly, she would learn how to keep customers happy. Kaylee also decided that she would take courses to learn more about the business. While she was learning the business, Kaylee could save money to buy her own flower shop.

Kaylee realized that she had to follow some rules while she worked toward her goal. She also knew how important it is to be responsible. Then her supervisor would put her in charge of other workers. That's how Kaylee would learn to supervise her own employees.

Your career plan will help you identify the steps you need to take. You will then know what you have to do to reach your career goal.

Set up a time line to help move your plans along. Decide about how much time each of your steps should take. You might measure this time in months or years. For instance, Kaylee might work at a flower shop for seven years before buying her own shop. Remember, this time line is just a guess. Many things can affect it. You may complete a step sooner or later than you had

The time line you set up now is just a guideline. It will change over time.

planned. You might need to add a step. As you work toward your goal, you might even skip a step.

Identifying any obstacles that could stop you from reaching your goal is important. Things can get in the way of meeting your goal. For example, Kaylee might have trouble saving enough money to buy her own shop. However, she might think of a way to overcome this problem. She could ask two of her friends to be her partners. Then they can help her buy the shop.

Write down any obstacles you might face. Then name some ways you could overcome each obstacle.

Identifying sources of help can help overcome obstacles. Decide who or what can help you reach your goal. You may think of supervisors, coworkers, or even customers who could help you. Kaylee's friends, for example, might be sources of help for her.

◀ *Learning the skills you need is an important step in reaching a career goal.*

Check your progress as you work toward a goal. Make any changes in your plan that you think will help you move closer to reaching your goal.

As you get closer to your goal, you may already have a new goal. Add it to your career plan.

Skills Practice

Talk with one or more people who have successful careers. They might be family members, neighbors, or staff at school. These people don't have to earn lots of money. They should just be happy with their work. That is success!

Ask them to explain the steps they took to get where they are now. Then draw some stair steps on a separate sheet of paper. Write each step the person took toward their goal. Share your steps and what you learned with the class.

Working toward Your Career Goal

Imagine your career goal is to be a toy designer. As your first step, you get a job in a toy factory. Your job is to put wheels on toy trucks. One day your supervisor offers you a **promotion.** A promotion is a new job with more responsibility and more pay.

However, in this new job you would not be designing toys. You would be selling them. You would travel around the country and show the company's toys to toy stores.

The problem with the promotion is that this sales job is not part of your career plan. You must decide what to do. As with all decisions, you need to think about the possible results of each choice. If you took the job selling toys, you would earn more money. You would also get to travel. But you might not be working toward your goal of being a toy designer.

You can decide to take a job that isn't in your original career plan. You need to be flexible so you can take advantage of new opportunities. A job in sales could take you in an interesting direction. It might also help you meet your career goal. By selling the toys, you might get ideas for new toys. You could take those ideas back to your company. Maybe you could design the new toys.

Earning Trust

Setting a career goal is important. It helps you plan where you're going in the future. However, you also need to make the most of any job, even if it's not part of your plan. To do that, you must earn your employer's trust.

When your employer trusts you, you will be more likely to get promotions and raises. When your employer knows you are responsible, you may be allowed to make more of your own decisions. Your employer may realize that you don't need to be closely supervised.

An employer must see that you can be trusted. Let's say you have been working for a delivery company. You ride with a driver and help him load and unload a small truck. One morning, this driver doesn't show up for work. Your supervisor needs another driver immediately. You volunteer to drive. You tell the supervisor you know you can do it. He takes a chance and gives you the driver's schedule. You follow it carefully and do a good job.

The next time your supervisor needs a driver, he might think to ask you first. You have proven that you can be trusted. Soon you might have your own truck to drive. However, it takes time to gain an employer's trust. It is your employer's decision when to give you a promotion, not yours. You cannot demand more responsibility or a promotion.

You might change your career goal as your interests and needs change. Don't ignore interesting new opportunities.

*Every job has ▶
opportunities to show
that you are trustworthy.*

There are certain guidelines that can help you gain
your employer's trust. Be reliable and responsible on
the job all the time, not just in front of a supervisor.
Prove that people can count on you. Always be on
time. Always do a little more than what's required in
your job. Don't make excuses for your mistakes.
Instead, fix them.

Another guideline to follow on the job is to stay
flexible. Offer to change your schedule and help
out in emergencies. Be willing to try new ways of
doing things. Being flexible is another way to be
cooperative.

Remember to be visible and confident. Let your
supervisor see you or your work. Take pride in your
work. Show that you know you can do the job. Ask to
take on new duties. Then handle them well. Look for
opportunities to prove yourself.

Skills Practice

Think about a job you would like to have. What could you do on this job to gain your supervisor's trust? Write your ideas on a separate sheet of paper. Then share your list with two other students.

Handling Job Reviews

After you have worked for several months, your supervisor may give you a **job review**. A job review is a rating of how well you are doing your job. The supervisor will describe what you are doing right. He or she will also explain what you need to improve. You will probably receive your job review in a meeting with your supervisor and in writing.

As part of your job review, you might receive a score for each responsibility you have at work. The responsibilities listed on your job review will depend on your job. For example, if you work as part of a team, you might be rated on how well you cooperate with team members.

During a job review, your supervisor will list your strong points. Remember these and continue to do them well. It's also important to listen carefully to areas where your supervisor thinks you need to improve. Try not to argue or give excuses. Show that you are eager and willing to improve.

Asking for a Raise or Promotion

A job review sometimes includes a promotion or a raise. This means that some people receive a promotion or raise without asking for it. However, many don't receive a promotion or raise during a job review. If you think you deserve a better job or more pay, find out about your company's policy. You might look for this information in your employee handbook.

Or call the human resources or personnel department. Ask someone there when the company makes promotions or gives out raises.

If you want to ask for a promotion or a raise, meet with your employer. Explain why you think you deserve a raise or a promotion. By asking, you show you are confident of your skills. Your supervisor may realize that you deserve that raise or promotion. However, he or she may disagree with you. In the end it is the supervisor's decision to give you a raise or promotion.

Skills Practice

Interview someone who works full time. Ask the person you interview the questions below. Write the answers on a separate sheet of paper. Share what you learn with the class.

1. How would someone get a raise or promotion where you work?

2. What good qualities have caused people to be promoted where you work?

When you ask for a ▶ promotion or a raise, remember to focus on the positive things you have done on the job.

Getting Ahead

Make the most of any job. Set a career goal and work toward it. To get ahead where you work now, show that you can do the job and work hard. Receive good reviews. Then maybe promotions and raises will follow.

Decisions, Decisions!

Read about the problem Ted is facing and help him decide what to do.

Ted has been working in a restaurant for a month. He is a kitchen helper and cleans up after the chef. One evening Ted forgot about a large plate of chicken that the chef had prepared. When he got to work the next day, Ted found the chicken. It had been on the counter all night. Now it was probably spoiled. No one should eat it.

Just then the chef came in. She asked Ted to get the chicken out of the refrigerator. She was going to make chicken salad. Ted wants the chef to trust him.

On a separate sheet of paper, follow the steps below to help Ted decide what to do.

Step 1: Identify the decision Ted must make.

Step 2: List Ted's choices.

Step 3: Cross out any choices that are harmful or might be against Ted's beliefs .

Step 4: Think about the possible results of each remaining choice.

Step 5: Select the best choice.

Step 6: Explain how Ted would carry out that choice.

Step 7: Describe the possible results.

Chapter Review

Chapter Summary

1. One way to make the most of your job is to set a long-term career goal. Setting a career goal can give you something to work toward. After you set this goal, you can start gaining the skills you'll need to reach it.

2. Your career goal should be realistic and specific. It should take into account your personal qualities, skills, interests, and needs.

3. Setting up a step-by-step career plan can help you reach your career goal. A career plan is like an action plan that you follow to meet a goal.

4. Getting ahead at work means earning an employer's trust. You earn trust when you are reliable, responsible, flexible, visible, and confident in your own abilities. Asking for new assignments and doing them well can also gain others' trust.

5. Job reviews help employees learn about their strengths and weaknesses. You should continue actions that are considered strengths. Try to improve any weaknesses.

6. One day you might want to ask for a raise or a promotion. Find out if the company makes them at certain times of the year. If not, politely ask your supervisor for a raise or a promotion. Don't be discouraged if you don't get it. Try again later.

Chapter Quiz

Answer these questions on a separate sheet of paper.

1. What are some things to consider in setting a career goal?

2. What if you don't know how to do the job you selected as your career goal? Do you have to choose a different goal? Why or why not?

3. Renata's career goal is to earn $25,000 a year. Is this a good career goal? Why or why not? How could her goal be improved?

4. What are the steps in creating a career plan?

5. After you set a career goal, should you stick to it, no matter what? Why or why not?

6. When you are faced with choices between two jobs in your career, what should you do?

7. Why is it important to gain your supervisor's trust?

8. What are some ways to gain a supervisor's trust?

9. What happens during a job review? How should you respond to a job review?

10. Your department is facing a major deadline. One employee is out sick. Is this a good time to ask for a raise or a promotion? Why or why not?

Putting Skills to Work

For the third summer, Elizabeth was working as a lifeguard at Camp Waterway's pool. In late July, the supervisor of the pool broke her leg. The camp director suddenly needed a new supervisor. Elizabeth wanted the job, and she knew she could handle it. However, the camp director did not seem to be considering her. What could she do?

In a small group, think of ways that Elizabeth might convince the director to give her the job. Then tell the class your ideas.

Skills Issues

Job reviews usually become part of each employee's work record. What if you thought your job review was unfair? Maybe you received a low score in an area in which you think you do well. What might you do? Talk it over with a partner. Then share your ideas with the class.

Unit Four Review

Answer these questions on a separate sheet of paper.

1. List some things about yourself that you should consider before looking for a job.

2. How can you find out what jobs are available in your community?

3. How can an informational interview help you choose a job?

4. What is a résumé? What information should it include?

5. What are at least four things you should do before or during a job interview?

6. List things to consider before you decide to take a job.

7. What are three actions that can help you keep your job?

8. How can good communication skills help you get along with people at work?

9. Josh has been working as a library assistant for a month. He likes his job. He doesn't think he needs to set a long-term career goal. Is he right? Why or why not?

10. Suni had a job review with her supervisor. The supervisor told Suni that she needed to be more polite to customers. Suni thought she was already polite enough. She didn't plan to make any changes. What should Suni do instead, and why?

Unit Five

Handling Your Money

Chapter 14

Banking Your Money

Chapter 15

Managing Your Money

Chapter 16

Being a Wise Consumer

Chapter 17

Using Credit Wisely

Chapter 14
Banking Your Money

Choose a bank that offers the services you need and has a branch near your home.

Chapter Learning Objectives
- Describe a checking account.
- Explain how to open and use a checking account.
- Explain how to fill out a deposit slip, a check, and a check register.
- Explain how to open and use a savings account.
- Explain the importance of keeping track of money in a checking or savings account.
- List some issues to consider when choosing a bank.

Words to Know

insufficient funds   not enough money in a checking account for the bank to pay the checks you write

checking account   money in a bank that can be taken out using a check or ATM card

deposit   money put in the bank

check   a written order directing a bank to pay a certain amount of money from the account of the person who signs it to the person named

minimum deposit   the lowest amount of money needed in an account

withdraw   remove something

interest   money that a bank pays you for keeping your money in a checking or savings account; also, a fee that you pay when you borrow money

fee   cost

ATM   an automatic teller machine; a machine that allows you to take money out of your checking or savings account using a special card

signature card   a card you sign when you open a bank account

deposit slip   a slip of paper you fill out that shows how much money you put in the bank

receipt   a slip of paper the bank gives you that shows how much money you put in or took from your bank account

check register   a small chart where you record the checks you have written and deposits you have made

balance   the amount of money in a bank account

cash   dollar bills and coins

savings account   money in a bank that gains interest; it can be taken out using an ATM card or withdrawal slip

withdrawal slip   a piece of paper used to take money from the bank

bank statement   a report that the bank sends you to show how much money is in your checking or savings account; lists any checks you wrote or deposits or withdrawals you made

The story below is about a girl named Carrie. She was excited to have her own checking account at a bank. However, she didn't really know how to use it. Read to find out the mistake Carrie made and the problems it caused.

At the grocery store, Carrie decided to pay for her groceries with a check. She carefully wrote out a check to the store for $23.56. A week later, the store manager called her at home. He said that Carrie's bank had returned her check to the grocery store stamped with the words *insufficient funds*. That meant Carrie did not have enough money in the bank to pay for the groceries.

The manager asked Carrie to bring $23.56 in cash to the store to pay for the groceries. The store was also charging her $15 more because her check was bad. Carrie was embarrassed and confused. How was she supposed to know how much money she had in the bank?

Carrie needs to learn how to use her new checking account. This chapter will help you learn how to use a checking account and other bank services. Then you won't end up embarrassed and confused, like Carrie.

How Checking Accounts Work

A **checking account** is money kept in a bank that can be taken out using a check or ATM card. To open a checking account, you put money in the bank. This money is called a **deposit**. Then you can write a **check** to pay for something. A check is a written order directing the bank to pay a certain amount to the person or company named on the check. That person or company sends or takes the check to the bank. The bank will **withdraw**, or remove, the amount of money written on the check from your checking account. The bank then gives this money to the person or company named on the check.

Think back to Carrie's problem with the bad check. She wrote a check for $23.56 for her groceries. Then the grocery store sent her check to the bank. However, Carrie only had $15.79 in her checking account. The bank stamped the words "**insufficient funds**" on the check because there was not enough money in the account. The bank sent the check back to the grocery store.

Before you write a check, you must know how much money is in your checking account. Later in the chapter, you will learn how to keep track of the money in your checking account.

Stores often charge you $10 or more if your bank sends back your check.

Shopping for Checking Accounts

Before you choose a bank, learn more about the checking accounts at the banks in your area. You should find some differences. Start with finding out what the **minimum deposit** is for a checking account at each bank. A minimum deposit is the lowest amount of money that you can use to open an account. This might be $5 or $50 or more. You can always open a checking account with more money than the minimum deposit. However, many banks will not let you open an account for less.

You should also find out if the bank pays **interest** on checking accounts. Interest is money that a bank pays you for keeping your money in that bank. Some banks pay interest on checking accounts; others do not.

Let's say you keep $100 in your checking account for a year. A bank might pay 3 percent interest on a checking account for each year. That means the bank will add $3 to your account at the end of that year. Then you will have $103 in your checking account.

A deposit is money you put in the bank. *Minimum* means "the lowest number." A minimum deposit is the smallest amount of money that you can use to open an account.

Fees for Checking Accounts

Many banks charge **fees** on checking accounts. A fee is a cost that you must pay. The fees for a checking account are often higher than the interest the bank might pay. It is important to know how much a bank charges for its services.

Some banks charge an extra fee if the money in your checking account falls below a certain amount. This fee is called a minimum balance charge. Another fee could be a check printing fee. To have a checking account, you need checks. They must be printed with your name and address on each check. Some banks charge a fee for printing these checks; other banks do not. Some banks charge a fee of $.10 to $.25 for each check you write. Others do not charge this fee if you keep a minimum amount of money in your account.

A bank may also charge a monthly or yearly fee just to keep your account open. Again, there may be no fee if you keep a certain amount of money in your account.

Another common bank charge is a fee each time customers use an **ATM**, or automatic teller machine. ATMs are machines that allow you to take money out of your bank account using a special card. ATMs are often located at banks, shopping malls, bus stations, supermarkets, and other public places.

Banks may also offer other services. Make sure you understand how much a bank charges for each of its services. Once you add up all the fees each bank charges, you can decide which is the best bank for you.

Skills Practice

With a partner, visit a nearby bank. Find out what fees it charges for checking accounts. Write them down. Share what you learn with the class. Discuss which nearby banks offer the lowest fees for checking accounts.

How to Open a Checking Account

To open a checking account, you must prove who you are. When you go to the bank, take identification with you. It should be something with your name, address, picture, and signature on it. You might use your driver's license or your school ID.

Some banks require proof of where you live. They may ask for a piece of mail that you received at your home address. Bring two letters or bills that you got in the mail with you when you go to open any account. Try to use mail that is one year old. The bank wants to make sure your address is real.

You will also need your social security number, address, phone number, and birthdate. You might need a minimum deposit to open the account. Find out the amount ahead of time. Call the bank before you go. Then take enough cash with you to open your account.

If you are less than 18 years old, the bank might put the account in your name and a parent's name. This means that both of you can put money into the account and take it out.

When you open your account, you will sign a **signature card**. This card shows the bank how you sign your name. Later, bank employees can check this card to make sure you are the one who signed your checks.

How to Fill Out a Deposit Slip

When you open a checking account, you will fill out a **deposit slip**. This piece of paper shows how much money you are putting in your account. Every time you put money in the bank, you will fill out a deposit slip.

A deposit slip shows how much money you are putting into your bank account.
▼

Look at the deposit slip on page 195. Carrie filled this out when she opened her checking account. She listed her paycheck for $39.80 in the space that says "Checks." She also listed the $10 bill she was depositing in the space marked "Cash." Then she added the numbers for the total of $49.80.

When you deposit money, the bank will give you a **receipt**. A receipt is a slip of paper that shows how much money you put into or took out of your account. Make sure the amount shown on the receipt is correct. Save your receipts in a special place at home. If you have questions about your account later, you can refer back to your receipts.

How to Write a Check

The bank will give you a set of checks. You may have to pay a fee for your checks. You might also have to wait a few days to get checks with your name and address printed on them. Some banks will give you temporary checks to use in the meantime. Look at the check on page 197 that Carrie wrote.

Always write checks with a pen, not a pencil. Someone could erase writing in pencil and change what you wrote on your check. Write the date on your check. Carefully and clearly write the name of the person or company that will cash the check.

Be careful when you write the amount of the check in words and in numbers. The two amounts must be the same. Remember to fill the whole amount line when you write the amount of the check in words. Start writing at the left end of the line. If there is space left over, fill it with a wavy line. That makes it harder for anyone to change the amount you wrote on the check. If you make a mistake, tear up the check. Write a new check. The bank might not cash your check if it has any crossed-out mistakes.

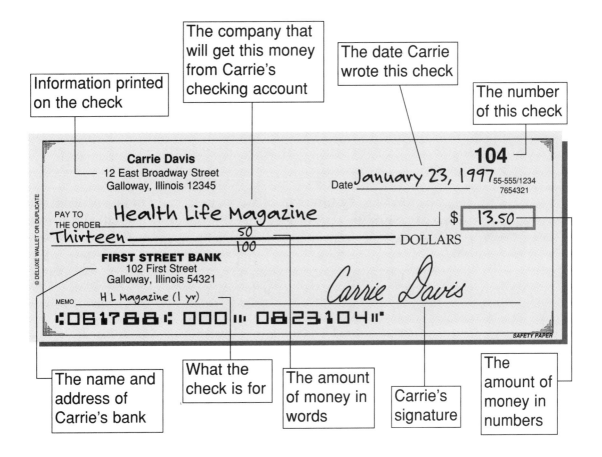

Information printed on the check

The company that will get this money from Carrie's checking account

The date Carrie wrote this check

The number of this check

Carrie Davis
12 East Broadway Street
Galloway, Illinois 12345

Date January 23, 1997

104

55-555/1234
7654321

PAY TO THE ORDER OF   Health Life Magazine $ 13.50

Thirteen   50/100   DOLLARS

FIRST STREET BANK
102 First Street
Galloway, Illinois 54321

Carrie Davis

MEMO   H L Magazine (1 yr)

⑆061788⑆ 000 ⑈ 0823104⑈

The name and address of Carrie's bank

What the check is for

The amount of money in words

Carrie's signature

The amount of money in numbers

Never sign a blank check. Someone could fill in the check with his or her own name and any amount of money. Also, if someone uses your checks you could lose all the money in your checking account. Also, never lend your checks to anyone. If someone else writes the check and signs it, the money will come out of your checking account.

Always sign your name the way you signed your signature card. Let's say a person signed his name as "Jeremy" on his signature card. He should not sign a check "Jerry." If he does, the bank might not accept the signature on the check. It might not get cashed.

Skills Practice

On a separate sheet of paper, answer these questions:

1. Where is Carrie's name on the check? Does it appear in more than one place? Why?

2. What bank name is on the check? Why?

How to Keep Track of Your Money

Every time you write a check, you must record it in a **check register**. A check register is a small chart where you record the checks you write and the deposits you make. It is part of your checkbook. Look at Carrie's check register below. See how she recorded a deposit and a check.

Notice the part of the check register marked **balance**. The balance is the amount of money in your checking account. Every time you write a check or make a deposit, your balance changes. When you write a check, you must subtract that amount from your balance. When you make a deposit, you must add that amount to your balance. Then you will know exactly how much money is in your checking account.

NUMBER	DATE	CHECKS ISSUED TO OR DESCRIPTION OF DEPOSIT	(−) AMOUNT OF CHECK	✔ T	(−) CHECK FEE (IF ANY)	(+) AMOUNT OF DEPOSIT	BALANCE
		PLEASE BE SURE TO DEDUCT ANY CHECK CHARGES OR SERVICE CHARGES THAT MAY APPLY TO YOUR ACCOUNT					
	10/97	TO/FOR Deposit				49.80	49.80
						BAL	49.80
104	11/97	TO/FOR Health Life Magazine	13.50				13.50
						BAL	36.30
		TO/FOR					
						BAL	
		TO/FOR					
						BAL	
		TO/FOR					
						BAL	

When you deposit a check, it must clear before you can use the money. For a check to clear, there must be enough money in the account of the person who wrote it to cover the amount of the check. That money is then put into your account.

Let's say that Carrie started her checking account by depositing $49.80. Carrie's balance was $49.80. When she wrote a check to pay for a magazine subscription, she subtracted it from her balance. $49.80 - 13.50 = $36.30. Her new balance is $36.30.

Carrie shouldn't write a check for more than $36.30. That is all the money she has in her checking account right now.

Skills Practice

On a separate sheet of paper, answer these questions:

1. What was Carrie's starting balance in her checking account?

2. Why did Carrie's balance change to $36.30?

3. If Carrie deposits another paycheck for $39.80, what will her new balance be?

Carrie has learned how to use her check register. Now she knows how much money is in her checking account. That means she shouldn't accidentally write a check for more money than she has.

Choosing a Bank

You could keep all your money in your wallet. Then you would have to pay **cash** whenever you bought something. Cash is paper money and coins. However, your wallet could get lost or stolen. Then your cash would be gone. Putting your money in a bank is much safer. Your money will be safe there until you take it out or write a check.

Let's say you have decided to put your money in a bank. Your community has several banks. Most banks have several offices. You must decide which bank is best for you. Don't choose a bank just because of an ad or because a friend goes there.

First of all, a bank should be easy to visit. Begin your search for a bank by checking the ones near your home or the place where you work. Find out how long they are open every day. Some are open in the evenings. Some are even open on Sundays. The more the bank is open, the easier it will be for you to put money in or take money out.

Skills Practice

With a partner, list all the banks you know of in your community. Share your list with the class. How many different banks are there? Then look in the phone book to find out how many offices each bank has. After you open a checking account at a bank, you can usually go to any of its offices. Which bank offices are near your school?

The next step in choosing a bank is learning about the services it offers. Some services are free, and some have a fee. Some banks charge for certain services. Other banks provide the same services for free. Shop around to find out.

How Savings Accounts Work

It's smart for you to save money for things you want. However, if you try to save your money in a drawer at home, you might spend it. If you put your money in a **savings account** at a bank, it won't be so easy to spend. A savings account is money kept in the bank that gains interest.

Banks almost never charge fees for having a savings account. In fact, if you put money in a savings account, you will earn money. All banks must pay interest on savings accounts. It's the law. The interest for a savings account is always higher than the interest for a checking account.

For example, a bank that pays 5 percent interest on a savings account might pay 1 percent interest on a checking account. That means the savings account pays five times more interest than the checking account. If you put $100 in this savings account and left it there, you would earn $5 at the end of a year. However, if you put $100 in this checking account and left it there for a year, you would earn only $1.

The longer you leave money in a savings account, the more interest you will earn. The more money you put in your account, the more interest you will earn.

However, you probably shouldn't put all your money into a savings account. You cannot write a check on the money in your savings account. You can get money out of your savings account by using your ATM card or by filling out a **withdrawal slip** at the bank. The money you take out is called a withdrawal. You can also move, or transfer, money from your savings account to your checking account.

Many banks set a limit on how often you can take money out of a savings account. At one bank, for example, you can take money out of a savings account only six times a month without paying a fee. However, you can make deposits in a savings account as often as you like.

How to Open and Use a Savings Account

Opening a savings account is like opening a checking account. You have to fill out forms and sign a signature card. You also have to bring a check or cash for the bank's minimum deposit for a savings account.

The bank may give you a small book, called a passbook, in which they will list each deposit and withdrawal. Or you may have a register, like a check register, in which you keep track of your account.

How much interest would your money earn if you saved it in a drawer at home?

Before you withdraw money from your savings account, ask yourself, "Do I really need to use this money now? Should I save it for another time?"

Your savings account will have a balance, just like your checking account. You will have to add your deposits to your balance. You will have to subtract your withdrawals. Keeping track of a savings account is like keeping track of a checking account.

Banking Benefits

A checking account can help you pay your bills. A savings account can help you save for things you want to buy in the future. Both kinds of accounts can be very helpful.

At the end of each month, your bank will send you a **bank statement**. A bank statement is a report that the bank sends you to show how much money is in your accounts. Most banks send a checking account statement at the end of each month. Your checking account statement will list your balance and any checks you wrote or deposits you made. It will also list any bank fees that have been taken out of your account. Use this information to make sure the balance in your check register is correct.

Banks also send bank statements to show how much money is in your savings account. Some banks send a statement every month. Other banks send these statements every three months, which is four times a year. A savings account statement lists your deposits and withdrawals. It also lists the amount of interest you have earned on your savings. You should look at the balance in your savings account register. Remember to add the interest the bank has paid you to the balance in your register.

Learning how to choose and use a bank is another part of preparing to live on your own. If you still have questions, ask a parent or someone else who knows how to use banks.

The tellers and other people who work at the bank can also help you. You can call the bank and get your questions answered. You are the customer, so a good bank should be glad to help you

---

Decisions, Decisions!

Read the situation below. Then help James decide which bank to choose.

James wants to open a checking account. He has a choice of keeping his money at Capital Bank or Branford Bank.

Capital Bank requires customers to keep at least $200 in their checking accounts at all times. If a customer's balance falls below the minimum, the customer must pay $.20 for each check he or she writes. James writes about ten checks a month. He has $300 for his first deposit. However, he will soon have to make a car payment of $125.

At Branford Bank, James can keep any amount in his checking account. He doesn't have to pay a fee for writing checks. However, he will have to pay a service charge of $5 a month on his checking account.

On a separate sheet of paper, follow the steps below. Help James decide which bank to choose.

Step 1: Identify the problem James must solve.

Step 2: List James's choices.

Step 3: Cross out any choices that are harmful or might be against James's beliefs.

Step 4: Think about the possible results of each choice. You will have to do some math for this step.

Step 5: Select the best choice.

Step 6: Explain how James would carry out this choice.

Step 7: Describe the possible results of James's choice.

Chapter Review

Chapter Summary

1. When you open a checking account, you put money in the bank. Then you can write checks. The bank gives the money to the person or company you wrote checks to.

2. You should never write checks unless you have enough money for them in your checking account.

3. Many banks have a minimum deposit for checking and savings accounts.

4. Banks often charge fees for checking and savings accounts. These could include check fees, service charges, ATM charges, and a charge for withdrawing money.

5. When you put money in your account, you fill out a deposit slip. On the slip you should list cash and checks separately.

6. You must fill out checks carefully and clearly using a pen. Also sign and date the check. Never sign a blank check.

7. Put money you wish to save in a savings account. Banks pay interest on your savings accounts.

8. A bank statement is a report of how much money is in your account. Use the information to make sure your balance is correct.

9. When you choose a bank, make sure it offers the services you need.

Chapter Quiz

Answer these questions on a separate sheet of paper.

1. Steven wrote a check to a shoe store for $46.78. However, he only has $17.18 in his checking account. What will happen?

2. Imagine the minimum deposit for opening a checking account is $50. Can you open the account with $40? Why or why not?

3. What is the difference between the interest banks pay you for keeping an account and a fee for an account?

4. When you open a checking account, what do you need to have with you?

5. What are three tips for writing checks?

6. What could happen if you do not keep track of the checks you write?

7. Karen wrote a check to her CD club. She also deposited her paycheck in her checking account. What should she add and subtract from her balance?

8. Where will your money earn more interest, in a checking account or a savings account?

9. How are writing a check and making a withdrawal alike?

10. What things should you consider when you choose a bank?

Putting Skills to Work

Talk with a parent or another adult who has a checking account. Find out why this person chose that bank. Does the bank pay interest on checking accounts? What fees does it charge for checking accounts? Take notes as you talk. Then share what you learned with the class.

Skills Issues

Most stores charge customers $10 or more if banks return their checks. However, most people don't write bad checks on purpose. They just don't know how much money is in their checking accounts. Do you think honest people should be charged for writing bad checks? Talk with a partner about this. Then share your opinions with the class.

Chapter 15

Managing Your Money

Managing your money carefully allows you to buy the things you really want.

Chapter Learning Objectives

- Explain the information shown on a paycheck.
- Explain the basic information on a paycheck stub.
- Describe how to cash a paycheck.
- Describe how to set up a budget.
- Explain why it's important to stay on a budget.
- List some reasons why people save money.
- Explain how to manage your money.

Words to Know

paycheck   a check for the money earned from a job

paycheck stub   a piece of paper attached to a paycheck; it lists important information about the paycheck

gross pay   the total amount of money an employee earns

deduction   money taken out of a paycheck for taxes, insurance, savings, or other reasons

net pay   the amount of money an employee receives after deductions are taken out of the gross pay

cash a check   to give a check to a bank and receive the amount of money written on the check

teller   a bank employee

endorse   to write your name on the back of a check

expenses   payments you must make, such as rent

budget   a plan for spending money

income   money earned

retirement   the years after a person stops working and earning income

Social Security   a government program that takes money out of each employee's paycheck; after the employee retires, he or she receives money from the government as a monthly Social Security check

Read the situation below and see if Keith sounds like anyone you know. Keith is earning money. Yet he is not managing it very well.

When Keith received his first paycheck, he felt rich. He bought himself a shirt he had wanted for a long time. He went to a couple of movies with his friends. He also stopped and had pizza after school a few times.

After only three or four days, Keith was broke. "I must have lost some of my money," he said. "I couldn't have spent it all!"

Keith needs to learn how to handle his money so it doesn't seem to just disappear. This chapter will help you learn how to manage your money. Then you will have some when you need it!

Understanding Your Paycheck

When you have a job and start earning money, you receive a **paycheck**. A paycheck is a check from your employer. It has your name on it. Your paycheck also shows the amount of money that your employer is paying you for your work.

Some employers pay their employees every week. Other employers pay them every two weeks. Some employers pay employees only once a month.

The amount of money in your paycheck depends on several things. It may be based on how much money you earn per hour and the number of hours you worked. Other types of paychecks are based on a set amount for a certain job.

Keith's paycheck is for $76.40. That is how much he earned for the hours he worked last week. Keith

Depending on where you work, you may receive a paycheck once a week or once a month. ▼

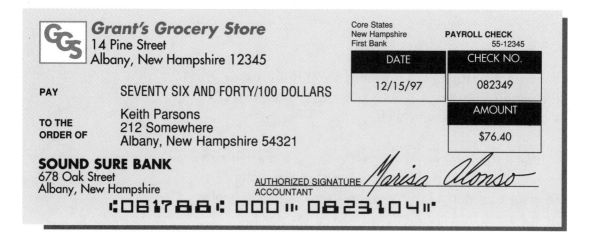

Grant's Grocery Store
14 Pine Street
Albany, New Hampshire 12345

Core States
New Hampshire
First Bank

PAYROLL CHECK
55-12345

DATE	CHECK NO.
12/15/97	082349

PAY   SEVENTY SIX AND FORTY/100 DOLLARS

AMOUNT
$76.40

TO THE ORDER OF
Keith Parsons
212 Somewhere
Albany, New Hampshire 54321

SOUND SURE BANK
678 Oak Street
Albany, New Hampshire

AUTHORIZED SIGNATURE *Marisa Alonso*
ACCOUNTANT

⑆061788⑆ 000 ⑈ 082310 4⑈

works at Grant's Grocery Store. This store keeps its money at Sound Sure Bank. That is why Sound Sure is the name printed on the bottom of Keith's paycheck.

The check also shows the date it was written. It was signed by Marisa Alonso. Ms. Alonso works at the store and writes its checks.

Skills Practice

Pretend you work for Grant's Grocery Store and write its checks. On a separate sheet of paper, draw a paycheck. Use a partner's name in place of Keith's. Show $35.60 as the amount your partner is being paid. Write the amount in numbers and in words, as on Keith's paycheck. Sign the paycheck with your name in place of Ms. Alonso's. Show this paycheck to your partner. Discuss whether you put the information in the right places.

Understanding a Paycheck Stub

A piece of paper is attached to Keith's paycheck. This is the **paycheck stub**. It lists a great deal of information. When Keith gets his paycheck, he looks at the stub to check that it is correct. First, he checks

Make sure your
▼ *paycheck stub is correct.*

Grant's Grocery Store

EMPLOYEE NUMBER	CURRENT HOURS		YEAR TO DATE				
	REGULAR	OVERTIME	Y.T.D. NET	F.I.T.	F.I.C.A	STATE TAX	SAVINGS
12345	15	00	76 | 40	5 | 30	3 | 70	2 | 90	1 | 70

CURRENT EARNINGS			YEAR TO DATE				
REGULAR	OVERTIME	SPECIAL	Y.T.D. GROSS	F.I.T.	F.I.C.A	STATE TAX	SAVINGS
90 | 00	| 00	| 00	90 | 00	6 | 70	4 | 35	2 | 95	1 | 77

CHECK NUMBER	DESCRIPTION	AMOUNT	DESCRIPTION	AMOUNT	TOTAL DEDUCTION
082349					$13.60
ENDING DATE 04/15/98					$76.40 NET PAY
CHECK DATE 12/15/97	AUTHORIZED DEDUCTIONS AND SPECIAL PAY ELEMENTS				

STATEMENTS OF EARNINGS AND DEDUCTIONS • DETACH AND RETAIN FOR YOUR RECORDS

the Current Hours box. He wants to see if it shows all the hours he worked last week. The Current Hours box on this paycheck is correct. It shows that Keith worked 15 hours last week, with no overtime.

Then Keith multiplies the number of hours he worked by his pay for each hour. Keith makes $6 an hour: 15 hours times $6 per hour is $90.00. Keith checks the Current Earnings box on his paycheck stub. The amount is correct: $90.00.

The total amount of money an employee earns is called **gross pay**. Look for the Current Gross box on Keith's paycheck stub. It shows $90.00, which is the total amount he earned. That is his gross pay.

But Keith received a check for only $76.40. This is because some money was taken out of his paycheck. Money taken out of a paycheck is called a **deduction**. A deduction is a subtraction. To deduct means to take away.

Below are the main kinds of deductions. Some are listed on Keith's paycheck stub. These deductions are all taxes. Most employees have these deductions taken out of their paychecks. Other paychecks may have other kinds of deductions.

F.I.T: Federal income tax

F.I.C.A: Social Security tax

State: State tax

Local: City tax

Each tax is shown twice on Keith's paycheck stub. The Year to Date numbers are the total taxes he has paid so far this year. The Current numbers are only for this paycheck. The Total Deductions box shows all the deductions for this paycheck: $13.60.

The amount of money an employee receives after deductions are taken out is called **net pay**. Find the Net Pay box on the paycheck stub. It shows $76.40. This is the amount of money Keith actually gets to keep. It is his net pay. To figure out net pay, subtract all deductions from the gross pay: $90.00 - $13.60 = $76.40.

Skills Practice

Answer these questions on a separate sheet of paper:

1. How much money was taken from Keith's paycheck for local taxes? How much has been taken out for local taxes so far this year?

2. What does Y.T.D. Gross mean?

Cashing a Paycheck

Keith turns his paycheck into money by cashing it. When you **cash a check**, you give it to a person at a bank or a business that cashes checks. That person gives you the amount of money written on the check. Keith could go to a check-cashing business. However, he knows that he must pay a fee to this business to cash his check.

Keith wants to keep all of the money he earned, so he goes to a bank. If he goes to the right bank, he can cash his check for free. Keith could go to the bank named on the check. That is Sound Sure Bank. If Keith had his own checking account, he could go to his own bank.

The Sound Sure Bank is near Grant's Grocery Store, so Keith goes there. The bank employee who works behind the counter is called a **teller**. The teller asks to see identification, or something with Keith's picture, signature, and name on it. The teller must be sure he is giving the money to the person whose name is on the check. Keith shows the teller his driver's license. It has his name, picture, and signature on it.

Keith must **endorse** the check. This means he must sign his name on the back of the check. The teller checks Keith's signature against Keith's signature on his driver's license. They look the same,

"What if you don't have a driver's license? Many Motor Vehicle Departments will make a photo ID card for you.

Always count your money before leaving a bank or ATM machine.

so the teller gives Keith $76.40 in cash. Keith counts the money to make sure it is the right amount before he leaves the bank.

Budgets Are Best

Think back to Keith's problem. He spent his money quickly and was unsure of what he had bought. Keith wants to be more careful about spending his money from this paycheck. However, he wants to buy new sneakers. Keith would use his whole paycheck if he bought the sneakers. He knows he has other **expenses**, or payments he must make. If he buys sneakers, he will not have enough money for his car payment, insurance, and gas.

Keith needs to set up a **budget** to help him manage his money. A budget is a plan for spending money. A budget is a way to take control of your money.

Maybe you don't have a job. The only money you have might be an allowance. A budget can still help you buy the things you want or need. Sticking to a budget will also keep you from wasting your money. You won't buy things you don't really want or need.

When you plan a budget, you find out that you can never get or do every single thing you want. But when you sit down and plan it out, you usually end up spending your money much more wisely.

A budget can keep your ▶ money from getting away from you.

Setting Up a Budget

To begin making a budget, list your expenses for each week or month. Below are the expenses that Keith must pay each month. Most of Keith's expenses are for his car.

Car payment	$110
Car insurance	75
Gas	60
Total	$245

Keith also sets aside $50 a month for movies, snacks, and other fun things. Keith might spend more or less than $50 on these things each month. Some of your expenses may change every month, too. However, Keith needs to stay on his budget in order to learn how to manage his money.

Here are Keith's total expenses for a month:

Car expenses	$245
Entertainment	50
Total	$295

The other part of setting up a budget is figuring out your **income**, or how much you earn. If Keith works 15 hours in a week, he gets a check for $76.40 for that week. In four weeks his income will be four times $76.40, or about $305. However, Keith needs most of his income to pay his expenses. After Keith pays these expenses, he has only $10 left over.

$305   income from his job

- 295   expenses for his car and fun things

$ 10

Setting up a budget is like planning your time. You only have a certain amount of money to spend. You need to decide the best ways to spend it. Wasted money is like wasted time. You can't get it back.

Different people have different expenses. These could include rent, phone bills, and credit card payments.

Skills Practice

Keith only has $10 a month left over. On a separate sheet of paper, answer these questions:

1. How many months would Keith have to save to buy sneakers that cost $80?

2. How many months would Keith have to save to buy a new tire for his car that costs $45?

Staying on a Budget

Keith still wants to buy new sneakers. However he wants to stay on his budget. So he will have to save for the sneakers. He must make his car payment. If he can't make payments, the company that sold him the car will take it back.

The law says he must have car insurance. If he doesn't pay his insurance bill every month, his insurance will be canceled. Then Keith won't be able to drive.

If Keith really wants those sneakers, he might be able to increase his income. Maybe he could work more hours at his job on weekends. Keith's grandmother gave him $10 for his birthday. He can add that to his savings for the sneakers.

Keith could also lower his expenses. For example, he could spend less than the $50 in his budget for movies and other fun things. He can put any money he didn't spend toward the sneakers. Keith must remember not to spend more than $50 on fun things. If he spends an extra $5 on pizza, he will have only $5 left over that month to save for the shoes.

Keith might also be able to save money by spending less on gas. Maybe he could walk places more often or ride with friends. He could also take the bus. If his car needs a new tire or a repair, Keith would have to spend some of the money he has saved to fix his car. Then he will have to wait even longer for his sneakers.

To save more money, try earning more or spending less.

Different Budgets for Different Needs

As Keith knows, having a car is very expensive. He spends most of his paycheck on his car. However, Keith really enjoys having a car. He is willing to spend most of his money on it.

Keith's friend Joy doesn't have a car. However, she still has to make a budget for her expenses. Joy is saving money from her job for something different. She has her heart set on going to college after she graduates from high school. Joy has set up a budget to help herself reach this goal. She wants different things than Keith does, so her budget is different from his. Here are Joy's monthly expenses:

Clothing	$60
Entertainment	40
Savings for college	200
Total:	$300

◀ *Staying on a budget can help you reach your goals.*

Joy's parents earn more than she does. However, they know it's still wise to manage your money, no matter how much you have. Like Joy, they have a budget. Here are their monthly expenses:

Home mortgage payment	$800
Electricity, gas, and water bills	150
Car payment	250
Car insurance	100
Gasoline	60
Credit card payment	100
Food	350
Entertainment	70
Clothing	120
Total expenses:	$2,000

Skills Practice

On a separate sheet of paper, plan a budget for a teenager who earns $400 a month. Then show your budget to a partner. Discuss how your budgets differ. Decide which budget you think is better. Share your budgets with the class.

Planning Ahead

Together, Joy's parents earn about $2,800 a month. After they pay their expenses of $2,000, they have $800 left over. Here is what they do with that $800:

Savings to send Joy to college	$250
Savings for their own retirement	350
Savings for emergencies	200
	$800

Joy's parents want to help her pay for college. However, they must also plan ahead for their own **retirement**. Retirement is the years after a person stops working and earning income. Many people retire at about the age of 65.

After Joy's parents retire, they will receive a check each month from the United States government. This check is called **Social Security**. While people work, a certain amount of money is taken out of their paychecks for Social Security. Recall that deduction on Keith's paycheck. When people retire, they get money back from the government in Social Security checks.

However, Joy's parents know the Social Security checks will not be enough to pay for all their expenses. That's why they are saving some of their income now for their retirement in the future.

Joy and Keith could start saving for their retirement now, too. However, it seems so far away that they have not given it much thought. It is best to start saving for retirement as soon as you can.

Joy's parents also set aside money for unexpected expenses or emergencies. Joy and Keith should do that, too. Then if Keith needs a new tire, he will be able to buy it. If Joy loses a library book, she will be able to pay for it. Planning ahead for emergencies and unexpected need is part of living on your own. If you have saved some money for emergencies, you will not have to ask your parents or others for help.

How Budgets Help You

Setting up a budget doesn't mean you have to save all your money. It doesn't mean you can't buy the things you want. Instead, a budget can help you keep track of your money and learn to spend it wisely. That way, your money won't seem to disappear from your wallet.

Having a budget also makes you think about how you spend money. You may think of more ways to save money. You may also find ways to buy more with whatever money you have.

For example, suppose you decide to spend less on movies each month in order to save more money.

Social Security is like a very long-term savings account for everyone who earns a paycheck.

Setting up a budget helps you learn to manage your money. Being able to manage your money is an important part of living on your own.

Then you might only go to two movies during the month. You might rent a videotape instead of going to a movie theater.

Setting up a budget can help you reach your goals. This is true whether your goal is buying sneakers or going to college. A budget helps you work toward your goal, step by step.

Money Decisions

Sometimes you have to make difficult decisions about money. Knowing what is important in your life will help you make these decisions.

The way you use money shows what is important to you. For example, you might decide to buy a small gift for a parent instead of something for yourself. Or you might give some of your money to a group that you think is important and would like to help.

You might even pass up a chance to work for pay. Instead, you might volunteer by donating your time. For example, you might help at an animal shelter or a day care center. Or you might do errands for a neighbor who is not able to handle them.

Everyone needs some money. However, don't ever let your need for money tempt you to do things that are harmful or go against your beliefs. For example, people who value honesty will return money if a store clerk gives them too much change. If they were paid for more hours than they worked, they would tell their employer. They wouldn't keep money they did not earn. They couldn't enjoy spending it.

Learning how to make decisions about money is part of preparing to live on your own. Being able to manage your money is a valuable skill. It will help you the rest of your life. Money is an important part of your life. Manage it well!

Decisions, Decisions!

Read the situation below. Then help Keith decide what to do.

Think back to Keith's problem at the beginning of the chapter. He was having trouble managing his money. Keith realized that he had to be more careful about what he spent his money on.

Keith still wants a new pair of sneakers that cost $80. However, he doesn't want to save $10 a month to buy them. He wants them as soon as possible so he can wear them at track practice.

Right now, business is slow at Grant's Grocery Store. That means Keith can't work extra hours at the store to make more money. He has to think of other ways to increase his income or lower his expenses.

On a separate sheet of paper, follow the steps below to help Keith make a decision.

Step 1: Identify the decision Keith must make.

Step 2: List Keith's choices.

Step 3: Cross out any choices that are harmful or might be against Keith's beliefs.

Step 4: Think about the possible results of the remaining choices.

Step 5: Select the best choice.

Step 6: Explain how Keith would carry out those choices.

Step 7: Describe the possible results of Keith's choices.

Chapter Review

Chapter Summary

1. Businesses pay their employees with paychecks.

2. A paycheck stub shows how much an employee earned. It also lists any deductions that were taken out.

3. To cash a check, you must go to a bank or check-cashing business and prove who you are. A driver's license is one form of identification you could use.

4. A budget is a spending plan. To set up a budget, you list your expenses and your income. A budget helps you see how much money you need for your expenses. It shows if you will have any money left over after you pay your expenses.

5. Staying on your budget is important. It helps you prepare to have enough money to pay your expenses.

6. People save money for small and large items. They save to meet their goals, such as continuing their education. People also save for retirement and for emergencies.

7. Setting up a budget gives you more control over your money. It helps you pay your bills and save for the things you want.

Chapter Quiz

Answer these questions on a separate sheet of paper.

1. What kind of information is on a paycheck?

2. What kind of information is shown on a paycheck stub?

3. Where can you go to cash a check?

4. Why do banks ask people for identification before they cash their checks?

5. Should you have a job before you set up a budget? Why or why not?

6. Should everyone set up the same budget? Why or why not?

7. What are two things you could do if you want to save more money?

8. What are three things that someone might save money to buy?

9. Why should you start saving for your retirement?

10. How can setting up a budget help you prepare to live on your own?

Putting Skills to Work

Pam gets an allowance of $10 every Sunday. However, she usually spends it all by Wednesday. Pam and her friends stop at a pizza place every day after school. Pam always buys a slice of pizza and a soda. On a separate sheet of paper, set up a budget for Pam. Help Pam stop spending all of her money before the end of the week. Think of ways she could have fun with her friends without spending her whole allowance.

Skills Issues

Some parents require their teens to save a certain part of their income. Talk with a partner about whether you think this is fair. Should teens be forced to save? Why or why not? Share your opinions with the class.

Chapter 16

Being a Wise Consumer

Don't buy something just because it is on sale. Think about the things you really need and find the best prices for them.

Chapter Learning Objectives

- Explain the difference between a want and a need.
- Explain how setting up a budget can help you be a wise consumer.
- Describe ways that ads try to convince people to buy things.
- List things that make someone a wise consumer.
- Explain what you can do if you are not happy with a product.

Words to Know

need something you must have

want something you would like but can do without

impulse a sudden act, done without thinking it through

unit pricing how much a product costs per unit of weight or volume

refund a return of your money when you bring back an item to a store

exchange a trade of one item for another

warranty a promise about how long a product will last without breaking

service contract a promise by a store or company to fix a product if it breaks within a certain time

You might have friends like Bonita and Shakira in the story below. They both have the same amount of money for clothing, but they spend it differently.

When school starts in the fall, Bonita looks like a magazine model. She has the newest style of jeans, shirts, and shoes, along with the latest haircut. By the end of the school year, Bonita is bored with her clothes. Yet she can't afford to buy the newer styles she wants.

Shakira has enough clothes to make her happy. No matter where she goes, Shakira has the right thing to wear. She always looks and feels comfortable. However, she never buys clothes she knows she will tire of easily.

Shakira is a wise consumer. Bonita spends her clothing money quickly, but Shakira knows how to make the most of her money. This chapter will help you learn how to become a wise consumer. You will learn when to buy and when not to buy something. You become a wise consumer of clothes, CDs, sports equipment, and anything else you want to buy.

Needs are things you must have. *Wants* are things you'd like but could live without.

Needs and Wants

Think about the last thing you bought. People buy things for many different reasons. We often tell ourselves that we need to buy something. Yet we often just want it; we don't really need it. People need food, water, and protection from the weather. As a student, you might also need notebooks, pencils, bus fare, and lunch money.

People want many other things. Students might want in-line skates or a haircut they saw in a magazine. Or they might want the latest jeans or a ticket to a rock concert. These are not needs. They are wants. A **need** is something you must have. A **want** is something you would like but can do without. Living without a want won't cause any harm.

Skills Practice

On a separate sheet of paper, list three things a teenager might need to buy. Then list three things a teenager might want to buy. Show your lists to a partner. Then discuss these questions:

1. What should a teenager buy first, the things he or she needs or the things he or she wants?

2. Do you think many teenagers should change the way they spend their money? If so, what changes should they make?

Needs, Wants, and Budgets

People have other kinds of needs besides physical ones. For example, people who buy a car need to make car payments. People who make long-distance phone calls need to pay their telephone bills. If they don't pay these bills, the companies will take back their cars or disconnect their telephone service.

Spending money on things you want is easy—too easy. Be sure you have enough money left to pay for the things you really need.

Of course, buying a car doesn't make that car a need. Steve bought a car he wanted. Now he needs to pay his car payments. The car Steve wanted has become a payment he needs to pay.

If you buy all the things you want, you may not have enough money for all the things you need. For example, if you spend all your money on the jeans you want, you may not have the bus fare you need to get to school or work. To avoid these problems you can set up a budget and stick to it.

Think back to Shakira from the beginning of this chapter. In August, Shakira's parents gave her money to buy school clothes. Shakira carefully looked over the clothes she already had. She decided what new clothes she needed. Then she made a budget. By keeping to her budget, she can buy the clothes she needs. Her budget also keeps her from wasting her money on fashions she knows will quickly go out of style. They are too expensive to be in Shakira's budget.

Bonita's parents gave her the same amount of money for clothes. However, Bonita did not have a budget. She started shopping by looking through

A budget is a plan for spending. First, you list your income. Then you subtract your bills and other expenses. These are your needs. You can spend any leftover money on your wants.

fashion magazines. Then she bought the latest styles until her money ran out. It didn't take long. The latest fashions tend to be very expensive. Bonita could only buy a few things. Now her friends and family have to hear her say, "I don't have a thing to wear!"

A Close Look at Ads

Bonita and others spend money without thinking. Sometimes we let ourselves be influenced by advertisements. Ads use many tricks to get us to buy things that we may not need.

An ad might try to make you feel that everybody else has a certain product. This kind of ad says you should buy something because everyone else has it. You don't want to be left out. Companies often sell a new product this way.

When you see an ▼ advertisement, ask yourself if it is telling the truth.

These sneakers have made me a star

★ ACCESS ★

I only give my grandchildren

Golden Goodness Oatmeal!

It's the best around. Everyone's drinking *Cool Juice*

Other ads use famous people to sell a product. A movie star or famous model might say a certain shampoo makes her hair shiny. Some people believe what these stars say. However, they are paid to say these words. The words were written by someone at the shampoo company.

Ads may say a product will make you more attractive. They suggest that certain products will make people look like models or movie stars. However, the models in their ads were born with clear skin, beautiful eyes, or big muscles. Most people are never going to look like the models in the ads. It doesn't matter how much skin cream, make-up, or exercise equipment they buy.

"Use this product and you'll have more fun" is another message ads use. Many food, drink, and cigarette ads use this approach. They show people having fun together. You are supposed to think they're having fun because they're eating a certain brand of snack or drinking a certain soda. You are not supposed to remember that too many snacks and sodas are not part of a balanced diet or that smoking cigarettes will cause health problems.

"We are your friends and we're telling the truth" is a feeling some ads try to give you. These ads use ordinary, friendly people, not fashion models. These people smile and tell you they weren't sure this product would work. Then they tried it, and it works! They wouldn't be happy without it. You need it, too! Trust them!

Ads find lots of ways to say their product is just what everyone needs, not just what everyone should want. The ads also make it appear that their product will solve any problem someone might have. Most people want to solve their problems, so they buy the product. When you read or hear an advertisement, ask yourself if it is telling the truth.

Skills Practice

Look for examples of the kinds of ads described on pages 226–227. You might find them in magazines and newspapers or hear them on television. Show or tell the class what you found. Discuss whether the ads convince you to buy the products.

Tips for Smart Shoppers

When you are thinking of buying something, ask yourself if you need it. If you don't really need it, check your budget. After you pay for what you need, decide if you have enough money left over to buy the item.

After you're sure you need something, gather information about it. If you plan to buy new jeans, check out different brands. Look for brands that are comfortable and attractive. Avoid any brands that might shrink, fade, or fall apart. Choose ones that you like.

These questions can help you shop:
- Do I need this?
- Will I use it?
- Can I afford it?
- Should I save this money for something else?

Don't let your friends talk ▶ you into buying something you really don't need.

Ask your friends which brands they like. Then ask *why* they like them. Do they like a brand because they can wear it for a long time? Do they like it because a favorite movie star wears it? Read newspaper ads. Find out if the item you want is on sale and compare prices.

Be careful if you go shopping with your friends. Don't let them talk you into buying things you didn't plan to buy. Don't buy something just because a friend wants you to get it. Later, you may be sorry you wasted your money.

When you shop, go to several stores and compare prices. Look for sales. If something on your list is on sale, buy it. But don't buy something just because it's on sale. You might decide later you really don't like it. Also, it might not be in your budget. You will be spending money that you need for something else.

A $100 sweater marked down to $50 might seem like a bargain, but it's not if you really don't like it. Remember, you're not saving money if you never use, wear, or eat what you bought.

Another way to make your money last longer is to shop at cheaper stores. Think about shopping at factory outlets or discount stores. These stores often sell designer clothing at lower prices. Usually, this clothing is not perfect. But the problem may be something no one will notice or that you can fix. Check a product carefully before you buy it.

Shopping at the Grocery Store

With so many different items to choose from, a grocery store can be a confusing place. Make a list of what you need and stick to it. Avoid **impulse** buying. An impulse is a sudden act, done without thinking it through. Grocery stores put magazines and snacks beside the checkout lines on purpose. While people wait, they see these things and buy them on impulse. To avoid wasting money, remember your budget. If you buy things on impulse, you may not be able to buy things you really need.

Think about what is important to you. Maybe you would rather buy something that will last a long time rather than wear the latest style.

Don't shop for food when you are hungry. All of the food will look good. Then you will buy things you don't need or want.

Another way of shopping wisely is to check the **unit pricing** on different items. Unit pricing is how much each product costs per unit of volume or weight. A unit could be an ounce, a pound, a serving, or a single item.

For example, one cereal might cost $.34 an ounce while another brand of the same cereal might cost $.47 per ounce. Unit pricing lets you compare brands to see which costs less. You can also compare small and large packages of the same brand to see which is a better buy. You will find a product's unit pricing on a small sign on the store shelf where the product is displayed.

Skills Practice

Let's say one box of cereal weighs 24 ounces and costs $3.60. A smaller box of the same cereal weighs 16 ounces but is on sale for $2.24. On a separate sheet of paper, figure out which box costs less per ounce.

Stores often sell their own brands of cereals, canned vegetables, soup, bread, chips, soap, and so on.

Buying store brands can usually save you money. Store brands are cheaper than the name brands. Store brands are usually just as good as other brands.

Try looking for "quick-sale" items. Many stores mark down meat or bread that must be sold quickly or be thrown away. Often you can save money by buying these items. Still, you must eat or freeze them right away. If you keep them without freezing them, they will spoil or get stale.

Buy food in large packages, which usually cost less than smaller ones. But check the unit price first to make sure it is cheaper. As soon as you get home, divide the food into meal-sized amounts. Then freeze it right away.

Other Ways to Stretch Your Money

When you want something, you don't always have to buy it. Borrowing from friends and family is one way to avoid spending.

For instance, if you buy a dress or suit for a special dance, you might wear it only once. Then it will just hang in your closet. Instead, borrow something to wear from a friend. However, remember to be responsible and have the clothing cleaned before you return it.

Trading is another way to save your money. Imagine you would like to type a report you just wrote. You don't have a typewriter or computer and can't afford to buy one. However, your friend Ann has a computer. Ann might let you use her computer if, in return, you washed her car.

Another way to save money is to shop at secondhand stores and garage sales. Slightly used things can be good bargains. You might find a sweater or even a computer at a very low price.

When Something Goes Wrong

Sometimes when you buy a product such as a hair dryer or a pair of shoes, you're not happy with it when you get home. The hair dryer might not work or the shoes might be too small. You don't always have to keep these things.

You can usually take an item back to the store and get a **refund,** which is a return of money. Or you

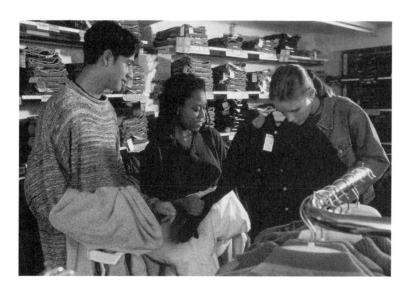

◀ *Sometimes when you buy an item, you're not happy with it when you get home. You can usually return the item for a refund.*

Sometimes you can exchange one item for a different item. This only happens if both items are the same price.

could ask for an **exchange,** which is a trade of the item for a different one. That way, you can get a hair dryer that works and shoes that fit.

If a hair dryer did not work, you might want to try another dryer of the same kind. Then you would ask for an exchange. However, if a shirt changed colors in the wash, others like it would probably do the same thing. In that case, you should ask for a refund. Then you can buy a different kind of shirt, maybe at a different store.

When you return something to the store, be polite. Remember that the store probably did not mean to sell you a dryer that doesn't work. The clerk didn't know that there would be a problem. Calmly explain why you don't want to keep the product. Then ask for a refund or an exchange. Be firm, but polite.

Successful Returns

Two ways to increase your chances of getting a refund are to save your sales slips and know the return policy. A sales slip proves you bought the item from that store. It shows when you bought it and how much you paid. If you don't have the sales slip, some stores will not give you a refund or exchange for what you bought.

Other stores may give you credit toward another purchase. This means you cannot get your money back. However, you can get something else in the store that costs the same. You will only get credit for what you paid.

Most stores insist that you have a sales slip to return an item. Some stores will only allow you to return items for a certain amount of time after you buy them. Some discount stores and secondhand stores might not allow any returns. You have to be sure you really want the item before you buy it.

There is another good reason to save your sales slips. You can use them to keep track of how you have spent your money. Receipts and sales slips help you when you are making your budget.

Skills Practice

Talk with a group about what happened when any of you tried to return things to stores. Were you happy about how the store treated you? What could you do differently the next time? Share one of the group's experiences with the class.

Warranties and Service Contracts

Imagine you used a hair dryer for a month and then it stopped working. In this case, a **warranty** might help. A warranty is a written promise that the product will work for a certain amount of time. Some warranties are for a year.

Many products that have motors also have warranties. The warranty might be printed on the box or on a paper inside the box. Sometimes you might have to fill out a card and mail it to the manufacturer to get a warranty on what you bought.

The warranty will explain what to do if the product stops working. You might have to take it back to the store or mail it to the manufacturer.

Before you buy an expensive product, read its warranty carefully. It might cover only part of the cost

▼ *Read the warranty carefully before you replace or repair an item. You may save a lot of money.*

IN-LINE SKATES

LIMITED WARRANTY
Completion of the warranty registration form gives you valuable rights. If you, the purchaser, complete your attached registration form and mail the original to us at IN-Line Skates, Inc. P.O. Box 082349, Somewhere, NJ 12345 within 10 days of your purchase or receipt of the skates as a gift, your IN-Line skates will be covered by the Limited Warranty described here. Limited Warranty. Subject to registration, your new IN-Line Skates are warranted by IN-Line dealer within six months of the purchase of your skates from the company. Skates furnished as replacements will continue to be covered under the Limited Warranty, until six months from the date of the original purchase.

of repairing the product. It might be wiser to buy something with a better warranty.

You might also buy something that would cost a lot to repair, such as a stereo or an air conditioner. Then the store may offer to sell you a service contract. A **service contract** promises to fix a product if it breaks within a certain time. One service contract may promise to fix the product for free if it stops working within a year. Another service contract might warranty a product for two or three years. Some contracts promise to replace parts that break, but you must pay the cost of the labor.

Think carefully before you buy a service contract. It might cost more than the actual repairs. If you don't need repairs during the time of the contract, you cannot get your money back.

Consuming Wisely

Being a wise consumer means buying what you *need* first. Then you can use any extra money to buy what you *want*. It also means remembering that ads are designed to get people to buy products. They are not written to explain anything bad about a product.

The tips in this chapter should help you make the most of your money. Learning to spend money wisely is one more way to get ready to live on your own.

Decisions, Decisions!

Read the situation below. Then help Anthony decide what to do.

Anthony and Kurt are at the mall. Anthony has found a pair of jeans he really likes that cost $45. Anthony has $50 in his budget for new jeans. However, Kurt wants Anthony to buy a different pair. Kurt likes the designer pair he saw someone wear in a movie. The designer jeans are on sale today for only $35.

On a separate sheet of paper, follow the steps below to help Anthony decide which pair to buy.

Step 1: Identify the decision Anthony must make.

Step 2: List Anthony's choices.

Step 3: Cross out any choices that are harmful or might be against Anthony's beliefs. For example, telling Kurt to mind his own business would be rude.

Step 4: Think about the possible results of the remaining choices.

Step 5: Select the best choice.

Step 6: Explain how Anthony would carry out this choice.

Step 7: Describe the possible results of Anthony's choice.

Chapter Review

Chapter Summary

1. A need is something you must have, like food. A want is something you would like to have but could do without, like new jeans.

2. Ads try to convince people to buy things. You must decide what you want and need to buy.

3. Before you shop, make sure you need or can afford what you plan to buy. Gather information so you know which brand to buy and where it is on sale. Make your own decisions. Don't let your friends influence you to buy something you don't want or need.

4. When you shop, don't buy something on sale if you don't really need it. Compare prices at several stores. Buy things based on what is important to you, such as style, cost, or fit.

5. Avoid impulse buying. Before you go to the grocery store, make a list of what you need. Be sure to check the unit pricing of items.

6. When you return something to a store, you might get a refund or an exchange. Find out a store's return policy before you buy anything. Save your sales slips to make returning things easier.

7. Read product warranties and service contracts carefully. Service contracts may cost more than they're worth.

Chapter Quiz

Answer these questions on a separate sheet of paper.

1. Give some examples of a need and some examples of a want.

2. What should you buy first, things that you need or things that you want? Why?

3. A magazine ad shows a beautiful young woman holding a bottle of perfume. She is surrounded by handsome young men. What does the ad want you to think? What is the truth?

4. An ad shows a friendly, happy person explaining how good a special cheese tastes. What do you think the ad wants you to think? What is the truth?

5. How can looking through the newspaper help you be a wise consumer?

6. When should you buy something that is on sale?

7. How can taking a list to the grocery store help you save money?

8. What is the difference between a refund and an exchange?

9. Why is it important to save sales slips?

10. If a store offers you a service contract, should you buy it? Why or why not?

Putting Skills to Work

Imagine you want to buy a new bike. Talk with a partner about three or four things you would do before buying the bike. List them on a separate sheet of paper. Then read your list to the class.

Skills Issues

The United States government has laws called "truth in advertising." That means companies are not allowed to say things about their products that aren't true. Find an ad that you think goes against these laws. On a separate sheet of paper, explain why you think the ad does not tell the truth about the product.

Chapter 17

Using Credit Wisely

Sometimes it is too easy to buy things with credit cards. Don't let credit cards cause you problems.

Chapter Learning Objectives

- Explain why it is important to pay bills on time.
- Describe how credit cards work.
- Explain what minimum payment and interest means in relation to credit cards.
- Describe the good and bad points of using credit cards.
- Explain a credit report.
- Describe how to get and keep a good credit report.

Words to Know

consumer   someone who buys something

bill   a written request for money for something you bought

due date   the date by which a bill should be paid

late fee   an extra charge when a bill is not paid on time

credit   money loaned to you by a bank, store, or credit card company to pay for things you buy

loan   money that is borrowed and must be paid back

interest   a charge for borrowing money

credit card   a card that lets you buy something now but pay for it later

minimum payment   the smallest payment that is accepted

plastic   a slang term for a credit card

apply   to ask for

credit report   a report of whether you paid your bills or loans on time

credit bureau   a business that puts together credit reports

cosigner   a person who agrees to pay for someone else's credit card bill if that person can't pay it

---

Sometimes people do not have enough money to pay all of their bills. Sometimes people forget to pay a bill. Read the situation below to find out what happened to Andy when he didn't pay a bill.

Andy belongs to a CD club. Each month he orders one or two CDs through the mail. He pays for them with money he earns by working at a grocery store.

A few months ago, Andy broke his hand while playing basketball. For a while, he wasn't able to work at the grocery store. However, Andy ordered another CD. The club sent him a bill for $17.50. Andy put the bill in a desk drawer in his room. He wasn't working, so he didn't have enough money to pay the bill.

When Andy's hand was better, he went back to work at the grocery store. He started earning money again, but he forgot about the bill for his CD.

The next month, Andy got another bill from the CD company. He still owed $17.50 for the CD. But the company charged him an extra $5 because he didn't pay his bill last month. His bill was now $22.50. Forgetting about the bill had cost Andy $5.

Everyone is a **consumer**. That means we buy things. After we buy things, we receive bills. A **bill** is a written request for money for something you bought. Paying people what you owe them is part of being responsible. It's an important part of living on your own. You may not receive many bills right now, but the older you get, the more bills you will get. Now is a good time for you to start learning good bill-paying habits.

A Date with a Bill

Paying bills on time helps make you a responsible consumer. Nearly every bill you receive will have a **due date** on it. The company expects you to pay the bill by this date. If your payment is late, the company may add a **late fee** to your bill. This is an extra charge for sending your payment in late. The company may add a late fee if you don't send a payment at all.

You may be charged a late fee for certain kinds of payments. These include payments for rent, telephone service, electricity, gas, and water. Many credit cards charge large late fees, sometimes $20 or more!

Usually, a company will not call and remind you to pay a bill the first month it is late. A late fee will just appear on your next bill. This is what happened to Andy.

School assignments are often due on a certain date. In the same way, a bill payment is due on a certain date.

Skills Practice

With a partner, think of ways that Andy could have avoided being charged the late fee. Write your ideas on a separate sheet of paper. Then share your ideas with the class. Discuss which ideas might work best.

Late Payments

If your payment is very late, you might have to pay more than a late fee. For example, the electric company may shut off your electricity if you don't pay your electric bill. Then you would have to pay a fee to have it turned back on again. This fee would cost much more than a late fee. Imagine if you had to pay this fee more than one time. This can get very expensive.

It's much cheaper and more responsible to pay your bills on time. When you receive a bill, check to see when it's due. Then pay the bill by that date. That way, you won't ever have to worry about late fees.

Understanding Credit

Some people buy things on **credit**. Credit is money that you borrow from a bank, store, or credit card company to pay for things you buy. You repay the money later.

A **loan** is one kind of credit. A loan is money you borrow from the bank to buy something special, like a car. You pay it back in monthly payments. You also pay the bank **interest**, a charge for borrowing money.

Another way to use credit is to have a **credit card**, a card that lets you buy something now but pay for it later. You can get a credit card from a bank or credit card company. Some department stores and gasoline companies also offer credit cards. If you have a credit card, you can buy things without using cash or checks.

Most bills include a customer service phone number you can call. If you can't tell when a bill is due, call customer service to ask. If you think there's a mistake on your bill, call as well.

Using a credit card is the same as borrowing money. You have to pay back what you borrow.

When you use a credit card, you are borrowing money from the credit card company. You are using that money to buy something from a store. The credit card company pays the store for what you bought. Then you pay the credit card company for what you bought.

When you use a credit card, you sign a slip of paper. Your signature is a promise to pay your credit card bill when it comes in the mail.

Buying With a Credit Card

It's easy to buy things with a credit card. You don't need to have any cash with you. You can get what you want right away. However, using a credit card can lead to problems.

Think back to Andy from the beginning of the chapter. He recently got a credit card in the mail. Andy used his new credit card to buy a pair of jeans. He had wanted the jeans for a month, and now he could finally get them. A few weeks later, Andy got a bill from the credit card company for $70.

If you don't pay your ▼ entire credit card bill, you will be charged interest on the amount remaining.

However, the bill said the **minimum payment** was only $10. Andy knew that a minimum payment is the smallest payment the credit card company would accept. That meant he could pay only $10 this month. He thought he could pay the other $60 later.

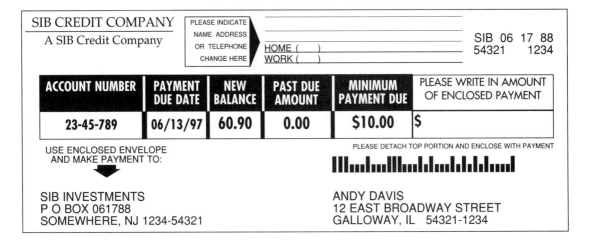

Andy had not set aside money in his budget to pay for the jeans. However, he did have $10 for the minimum payment. Andy decided to send the company a check for $10.

The next month, the credit card company sent Andy a second bill. It was for $60.90. The extra $.90 was for interest. This kind of interest is money you pay to a credit card company when you borrow money. It is different from the interest a bank pays to you when you have a savings or checking account.

Skills Practice

Look at the bill on page 242. Then answer these three questions on a separate sheet of paper:

1. When is Andy's next payment due?

2. What is the least amount of money Andy can pay on this bill?

3. What is the full amount of the bill?

The minimum payment on the second bill was still $10, so Andy paid that. Andy thought his next bill would be for $50.90. But it was for $51.66. The credit card company was adding more interest every month! Andy began to think he would never be able to pay for those jeans.

Andy was still borrowing money from the credit card company. As long as Andy owed the credit card company money, he would have to pay interest on the amount he owed.

You can avoid paying any interest on a credit card. You just have to pay the entire amount you owe when you get the bill every month. Then, the credit card company will not charge you interest.

Credit Card Costs

Credit card companies are in business to make money. They do this by charging three main fees. The first is an annual fee. This is a fee you pay the credit card company every year to use its card. This fee might be $10 to $30 or more. Not all credit card companies charge an annual fee. You can save money if you find out which companies don't charge an annual fee. Credit cards from department stores and gasoline companies often do not charge an annual fee.

Credit card companies make most of their money by charging interest. The companies hope you will not pay your entire bill every month. If you pay the whole amount, they can't get any extra money from you. However, many people just make the minimum payment. Then the credit card company charges them interest on the rest of their bill.

Remember, interest is another way credit card companies make money. Different cards charge different amounts of interest. It can be as low as 5.9 percent or higher than 18 percent. You can save money by looking for a credit card with a low interest rate.

Many credit card companies also charge late fees. A late fee can be higher than a minimum payment! Let's pretend that Andy had no money when he received the $70 bill for his jeans. He couldn't even make the minimum payment of $10.

The next month Andy would receive another bill from the credit card company. Now he would have to pay interest on the $70 he owed. For Andy's card, that would be about $1.05. Then the credit card company would probably add a late fee of $15. Now Andy would owe:

$70.00   for the jeans
  1.05   for interest on the $70
 15.00   for a late fee
$86.05

Many people are confused by the two types of interest. Interest from a bank is money the bank *pays you* for having an account there. Interest on a credit card is a fee *you pay* to borrow money from the credit card company.

When you are choosing a credit card, try to avoid cards with an annual fee. If you don't pay your bill each month look for a card with a low interest rate. Both of these will save you money.

Problems with Plastic

Credit cards are sometimes called **plastic** because that's what they're made of. Some people buy too many things with their plastic. Maybe they don't have a budget. If they have a budget, they ignore it. They don't plan how they will pay for the things they buy on credit.

Some people use several credit cards. Every month, they get bills from several credit card companies. These bills are often more than they can pay. So these people make only the minimum payment on each bill. Then they must pay interest on the money they still owe on each bill.

People can develop huge credit card bills. Companies will usually cancel credit cards if people can't make the minimum payments. You can avoid these problems if you learn how to manage your money.

Credit Card Advantages

There are many advantages to having a credit card. You don't have to carry a lot of cash with you. You can also buy things through the mail or by phone. Credit cards can be useful in an emergency. If you don't have the money at the time and you need something badly, you can use your plastic.

Skills Practice

Work with a partner to think of three reasons why someone your age should and should not get a credit card. Write them on a separate sheet of paper. Share your lists with the class. Discuss whether credit cards are a good idea for people your age.

How to Apply for a Credit Card

If you want a credit card, you usually have to **apply** for one. That means you will have to ask a bank or credit card company to give you one. To do this, you will have to fill out an application form.

Most credit card applications ask for your name, address, phone number, Social Security number, and birthdate. They also want to know where you work and how long you've worked there. The companies want to know how much you earn each month or each year. They may also ask for your checking or savings account numbers and if you have any other credit cards.

Skills Practice

Get a credit card application and fill it out. Your teacher or a parent might help you find one. Then talk with a partner about the application. Discuss any parts that were confusing.

The credit card company will check what information you put on your application. It might call your bank and your employer to make sure what you wrote down was correct. The credit card company wants to make sure that you earn enough money to pay your credit card bill.

If the company gives you a card, it may set a limit on how much you can charge on the card. The less income you have, the less you will be able to charge. The more income you have, the more you will be able to charge.

Credit Reports

The credit card company wants to know if you pay your bills on time. To find out, the credit card company will check your **credit report**. A credit report tells whether you have paid your bills or loans on time. Each time you are late on a payment or have a credit card canceled, it is on your credit report.

A business called a **credit bureau** collects the information about how people pay their bills. The credit bureau puts together a credit report on each person. A credit card company can get your credit report from the credit bureau. You can also request a copy of your credit report from the credit bureau.

If you are applying for your first credit card, there is probably no credit report for you. In this case, the credit card company may ask you to have a **cosigner**. A cosigner is usually a family member who already has a good credit report. You and your cosigner both sign your credit card application. This means that your cosigner agrees to pay your credit card bill if you can't.

How to Get a Good Credit Report

Over time, you can get a good credit report. But you have to start somewhere. To start to build a good credit report, apply for a credit card from a local store. If you need a cosigner, get one. Then buy some items with your new credit card. But don't buy more than you can afford! Be sure to pay your entire bill when it comes in the mail. This will be reported to the credit bureau. After a period of time your credit report will show that you are a responsible person.

To keep your good credit report, you must continue to pay your bills on time. At some point, you will probably want to get a loan to buy a car. If you have paid your bills on time, a bank will be much more willing to give you a loan. They will know you are a responsible person!

People who miss credit card and loan payments or pay bills late have bad credit reports. Banks and credit card companies read these reports. They often turn these people down when they ask for a loan or credit card.

If a company won't give you a credit card, you can find out why. You can get a copy of your credit report. The credit bureau will charge you a fee of $3 to $30 for a copy.

Protecting Your Credit Card

If your credit card is lost or stolen, other people might buy things with your card. You need to protect your credit card. Write down the card number and the name of the credit card company for each of your cards. Save this information in a safe place.

If your card gets lost or stolen, call the credit card company right away. Then someone else won't be able to charge things on your card. If someone has used your card, you won't have to pay for those things.

Save your credit card slips. On your monthly bill, the credit card company will list what you bought. Make sure only the things you bought are listed. If you see a mistake, call the company.

Do not tell your credit card number to anyone who calls you on the telephone. You don't know for sure who is calling you. Never lend your credit card to anyone. Your name is on the card, so you are responsible for the bills.

Finally, if you get a new credit card, cut up the old one and throw it away. Then no one can use it.

Decisions, Decisions!

Read the situation below and help Andy decide what to do.

Andy wants to buy a set of weights so he can work out at home. He found one set that costs $200. He only has $103 now. He makes $50 a week at his part-time job. Andy wants the weights right away, so he is thinking about buying them with his credit card. On a separate sheet of paper, follow the steps below. Help Andy decide the best way to pay for the weights.

Step 1: Identify the problem Andy must solve.

Step 2: List Andy's choices.

Step 3: Cross out any choices that are harmful or might be against Andy's beliefs.

Step 4: Think about the possible results of the remaining choices.

Step 5: Select the best choice.

Step 6: Explain how Andy would carry out this choice.

Step 7: Describe the possible results of Andy's choice.

Chapter Review

Chapter Summary

1. People who pay their bills late often have to pay extra fees or lose services.

2. When you buy something with a credit card, you are borrowing money from the credit card company.

3. Interest is a fee the credit card company charges for borrowing its money.

4. You can make a minimum payment on a credit card bill. However, you will then have to pay interest on what you still owe.

5. Some people buy too many things with their credit cards. Then they are unable to pay their credit card bills.

6. Credit cards can be helpful if you use them wisely. You don't have to carry lots of cash all the time.

7. You must fill out an application to get most credit cards. The credit card company checks the information. It decides whether you can afford to pay a credit card bill.

8. A credit report tells whether you are a responsible person and paid your bills on time in the past. Companies check people's credit reports before giving them credit cards and loans.

9. Protect your cards to prevent others from using them.

Chapter Quiz

Answer these questions on a separate sheet of paper.

1. What can happen if you pay your bills late?

2. Imagine you bought shoes with your credit card. Who will pay the store for your shoes?

3. When you sign a credit card slip, what are you promising to do?

4. Winona received a large credit card bill. She cannot pay all of it. Should she make a minimum payment, or should she just ignore the bill? Why?

5. Who receives the interest from a credit card payment?

6. Why do some people have a problem with their credit cards?

7. What are some ways that credit cards are helpful?

8. What are some ways you can keep others from using your credit card?

9. How do people develop a good credit report?

10. What can happen to people who have a bad credit report?

Putting Skills to Work

Find a partner and make up some rules for paying bills and using credit cards. Think of three to five rules. Write them on a separate sheet of paper. Discuss your rules with the class.

Skills Issues

It's easy to buy things with credit cards. Some people spend more than they should. Some people believe that young people tend to spend more because they have less experience managing money. Do you think that no one under the age of 21 should be allowed to have a credit card? Share your opinions with the class.

Unit Five Review

Answer these questions on a separate sheet of paper.

1. What is the difference between gross pay and net pay? Which one should you use when planning a budget?

2. Jamal is thinking about buying a leather coat that costs nearly $300. He doesn't know if he can afford it. How could setting up a budget help him?

3. You want to write checks to pay your bills. Should you open a checking account or a savings account? Explain your answer.

4. When Mandy writes a check or makes a deposit, she subtracts the amount from her balance. What mistake is she making?

5. A bank pays 2 percent interest on money in its checking accounts that keep a minimum balance of $500. That means you would get $2 for every $100 you left in your account for a year. This bank also charges $.25 for each check that you write. Is this a good place for someone to open a checking account? Why or why not?

6. Should you study ads to decide what to buy? Why or why not?

7. Let's say you buy something and decide you don't like it. Do you have to keep it? Explain your answer.

8. How is the interest on a savings account different from the interest on a credit card account?

9. Why do credit card companies charge interest if you don't pay your whole bill each month?

10. How can you avoid paying interest on your credit card bill?

Unit Six

Living on Your Own

Chapter 18
Getting Places

Getting around can be easy, if you know how. Think about the types of transportation in your community.

Chapter Learning Objectives

- List reasons not to buy a car.
- Describe the benefits of using public transportation.
- Explain how to read a bus schedule.
- Explain how to choose a car.
- Describe the costs of owning a car.
- Describe how to get a driver's license.
- Describe a responsible driver.

Words to Know

public transportation   buses, trains, and subways that are available to everyone for a fee

car pools   groups of people who share rides in each other's cars

schedule   a list of when things happen

route   a certain path or direction

temporary learner's permit   permission to practice driving with a licensed driver in the car

warranty   a promise that the dealer or manufacturer will pay for certain repairs for a certain period of time

mechanic   a person who works on car engines

service   to take care of a car's repairs or other needs, such as changing the oil and adjusting the engine

down payment   the first payment on a large purchase, such as a car or house

car insurance   money you pay a company each month so that the company will pay for repairs after an accident

reckless   careless and dangerous

Living on your own can be difficult. Read the story below to find out what is worrying Greg.

Greg had been reading the newspaper want ads for an hour. He was looking for a job. He saw lots of jobs that interested him. Greg's problem was that he couldn't get to many of them.

"If I had a car, I could drive anywhere," he told himself. "Then I could apply for more jobs." However, Greg couldn't afford to buy a car because he didn't have a job. But he couldn't get a job unless he could find a way to get there.

One of the challenges of living on your own is getting where you need to go. If you don't have a car, this might seem difficult. However, you don't always need to have car to get around. This chapter will help you explore other ways to get places. You will also learn how to get a driver's license and a car—if that's what you want.

Transportation for Everyone

Many people do not have cars, for many reasons. Some people want a car but can't afford one. Other people choose not to get a car. Cars are expensive to buy. Cars also cost a lot after you buy them. You must pay for insurance, gas, and repairs. There are other costs as well.

In large cities, people may not have any place to park a car. They often have to pay to park their cars in a parking lot.

Most cities have **public transportation**. Public transportation is a system of buses, trains, and subways that everyone can use for a small fee. Tax money helps pay for these buses, trains, and subways. This keeps the cost for riders low.

Millions of people use public transportation every day. They go to work, school, stores, and friends' homes. In fact, they go almost every place a car would take them within the city.

Finding Public Transportation

You can use the phone book to find out if your community has public transportation services. Look in the government pages of your local phone book. You can find the telephone number for your town or city and call the general number. Then you can ask what public transportation is available. Only the largest cities, such as New York City, Boston, and Washington, DC, have subways or trains. Small towns

Many people use public transportation instead of buying a car.

may not even have their own bus service. However, many cities do have some type of public transportation to help you get around.

If your town doesn't have its own buses, maybe buses from a nearby city pass through your town each day. Or maybe your town has set up **car pools**. Car pools are groups of people who share rides in each other's cars. You can sometimes get information on car pools by calling your local government office.

Skills Practice

Find out what public transportation is available in your town or city. Tell the class what you learn about getting around in your community.

Reading a Bus Schedule

Before you can use a bus, you have to know where to find one and where it is going. Begin by getting a bus **schedule**. A schedule is a list of when things happen. A bus schedule explains when and where the buses go. Your library might have copies of local bus schedules.

You can also call bus companies and ask how to get a bus schedule. Look in the Yellow Pages in the telephone book. Look under Bus for the telephone numbers of different bus companies. If you know the name of the bus company, look in the white business pages of the telephone book. Look under the name of the bus company for the telephone number.

Bus schedules look different in different cities. However, they all show the **route** the buses travel through the city. A route is a certain path or direction.

Look at the bus route map on the next page. The dark line is the path the bus follows. Streets that cross over the bus route are shown. That way, you can find where you can get on and off the bus.

Information on when buses come are on the back of this map. It shows that two buses follow the same route. Bus A starts out about 20 minutes before Bus B.

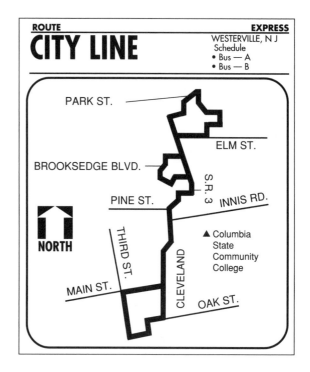

Below is part of the schedule for Bus A and Bus B. It is located on the back of the bus route map.

Monday–Friday: GOING NORTH in the mornings:

	Oak St.	Main St.	Pine St.	Elm St.	Park St.
Bus A	7:04	7:07	7:11	7:21	7:23
Bus B	7:23	7:26	7:30	7:40	7:42

Skills Practice

Use the bus route on page 258 to answer these questions:

1. If you wanted to go to Innis Road, at which stop would you get off?
2. If you had to be at Elm Street by 7:30, would you take Bus A or Bus B?
3. If you got on Bus A at Oak Street, how long would it take you to get to Elm Street?

Getting a Driver's License

If you want to drive a car, you need a driver's license. A driver's license allows you to drive a car legally. It also proves who you are. It's a form of identification, or ID. A driver's license with your name, picture, and signature can also help you cash a check or use a credit card.

To get a driver's license in many states, you must be at least 16 years old and pass two tests. One is a written test, and one is a driving test.

Begin by getting a copy of the booklet that explains your state's traffic laws and signs. You might get this booklet at a Driver's License Exam Center or a highway patrol post. These places may be listed in the government pages of the telephone book. Find the listing for your state and look under Public Safety Department, Department of Motor Vehicles, Highway Patrol, or similar words. Call to ask if they have the booklets.

You can study the driver's booklet at home to learn the driving laws and signs. You can study for as long as you want. Then you will have to go to the Driver's License Exam Center. There you will fill out an application for a driver's license.

The application asks for lots of information about you. Before you go to the Exam Center, call and find

To get a driver's license, ▶
you must pass a written
test and a driving test.

Be sure to study the
driver's booklet and learn
the driving laws and road
signs. It will help you
pass the written test.

out what you need to bring. You will probably need your birth certificate or Social Security card. You may also need other forms of ID. If you are under 18, a parent or guardian may also have to sign your application.

Someone at the exam center will test your eyesight. If you wear glasses or contacts, make sure you wear them for the test. You need to prove you can see well enough to drive.

Now it's time for you to take the written test on driving laws and traffic signs. If you do not pass the test, you can take it again. If you do pass, you will receive a **temporary learner's permit**. This allows you to practice driving for six months. However, while you practice, a licensed driver must sit beside you in the car.

When you are ready to take the driving test, you must make an appointment at the examination station. During the test, an examiner will sit beside you as you drive. The examiner will tell you what route to travel. You must prove you can drive safely and obey the traffic laws. The driver's booklet explains what you need to know for your test.

If you pass the driving test, you will get your license. Don't be discouraged if you don't pass the test the first time. Many people try several times before they pass the driving test.

Skills Practice

Talk with a friend or family member who has taken the written driver's test. Ask which parts of the test the person thought were difficult. What does this person think would help someone pass the test? Share what you learn with the class.

Getting Your Own Wheels

Cars mean freedom for many young people. They can go where and when they want without asking for a ride. But cars cost a lot of money. Cars are also a big responsibility. Before you decide to get a car, decide if you really need a car or just want one. Look into other ways to get places.

If you're sure you need a car, you have to decide between a new car and a used one. Almost everyone dreams of buying a brand-new car. A new car comes with a **warranty**. A warranty is a promise that the dealer or manufacturer will pay for certain repairs for a certain period of time. For example, the warranty might say that the dealer will fix any part that breaks during the first year or the first 12,000 miles.

A used car can be a better buy. A used car costs less than a new car. That means you don't have to save as long to get it. Some used cars come with a limited warranty. This would cover a few repairs, but usually just for the first few months that you own the car.

You take a chance when you buy a used car. You often can't tell if there are hidden problems in the engine. Cars last only so long. The one you buy might be near the end of its life.

If you are considering buying a used car, have a **mechanic** check it over. A mechanic is a person who works on car engines. You can take a mechanic with you the first time you look at the car or take the car to a car repair shop. This service may cost around $25 to $50, but it's worth it. It will give you a better idea of what you are buying. A mechanic will know what to check in a car engine. If there is a problem he or she will be able to find it. You don't want to buy a car that will cost a lot in repairs.

Choosing a Car Model and a Car Dealer

You might have already chosen the model of car you want. Even so, look through magazines that compare cars, such as *Consumer Reports*. There are also magazines that put out guides to used cars. Find out what experts think of the car you have in mind. Another car might have features that you want, but it might cost less and be safer to drive.

If you are buying a new car, visit car dealers that sell the car you want. You need to choose a car dealer by its reputation as well as its prices. Ask friends, neighbors, and family members which car dealers have treated them fairly.

Find out what kind of service the car dealers provide after you buy a car. New car dealers should be happy to fix anything that doesn't work right. Used car dealers may not have service departments.

Be sure to think about a car dealer's location. If you buy a new car, the warranty might require you to have the dealer **service** it. To service a car, the dealer changes the oil, adjusts the engine, and fixes other problems as well.

You may have to take the car to be serviced every 3,000 to 5,000 miles. If the dealer is far away, that can be a problem. If something is wrong with the car, you will need to take it back to the dealer. It may be easier if the dealer you choose is nearby.

Paying for a Car

Most people get loans to buy a car. That means they borrow money and have to pay it back over time. Most loans come from banks, but some car dealers can arrange loans for their customers.

You have to apply for a loan. That means you might not get it. If you have a good credit report, you have a better chance of getting a loan. A good credit report means you have been paying your bills on time.

To pay for a new or used car, you will probably make a **down payment**. This is the first payment you make when you buy a car. It will be about 20 percent of the total cost of the car. If a car costs $12,000, the down payment might be $2,000.

You will most likely borrow money to cover the rest of the cost. To repay this loan, you will make monthly payments for three or four years, sometimes more. You don't own the car until you have paid all of the loan payments.

Your monthly payments will include interest on whatever money you still owe. Let's say you buy a new car for $12,000 and make a down payment of $2,400. Then you get a loan for the remaining $9,600 for three years.

The bank will figure out how much interest you will have to pay over the three years. They will add that amount to your loan of $9,600. Then they will divide that amount by 36, which is the number of months in three years. That will be the amount of money you will have to pay the bank each month. So, your car will cost more than $9,600.

If you repay the loan over a five-year period, you will pay more in interest. Your monthly payments will be less, but you will pay more since you are borrowing money longer.

You don't always have to make a down payment. If you don't, you will pay the whole cost of the car in monthly payments. That will make the payments higher.

Skills Practice

With a partner, discuss the questions below. Then share your answers with the class.

1. How should you look for a used car?
2. Why is it better to make a large down payment on a car?

Getting a Loan

After you choose a car, the dealer will give you a paper showing how much the car costs. You can take that paper to the bank and ask for a loan. The bank will decide whether to lend you money for the car.

Applying for a loan is like applying for a credit card. You will need to fill out forms explaining where you work and how much you earn. The bank wants to make sure you can pay back any money you borrow. You might have to ask a parent or a good friend with a job to cosign your application. By cosigning for your loan, your parent or friend is promising to make your car payments if you can't.

If the bank gives you a loan, it will pay the dealer for your car. The bank now owns your car. If you miss a number of payments, the bank can take your car.

If you don't make your payments on time, the bank may charge you a late fee. A late fee could be 10 to 20 percent of your payment for the month. If your monthly payment was supposed to be $200, it could increase to $220 or $240. If you are often late in paying, your credit report will show this. The next time you ask for a loan or a credit card, you might not get it.

Car Insurance

Imagine another driver runs into your car. Your car is badly damaged. Someone must pay for the repairs on your car. Repairs can be very expensive. That's why most states require all drivers to have **car insurance**. Car insurance pays for damage that happens in an accident. You pay an insurance company a certain amount of money each month. If you have an accident, the insurance company pays for repairs.

You can get insurance to repair your car even if an accident is your fault and doesn't involve another car. Most states do not require this kind of insurance. However, if you get a loan, the bank might require you to have this insurance. Don't forget, it is really the bank's car until you pay off your loan.

Car insurance is a big expense. It can be $75 to $100 or more a month for young people. This is in addition to your monthly car payment! The cost of insurance depends on many things. Because teenagers usually have more accidents than older people, they pay higher insurance rates. Men are more likely than women to have an accident, so their insurance costs more.

Expensive cars have higher insurance rates because they cost more to repair. Your driving record affects the cost of your insurance. The more accidents you have or tickets you get, the more you pay for insurance. Finally, people who live in large cities have more accidents than people who live in small towns. So, people in big cities pay more for insurance.

Reckless or Responsible

After you get a car, driving is a big responsibility. A driver should be safe and not **reckless**. Reckless means careless and dangerous. A reckless driver takes chances, such as speeding or turning sharply in front of other cars. Reckless drivers often have accidents.

Responsible drivers realize that safe driving is a matter of life and death. They follow the traffic laws and look out for traffic signs. They know these laws and signs help cars share the road. The laws help keep cars from crashing into each other.

Responsible drivers are also polite. They wait for

their turn to pull out onto a road. They know that cutting in front of other cars causes accidents. They watch and wait until it's safe to pull out onto the road or pass another car.

Responsible drivers take care of their cars. They make sure their cars are safe to drive. They get new tires when they need them. They have their brakes checked to make sure they work. They also make sure all their lights are working.

Don't Drink and Drive

When you are driving, a mistake can cause anything from a dent in your bumper to a death. People who drink alcohol and drive greatly increase their chances of having an accident. Alcohol slows down the way we think and move. For example, if you have been drinking, you may not realize you are driving into the path of another car. You may not be able to turn your car fast enough to avoid an accident.

Police watch for how people are driving. If they think a driver has been drinking, they will stop the car. The police may ask a driver to take a test to see if the driver has been drinking. It might be a breath test, which tests the alcohol level on a driver's breath. If it is over a certain amount, a driver will be considered drunk. There is also a test to see whether the driver can walk a straight line.

If drivers refuse to take the test or fail it, they will be arrested. Drunk drivers may lose their driver's license and have to pay a large fine. Many are sent to jail. Don't ever drink and drive.

Remember to never ride with a driver who has been drinking. Find another way home. Just don't get in the car. If possible, stop the drinking person from driving. You may be saving a life.

Getting Places

Finding the best way to get places can be a challenge. Some people use public transportation their whole lives. Others buy a car as soon as possible. Both approaches have problems and benefits.

Now you know more about getting places. You can understand a bus schedule. You know how to get a driver's license. You have a better idea of whether or not you can afford to buy a car. Now you can work toward making a responsible decision about how you want to get around. All this brings you one step closer to living on your own!

Decisions, Decisions!

Think back to Greg from the beginning of the chapter. He was looking for a job. He just found a job that is a 15-minute drive from his home. Greg still doesn't have a car, but his city has buses. Also, one of Greg's neighbors works for the same company and has a car. Follow the steps below to help Greg decide how to get to his new job.

Step 1: Identify the decision Greg must make.

Step 2: List Greg's choices.

Step 3: Cross out any choices that are harmful or might be against Greg's beliefs.

Step 4: Think about the possible results of the remaining choices.

Step 5: Select the best choice.

Step 6: Explain how Greg would carry out those choices.

Step 7: Describe the possible results of Greg's choices.

Chapter Review

Chapter Summary

1. Many people use public transportation instead of cars to get places.

2. Bus schedules show the routes buses take and the times when they arrive at each stop.

3. To get a driver's license, you must pass a written test and a driving test.

4. Used cars usually cost less than new cars. However, used cars may have hidden problems and may not last as long as new cars.

5. When you buy a car, choose a car dealer that is nearby and has a good reputation.

6. Many people make a down payment when they buy a car. Then they borrow money from a bank to pay the rest of the cost. They must make monthly payments with interest to pay back the loan.

7. If people make loan payments late, they are charged late fees. If they stop paying, the bank may take back the car.

8. By law, all drivers must have car insurance.

9. Responsible drivers follow the traffic laws and signs.

10. Responsible drivers do not drink and drive.

Chapter Quiz

Answer these questions on a separate sheet of paper.

1. Why might some people choose to use public transportation?

2. What can a bus schedule tell you?

3. What should you do before you take the written test for a driver's license?

4. What do you do during the driving part of the test for a license?

5. What can you do to avoid buying a used car with problems?

6. When you buy a car with a bank loan, who owns that car? Why is that?

7. Is not making a down payment a good idea when buying a car? Why or why not?

8. What are some things that affect the cost of car insurance?

9. How does drinking alcohol affect drivers?

10. What are some of the rules you must follow to be a responsible driver?

Putting Skills to Work

Get a copy of the booklet that describes your state's traffic laws and signs. Using the booklet, work with a partner to make up your own written test. Write your questions on a separate sheet of paper. List ten questions on the driving laws and signs. Then trade tests with other students. See if you can answer each other's questions correctly.

Skills Issues

Discuss these questions with a small group:

1. Why do so many teenagers want their own cars?

2. Is having their own cars good for teenagers? Why or why not?
   After you decide what you think, share your opinions with the class.

Chapter 19

Finding Housing

Finding a new place to live can be challenging and exciting.

Chapter Learning Objectives

- Name some housing choices.
- Describe issues to consider when renting a room or an apartment.
- Explain how to use classified ads to find an apartment.
- List what to find out before renting an apartment.
- Describe ways to furnish an apartment with little money.
- Provide tips on keeping an apartment clean.

Words to Know

housing   places where people live

rent   to pay to live a certain place for a while; also, the money paid to live in a certain place

studio apartment   a one-room apartment

mortgage   a loan used to buy a place to live

security deposit   money that renters pay in case they damage an apartment

landlord   someone who owns a house or an apartment and rents it to others

rental agreement or **lease**   a written agreement between a renter and a landlord

classified ads   advertisements listed in a special section of the newspaper

An important part of living on your own is finding a place to live. Someday, you might face a situation like Maria's.

Maria graduated from high school a year ago. Since then, she has been living with her family and working. Maria wants to get a place of her own.

One of Maria's friends moved into an apartment right after high school. But now that friend has moved back with her family. She couldn't afford to pay the rent on her apartment. Another friend has also moved out of his apartment. It was too noisy. He couldn't study for the classes he was taking.

Maria doesn't want to make these mistakes. Yet she doesn't know how to avoid them.

This chapter will help you learn more about **housing** choices. Housing means places where people live. The chapter will also help you understand what is involved in renting an apartment. In addition, you will learn about taking care of a place of your own.

Housing Choices

You can **rent** or buy housing. When you rent housing, you pay to live a certain place for a while. When you buy, you own the place where you live.

Sometimes, families rent out rooms in their houses. In some houses, renters have their own bathrooms. In other houses, renters might share a bathroom with another renter or with the family that lives there. Renters might also be allowed to use the kitchen in the home.

A **studio apartment** is usually one large room. Studios have a small kitchen and space for a bed, a couch, and some other furniture. Most studio apartments include a bathroom that is connected to the main room. A studio apartment might be in someone's house or in an apartment building. Studio apartments are also called efficiency apartments.

Larger apartments are named by how many bedrooms they have. For example, a three-bedroom apartment would have three bedrooms. The number of rooms an apartment has affects the cost.

Apartments also come in different types, such as condominiums, townhouses, and family-style houses. Condominiums are apartments that people buy and own. People might rent or buy a townhouse. A townhouse usually has two floors and is connected to other townhouses on one or both sides. A single-family house is a house where one family lives. The family might rent or own their house.

Eliminating Some Choices

People looking for their own place to live for the first time usually don't have much money to spend. They must think carefully about housing choices and decide what fits their budget.

Why is a small one room apartment sometimes called an efficiency? Because it makes good use of a small space.

Many people cannot afford to make a down payment of several thousand dollars on an apartment, house, or condominium. Buying a house or condominium means making large monthly **mortgage** payments of several hundred dollars or more. A mortgage is a loan used to buy a place to live.

A mortgage is similar to a car loan. People who want to buy a house ask a bank to loan them money. If they have a good credit report and enough income, the bank may loan them the money. Then the new homeowners must pay back the money they borrowed, plus interest. They do this by making mortgage payments to the bank every month. The bank tells them what their monthly payments will be.

Renting Housing

Most people begin living on their own by renting their housing. Renters do not pay a mortgage. Instead, they pay monthly rent. Sometimes renters also have to pay their last month's rent in advance. They also pay a **security deposit** when they move in, along with the first month's rent. A security deposit is money that renters pay in case they damage their housing. If they cause damage, that money will be used to pay for repairs. If the renter doesn't cause any damage, the money is returned to the renter when they move out. The **landlord** keeps the security deposit in case of damage. A landlord is someone who owns a house or apartment and rents it out to other people. Let's say renters make a hole in a wall. The landlord will use the security deposit to pay to fix the wall.

Take care of your apartment. Then you will get your whole security deposit back when you move.

More about the Cost of Renting

The amount of rent you pay usually depends on several different things. A bigger apartment is usually more expensive than a smaller one. A new apartment in very good condition usually costs more money than an older apartment that shows some wear.

The location of an apartment and what is included also affects the rent. Apartments in some areas cost more than apartments in other areas. Some rents are higher because they include parking, air conditioning, or a washer and dryer. Some rents include the cost of heating the apartment. The more included, the higher the rent.

In addition to rent, you will have to pay for telephone service. You might also have to pay for electricity, gas, and water. An apartment can be very expensive.

One way to lower these costs is to share an apartment. Then you will each pay part of the rent and bills. If you do decide to share an apartment, choose someone you can trust. Find someone who will be responsible about paying bills and taking care of the apartment. You will be living in a small area and making many decisions together. If you cannot get along, living together will be difficult.

Skills Practice

Check out how much it costs to rent apartments in your community. Each student could find out the rent for several apartments. Your community might have a free booklet describing apartments in your area. Look for the booklet in banks and grocery stores.

Find out the size of the apartment and what it includes. Find out what costs are included in the rent. Share what you learn with the class. Which apartment costs the most? Which costs the least?

Signing a Rental Agreement

Renters must sign a **rental agreement**, or **lease**. This is a written agreement between a renter and a property owner that is signed by both. If two people share an apartment, they often both sign the rental agreement. The rental agreement usually includes the amount of the rent and the security deposit you would pay, when and to whom the rent must be paid each month, who pays the electricity and water bill, and how long you are renting the apartment. The rules that renters must follow should also be in the rental agreement.

The rental agreement is usually for a period of one year. It also states when you have to tell the landlord if you plan to move out. For example, you may have to give the landlord a written note 30 days before you move. Sometimes the rental agreement says renters have to pay rent for the entire period of the lease. They have to pay for the whole year, even if they move out.

Finding a Place

When it's time to look for a place of your own, talk to your friends and family members. Find out what kind of housing they have. Ask what they like about where they live. Ask what they don't like about it.

Many times, the **classified ads** are the best way to help you find an apartment. These ads are in a special section of the newspaper. They list properties that are for sale or for rent. They are near the Want Ads that help people find jobs.

People shorten words in classified ads to save space. Sometimes the same word is shortened different ways in different ads. For example, look at the ads on page 276. One ad shortens *laundry* to *laun*. Another ad shortens *laundry* to *lndry*. Sometimes people make up their own spellings.

Here are other shortened words:

RM	room	apt	apartment
BR	bedroom	A/C	air conditioning
TH	townhouse	fr	from
mo	month	furn.	furnished
dep	deposit	W/D	washer/dryer
cpt	carpeted	w/yd	with yard

Reading classified ads ▲ is an important part of finding a place to live. Take some time to learn how to read them.

Here are the meanings of other shortened words and phrases:

off st. prkg. off-street parking, which is parking in a driveway or a parking lot

appls. appliances, which are usually a stove and refrigerator, maybe a dishwasher

utils. utilities, which are electricity, gas, water; if the ad says *utils.* or *utils. incl.,* the landlord pays for these services

Skills Practice

Choose one of the ads on page 276. Figure out what the shortened words mean. Then explain the ad to a partner.

Pretend you have an apartment to rent out. Decide what is included in the rent and where your apartment is located. Think about what affects the cost of rent. Write a classified ad for the apartment.

Location

Along with the rent and services, you need to think about the location of your new place. You might want to live near your school or job. If you ride the bus, you might want a place near a bus stop. You also want to live in a safe neighborhood.

Most classified ads give the location of the apartment or house. For example, the ad might say *NE* for northeast area of your city or *SW* for southwest. Some ads give the address. Booklets that list rental housing may use maps to show locations. Use this information to find places in the area where you want to live. Make a list of the ones you might consider.

If an apartment sounds good, find out where it is. Most ads include a phone number. Call and ask for the address. If the landlord won't tell you, cross that place off your list. There must be something wrong with its location.

What to Find Out before You Rent

After you have several places to consider, call for information on each one. Ask if the place is furnished. Some apartments and houses come with furniture, dishes, and even sheets and towels. However, they cost more than unfurnished places. Unfurnished places do have a stove and a refrigerator. However, you have to supply everything else you will need to live there. Think about what you will need. If there is no washing machine, find out if there is a laundromat nearby.

Find out how much the rent and security deposit are for the apartment. The deposit might be one month's rent or more. Sometimes it is less than a month's rent. Find out what the rent includes and what costs you will have to pay yourself.

Visit the places that sound good to you. The classified ads might have left out something you really like or don't like. Many times an ad makes an apartment sound wonderful. When you go there, however, you may see that it has many problems.

See if the outside areas are well lit. Check if the doors and windows have strong locks. Find out if there is a lot of crime in the area. You need to feel comfortable walking around the neighborhood.

Find out what the neighbors are like. You might not make many new friends if all your neighbors are quite a bit older than you. However, if they are all young, they might be noisy.

While you're at the apartment, write down what you like and don't like about the place and the neighborhood. If you look at several places, you may soon forget which one is which. Your notes will help you remember.

Once you have gathered information, you should be ready to make a decision. Rent the place that you can afford and that you like best.

The landlord might also have some questions for you. He or she may ask where you work and how much you earn. The landlord may ask you to prove how much you earn. He or she wants to make sure you can pay the rent. You may have to show a landlord pay stubs to prove you can pay your rent.

Furnishing Your New Home

To live in your new place, you will need something to sleep on, sit on, and eat on. There are many ways to get what you need without spending a lot. You might ask your parents, other family members, neighbors, and friends if they have things they don't want anymore. Many people have furniture, dishes, and other things they no longer use. They might give them to you.

Another way to furnish a place is to buy things cheaply at garage sales, tag sales, and secondhand shops. Used furniture is a good way to get started. Thinking of new ways to use the furniture you have could save money. Use a card table for a kitchen table. Use your bed as a couch during the day. The less you spend on furniture, the more you'll save for the future.

Skills Practice

Work with a group to list things someone would need for a small apartment. Don't forget pots and pans, towels, lighting, and cleaning supplies. Your teacher will help the groups combine their lists into one list. Discuss whether the final list is longer or shorter than you expected.

Taking Care of Your Home

If you take care of your place, you will feel more comfortable there. Cleaning is easy if you have the right tools. Be sure to get sponges, a toilet brush, a broom

◀ *Garage sales are great places to buy useful things at low prices.*

and dustpan, a mop, and a bucket. If you have a carpet, get a vacuum cleaner. Also, buy cleaning products such as soap for the dishes, detergent for clothes, and cleaners for the bathroom.

Cleaning is also easier if you set up a schedule. If you have a schedule, you are less likely to forget to clean. Some things should be done every day. Wash the dishes and wipe off the table and kitchen counters every day. Sweep or vacuum the kitchen floor so crumbs don't attract bugs. If you put away clothes and shoes and make your bed every day, your apartment will look tidier.

Things don't get clean ▶
unless you clean them.

Some things you'll do at least once a week. Change the towels in the bathroom. Sweep or vacuum all the floors. Remember to take out the garbage. Change the bed sheets and clean the bathroom, including the toilet. Dust the furniture and wash the kitchen floor.

Are You Ready?

Having a place of your own can be both exciting and difficult. Don't rush into it. Consider all your choices before making any decisions.

Decisions, Decisions!

Think back to Maria from the beginning of the chapter. She was thinking of getting a place of her own. Her friend Elise has an apartment and wants Maria to live with her. However, the apartment is not near a bus stop. Maria doesn't have a car. She would have a long walk to catch a bus. On a separate sheet of paper, follow the steps below to help Maria decide what to do.

Step 1: Identify the decision Maria must make.

Step 2: List Maria's choices.

Step 3: Cross out any choices that are harmful or might be against Maria's beliefs.

Step 4: Think about the remaining choices.

Step 5: Select the best choice.

Step 6: Explain how Maria would carry it out.

Step 7: Describe the possible results.

Chapter Summary

1. Housing choices include room rentals, apartments of different sizes, townhouses, condominiums, and houses.

2. Buying housing requires a large down payment and a monthly mortgage payment.

3. Young people usually start out by renting a room or an apartment. Renters must pay a security deposit and monthly rent. They also sign a written rental agreement or lease. It states the rent and deposit the renters will pay, how long they will stay, and the rules they will follow.

4. Friends' recommendations and classified ads can help you find and choose a place to live.

5. When choosing a place to live, consider the rent, size, and location. Ask what things are included. Consider safety features in the neighborhood, laundry, and parking.

6. You can furnish your apartment by asking friends and family for things they no longer use. You can also shop at garage sales and secondhand shops.

7. To care for an apartment, buy cleaning supplies and set up a cleaning schedule.

Chapter Quiz

Answer these questions on a separate sheet of paper.

1. What kinds of payments may be required to buy a house or condominium?

2. What kinds of payments should renters expect to make?

3. What things affect the rent for an apartment or house?

4. What information is included in a rental agreement?

5. What words are often shortened in classified ads for housing?

6. Why should you see a house or apartment before renting it?

7. Why is location important?

8. What should you find out before renting a place?

9. How can you get furniture for your new place?

10. Why is it helpful to have a cleaning schedule?

Putting Skills to Work

Pretend that you have a cousin. Make up details about your cousin's life and needs. Imagine that your cousin is graduating from high school next year. This cousin is thinking about getting an apartment. On a separate sheet of paper, write your cousin a letter. Explain whether you think he or she should get an apartment right after high school.

Skills Issues

With a group, list skills you are learning in school that will help you live on your own. One example is math, which will help you figure out if you can afford an apartment. Then list things you haven't learned that you need to know. Share both lists with the class. Talk about how you could find the information or learn the skills you still need.

Unit Six Review

Answer these questions on a separate sheet of paper.

1. Stella is taking the bus to work and saving her money for a car. Kim already bought a very old car with a little money she had saved. Which girl do you think made the better decision? Why?

2. Why does it matter which car dealer you buy from?

3. Erik hasn't been making his car payments. What will happen?

4. Monica's car was damaged badly in an accident. She is worried because she cannot afford to repair her car. Should she worry? Why or why not?

5. Martin doesn't care what the other drivers do. He drives the way he wants. Is he being responsible? Why or why not?

6. Keisha is looking for an apartment. What are some things Keisha should consider?

7. Leon read a classified ad about an apartment that sounded great. When he called the landlord, he immediately said he'd take it. Did Leon make a wise decision? Why or why not?

8. Steve has ruined the carpet in his apartment. He says he doesn't care. He'll be moving out soon anyway. What will Steve's landlord probably do?

9. Austin decided to leave his own apartment and move in with friends. One Saturday morning he packed his things and moved without telling his landlord. What should Austin have done instead, and why?

10. Natalie wants her first apartment to be perfect. She has decided to sit on the floor until she can buy the chair she wants. What is another way Natalie could furnish her apartment?

You and Your Community

Chapter 20
Being a Good Citizen

Voting in an election is an important part of being a good citizen.

Chapter Learning Objectives

- Explain the purpose of a Social Security card.
- Explain how to register to vote.
- Describe how to learn more about candidates.
- Explain taxes.
- Explain what to do if you receive a jury summons.
- Describe volunteer opportunities in the community.

Words to Know

citizen   someone who lives in a certain city or nation

maiden name   a woman's last name before she is married

register   to sign up to vote

issue   a question the community must make a decision on

candidate   a person running for an office in an election

income tax   money that everyone who works pays to the government

federal   national

tax deduction   a cost that can be subtracted from your income when you figure out your taxes

standard deduction   an amount of money set by the government; it can be subtracted from your income

exemption   a tax deduction for each person in a family

withheld   held back or taken out

jury   a group that decides the outcome of a trial

summons   a legal request

You might know someone like Kim. She often decides that if something is too much trouble, she won't bother with it. The conversation below shows how Kim goes through life.

"So, who do you want for President? Who are you going to vote for?" Henry asked.

"Vote?" Kim said. "I'm not going to vote. It's way too hard to sign up to vote. I hate filling out forms. I don't even know what this election is about. Are you going to vote for President?"

Kim is not being a good **citizen**. A citizen is someone who lives in a certain city or nation. But being a good citizen means more than living in a certain place. It means doing your part and taking an active role. Good citizens vote. They also know what they're voting for and who the candidates are in an election. They pay their taxes, serve on juries, and volunteer their time to the community. In addition, they obey the laws. This chapter and the next one explain how to be a good citizen.

Getting a Social Security Card

Part of being a citizen is getting a Social Security card. You might already have one. Your parents might have gotten one for you when you were born. Children born in the United States must have a Social Security card before they are the age of one.

What is really important about a Social Security card is the number on your card. You are the only person who will have that number. The number identifies you. You will have the same number for your entire life. You will need this number when you apply for many things, such as credit cards and loans. Many forms ask for this number.

When you start working, you will need your Social Security number. Employers use the numbers to report each person's income to the government.

If you are under 18 and don't have a Social Security number, your parents should get one for you. If you are over 18, you must apply at a Social Security office for a number. These offices are listed in the government pages of the telephone book. Look under U.S. Government, Social Security Administration. There is no charge for getting a Social Security number.

When you apply for your Social Security number, you need to prove who you are. Take your original birth certificate and one other piece of identification. This could be your driver's license or a school ID. If you were not born in the United States, you will need your foreign birth certificate or passport and the papers you received from the Immigration and Naturalization Services.

Keep your Social Security card in a safe place.

SOCIAL SECURITY ADMINISTRATION
Application for a Social Security Card

INSTRUCTIONS	• Please read "How To Complete This Form" on page 2.
	• Print or type using black or blue ink. DO NOT USE PENCIL.
	• After you complete this form, take or mail it along with the required documents to your nearest Social Security office.
	• If you are completing this form for someone else, answer the questions as they apply to that person. Then, sign your name in question 16.

1 NAME
To Be Shown On Card

▶

FIRST   FULL MIDDLE NAME   LAST

FULL NAME AT BIRTH
IF OTHER THAN ABOVE

FIRST   FULL MIDDLE NAME   LAST

▶

2 MAILING ADDRESS
Do Not Abbreviate

STREET ADDRESS, APT. NO., PO BOX, RURAL ROUTE NO.

CITY   STATE   ZIP CODE

3 CITIZENSHIP
(check one)

☐ U.S. Citizen ☐ Legal Alien Allowed To Work ☐ Legal Alien Not Allowed To Work ☐ Foreign Student Allowed Restricted Employment ☐ Conditionally Legalized Alien Allowed To Work ☐ Other (See Instructions On Page 2)

4 SEX

☐ Male ☐ Female

5 RACE/ETHNIC DESCRIPTION
(Check One Only - Voluntary)

☐ Asian, Asian American Or Pacific Islander ☐ Hispanic ☐ Black (Not Hispanic) ☐ North American Indian Or Alaskan Native ☐ White (Not Hispanic)

6 DATE OF BIRTH _____
MONTH DAY YEAR

7 PLACE OF BIRTH _____
(Do Not Abbreviate)   CITY   STATE OR FOREIGN COUNTRY

Office Use Only   FCI

8 MOTHER'S MAIDEN NAME
FIRST   FULL MIDDLE NAME   LAST NAME AT HER BIRTH

9 FATHER'S NAME
FIRST   FULL MIDDLE NAME   LAST

10 Has the Social Security number previously assigned to the person listed in item 1?

☐ Yes (If "yes," answer questions 11-13.)   ☐ No (If "no," go on to question 14.)   ☐ Don't Know (If "don't know", go on to question 14.)

11 Enter the Social Security number previously assigned to the person listed in item 1.

☐☐☐ — ☐☐ — ☐☐☐☐

12 Enter the name shown on the the most recent Social Security card issued for the person listed in item 1.

FIRST   MIDDLE   LAST

13 Enter any different date of birth if used on an earlier application for a card. _____
MONTH DAY YEAR

14 TODAY'S DATE ▶ _____ **15 DAYTIME PHONE NUMBER** ▶ ( ) _____
MONTH DAY YEAR   AREA CODE

DELIBERATELY FURNISHING (OR CAUSING TO BE FURNISHED) FALSE INFORMATION ON THIS APPLICATION IS A CRIME PUNISHABLE BY FINE OR IMPRISONMENT, OR BOTH

16 YOUR SIGNATURE

▶

17 YOUR RELATIONSHIP TO THE IN ITEM 1 IS:

☐ Self ☐ Natural or Adoptive Parent ☐ Legal Guardian ☐ Other (specify) _____

DO NOT WRITE BELOW THIS LINE (FOR SSA USE ONLY)							
NPN		DOC	NTI		CAN		ITV
PBC	EVI	EVA	EVC	PRA	NWR	DNR	UNIT
EVIDENCE SUBMITTED				SIGNATURE AND TITLE OF EMPLOYEE(S) REVIEWING EVIDENCE AND/OR CONDUCTING INTERVIEW			
							DATE
				DCL			DATE

Form SS-5 (9/89) 5/88 edition may be used until supply is exhausted

You will have to fill out a form to get a Social Security card. The form asks for basic information about you. It asks for your name, address, citizenship, sex, and date and place of birth. It also asks your father's name and your mother's maiden name. A **maiden name** is a woman's last name when she is born. If you lose your card, you will have to fill out the form again. You must also prove who you are again. To replace a lost card, you can use a driver's license, school record, passport, or health insurance card for identification.

Skills Practice

Look over the Social Security card application form shown on page 289. On a separate sheet of paper, fill in all the information you would put on the form.

Registering to Vote

Another part of being a good citizen is voting. In every state except North Dakota you must **register** before you can vote. To register means to sign up to vote. When you register to vote, you fill out a voter registration form. To register, you must be a citizen of the United States and at least 18 years old.

It's easy to register to vote. You can register to vote at any Bureau of Motor Vehicles. You can also register to vote by mail. You can get a registration form at most post offices, libraries, and the board of elections office. You must mail the form to the address printed on the form.

Each time you move, you should register to vote. Every state has its own rules about how and when to register. Find out the rules in your state. You can call the Board of Elections for registration information.

After you register, the Board of Elections will mail you a Voter Notification Card. You will be assigned a place to vote near your home. It might be a school or a library. On election day, go to that place, show your Voter Registration Card, and sign your name. Then you can vote.

In the United States, your vote is secret. No one will know who you vote for. You have the right to vote for any person you choose. Remember, if you don't want to tell anyone how you voted, don't.

Voting Choices

When you vote, you help shape the government. You help choose your own leaders, such as mayor, senator, and President. To be a good citizen, you need to know who the candidates are and what you're voting for in each election.

You might also vote on **issues**. An issue is a question that the community must make a decision on. For example, you might be asked to vote on whether there should be a new tax to pay for a new school.

Preparing to Vote

Just before an election, you will see many advertisements on television, hear them on the radio, and read them in newspapers. These ads will try to get you to vote in a certain way.

Ads only give you one side of an issue. They try to make one candidate look good and the others look bad. A **candidate** is someone who is running for an office, such as mayor or President.

Before you vote, gather information. Be sure to read materials that give the facts and don't tell you how to vote. Consider your choices carefully. Then you can make your own wise decision. Don't let anyone decide who you should vote for. It's your decision.

During an election, you need to find out facts about the candidates and issues.

Skills Practice

Read this ad for a new school tax called Issue 37:

Vote for Issue 37! The future is in your hands! Without your help, our children will spend their days in school buildings that are falling apart. A vote for Issue 37 is a vote for our community's future!

Answer these questions on a separate sheet of paper:

1. Does this ad give any facts? If so, what are they?

2. What else would you want to know before you voted for or against Issue 37?

Taxes

Good citizens pay taxes. We all benefit from the services that taxes give to our communities. Money from taxes pays for police officers and firefighters. It pays for roads, parks, and schools. Taxes also pay part of the costs of community and state colleges.

Income tax is money that everyone who works must pay to the government. The amount people pay is based on their income. Income is the amount of money a person earns. People pay income taxes to the city, state, and federal government. **Federal** is another name for national. The federal government is the **United States government.**

Different people pay different amounts of taxes.

It is against the law to refuse to pay income taxes. People who do not pay their income taxes can go to jail. Good citizens also pay a smaller amount of taxes to their state governments. Then they pay an even smaller amount of taxes to their city or town governments.

The amount one person pays in taxes will be different from the amount someone else pays. Many things affect how much a person pays in taxes for each year.

Tax Deductions

You don't have to pay taxes on all the money you earn. Everyone gets a **tax deduction**. Tax deductions are certain costs that you have paid during the year. You can subtract these costs from your income when you figure out your taxes. Then you owe taxes on the amount of income that is left. Some common tax deductions include city and state income tax, property taxes, interest on a home mortgage paid to a bank, and donations to religious groups and charities.

You can list each deduction on your tax return. However, many people do not. Instead, they take a **standard deduction**. The standard deduction is an amount of money set by the government each year for each income level.

Standard deductions may change every year.

In 1995, the standard deduction was $3,900 for a single person. It was $6,550 for a married couple. This means single people could subtract $3,900 from their incomes in 1995. They did not have to pay taxes on that $3,900.

Exemptions

Workers can also subtract money from their incomes for **exemptions**. An exemption is a tax deduction for members in your family. You get one exemption for each person in your family who you support. The government sets the amount of these exemptions. In 1995, the amount for each exemption was $2,500.

You get one exemption for yourself. Married couples get two exemptions, one for each other. A single parent or a married couple also gets one exemption for each child. Here is how a single person could use the standard deduction and one exemption:

Income	$20,000
Standard deduction	- 3,900
One exemption	- 2,500
	$13,600

This person would owe taxes on $13,600. The amount of taxes would be 15 percent of $13,600. That is about $2,040. However, a person doesn't pay the $2,040 all at once.

Skills Practice

On a separate sheet of paper, figure out the amount of taxes James and his wife June owed in 1995. James made $17,000 that year. They took the standard deduction for a married couple. Their tax rate was 15 percent.

Withholdings

During the year, your employer subtracts income tax from each of your paychecks. Then in January, your employer sends you a W-2 form. This form shows the amount of money you earned during the past year. It also shows the amount of income tax that has already been **withheld** from your paychecks. Withheld means held back or taken out.

Because of the system of withholding, most of your income taxes have already been paid. All you normally need to pay is the amount you still owe. Some people have more income tax withheld than they owe. They will receive tax refunds, or get money back from the government after filling out their tax forms.

The W-2 form shows you ▼ *the amount of money you earned during the year. Below is a blank copy of a W-2 form.*

a Control number		Void ☐	For Official Use Only OMB No. 1545-008	
b Employer's identification number			1 Wages, tips other compensation	2 Federal income tax withheld
c Employer's name, address, and ZIP code			3 Social security wages	4 Social security tax withheld
			5 Medicare wages and tip	6 Medicare tax withheld
			7 Social security tips	8 Allocated tips
d Employee's social security number			9 Advance EIC payments	10 Department care benefits
e Employee's name (first, middle initial, last)			11 Nonqualified plans	12 Benefits included in box 1
			13 See Instrs. for box 13	14 Other
f Employee's address and ZIP code			15 Statutory Deceased Pension employee plan ☐ ☐ ☐	Legal Hshld. Subtotal Deferred rep. emp. compensation ☐ ☐ ☐ ☐
16 State Employer's state I.D. No.	17 State wages, tips, etc.	18 State income tax	19 Locality name	20 Local wages, tips, etc. 21 Local income tax

Filing a Tax Form

The Internal Revenue Service, which is usually called the IRS, sends you a tax form each year. If you have never filed a tax form, you may have to get one at the post office or other government office. The tax form is really a worksheet. You may receive Form 1040EZ for doing your taxes.

Tax forms have a place to list your income. It tells you to subtract your deductions and exemptions. It reminds you to subtract the taxes you have already paid. Tables in the instruction booklet help you figure out what you owe. Read the instruction booklet carefully to help you fill out your tax return carefully.

You must complete your tax form each year and send it to the IRS by April 15. If you have trouble filling out the forms, get help. Libraries are excellent resources for helping with tax forms. Libraries have copies of tax forms. They also have instruction booklets and tapes. A few libraries even offer help in completing the forms. It is also possible to call the IRS using the toll-free phone number on your tax booklet.

The 1040EZ form comes with an instruction booklet to help you fill out your tax return. ▼

Figure your total income (See page 20.) Attach Copy B of your Forms W-2 and 10099-R here. If you didn't get a W-2, see page 25. Enclose, but do not attach, any payment with your return.	7	Wages,salaries, tips, etc. This should be shown in box 1 of your W-2 form(s). Attach Form(s) W-2			7	
	8a	**Taxable** interest income (see page 25). IF OVER $ 400, attach Schedule 1.			8a	
	b	**Tax-exempt** interest. DO NOT include on line 8a.	8b			
	9	Dividends. If over $400, attach Schedule 1			9	
	10a	Total IRA distributions 10a	**10b**	Taxable amount (see page 27)		
	11a	Total pensions and annuities. 11a	**11b**	Taxable amount (see page 27)	11b	
	12	Unemployment compensation (see right page 30).			12	
	13a	Social security benefits. 13a	**13b**	Taxable amount (see page 31).	13b	
	14	Add lines 7 through 13b (far right column). This is your total income			**14**	
Figure your adjusted gross income	15a	Your IRA deduction (see page 34).		15a		
	b	Spouse's IRA deduction (see page 34).		15b		
	c	Add lines 15a and 15b. These are your **total adjustments.**			15c	
	16	Subtract line 15c from line 14. This is your **adjusted gross income.** If less than $25,296 and a child lived with you (less than $9,000 if a child didn't live with you), see "Earned income credit" on page 44			16	

Some businesses will also fill out the forms for you. However, they charge a fee. Look under Tax Preparation in the Yellow Pages.

Serving on a Jury

In the United States, each person who is accused of a crime has the right to a trial. During the trial a **jury**, or a chosen group of people, listens to both sides of the case. Then the jury decides whether the person is innocent or guilty. Serving on a jury is a duty of a good citizen.

Some day you may get a **summons** for jury duty. A summons is a legal request that you must follow. It will tell you when and where you must appear for jury duty. If you cannot be there then call the phone number on the summons. If you ignore a summons, you may get into serious trouble. It is against the law to refuse jury duty.

People are excused from jury duty only for serious reasons. If you are called for jury duty, your employer must give you time off from work. Jurors receive a small amount of money for each day they serve.

If you have been called for jury duty, be sure to arrive on time. The judge or lawyers who are part of a trial might ask you questions. They might decide to excuse you, or let you go, from jury duty for any number of reasons. If you are chosen for a jury, listen closely during the trial. Then when you are asked to make a decision, think carefully about what you heard.

Volunteering

Another way to be a good citizen is to volunteer. Volunteering is giving your time to help others. There are many ways to do this. You might cut a neighbor's grass. Or you might give your time to a group. For example, you could help *Meals on Wheels*. This group delivers lunches to people who can't leave their homes.

Skills Practice

Talk with a small group of your classmates. Think of ways to volunteer in your community. Then share your group's ideas with the class. Try out one of your ideas. Volunteering not only helps others in your community, but it also helps you.

You have many opportunities to be a good citizen. Some are required, like paying taxes or serving on a jury. Others you can choose, like voting and volunteering. You can be a valuable part of the community if you do your part!

Decisions, Decisions!

Read the story below and help Sam make a wise decision.

Sam's neighbor, Milo Stanfield, is running for the school board. He has asked Sam and his family to vote for him. Sam thinks Milo Stanfield is a nice person. However, he wants to close one of the local high schools to save money. He thinks it has too few students. Sam doesn't know the other candidate. However, he does know she's against closing the high school. Follow the steps below to help Sam decide which person to vote for.

Step 1: Identify the decision Sam must make.

Step 2: List Sam's choices.

Step 3: Cross out any choices that are harmful or might be against Sam's beliefs.

Step 4: Think about the possible results of the remaining choices.

Step 5: Select the best choice.

Step 6: Explain how Sam would carry out that choice.

Step 7: Describe the possible results of Sam's choice.

Chapter Review

Chapter Summary

1. Each person is required to have a Social Security number. It is used as a form of identification for your whole life. You need it for many things, including loans and credit cards.

2. To apply for a Social Security card, you must go to a Social Security office. Take along two forms of identification.

3. Voting is an important part of being a good citizen. You can register to vote at any Bureau of Motor Vehicles. You can also register by mail.

4. Before you vote, learn about the candidates and the issues.

5. Money from income taxes pays for many community services. These include schools, highways, and firefighters.

6. Income tax forms help you figure out what you owe. Use a tax instruction booklet to fill out the form.

7. If you receive a jury summons, follow the directions on it. Serving on a jury is a serious matter and part of being a good citizen.

8. Volunteering is one way to be a good citizen. You can cut a neighbor's grass or join a group like *Meals on Wheels*.

Chapter Quiz

Answer these questions on a separate sheet of paper.

1. Why should you get a Social Security number?

2. Where can you apply for a Social Security number?

3. How do you register to vote?

4. Julio didn't know anything about the candidates or the issues. But he thought he should vote anyway. What should he do?

5. Elena thinks she shouldn't have to pay taxes. She thinks it's like throwing money away because she doesn't get anything for it. What would you tell her?

6. What is a tax deduction? What is an exemption?

7. Do most people pay their income taxes all at once? Explain.

8. Where could you find help in filling out your income tax form?

9. If you receive a jury summons, will you be part of a jury? Why or why not?

10. What are some ways that young people in your community can volunteer their time?

Putting Skills to Work

Find copies of the 1040EZ tax form. Work with a small group to make up an imaginary taxpayer. Don't create a person with children. A taxpayer with children can't use this form. Decide on the taxpayer's income and whether he or she is married. Then fill out the form by following the instructions on the back. If your class has questions about the form, think of ways you could find the answers.

Skills Issues

Sometimes people do not like the way the government spends their tax money. Work in a small group to think of ways ordinary people could influence how the government spends money. Then share your group's ideas with the class.

Chapter 21

Obeying Laws

Part of being a good citizen is obeying the law. Take the time to learn the laws in your community.

Chapter Learning Objectives

- List traffic laws.
- Describe steps to take if you have a car accident.
- List safety rules for riding a bicycle.
- Explain laws about curfews, littering, and making a false alarm.

Words to Know

traffic   the movement of cars and trucks

fine   a fee paid by someone who breaks a law

defensive driving   driving carefully to avoid accidents

pedestrian   someone who is walking, running, or jogging

curfew   a time by which people must be home or off public property

public property   streets, highways, parks, playgrounds, and buildings that are open to all people

littering   leaving trash or garbage on public property or on someone else's else's property

false alarm   a warning about a danger that is not real

Read the story below to see what happened to Jake.

Manuel drove to Jake's apartment. Jake was waiting for him, holding a bag full of garbage. "What are you going to do with that?" Manuel asked.

"Let's stop at the park," Jake said. "I'm going to put it in the park's trash can. The trash cans at my apartment building are full."

"Are you sure that's okay?" Manuel asked.

"Of course!" Jake said. "Parks are for everyone, so I can use them any way I want."

A few days later, a police officer gave Jake a ticket for littering. Park employees had found Jake's garbage bag and opened it. They found Jake's name on some mail in the bag and called the police.

"It's against the law to leave garbage from your home on public property," the officer explained. "That's true even if you put it in a trash can."

You know that it's against the law to steal or to hurt other people. But there are other laws you might not know about. This chapter will explore some of those laws. You are responsible for knowing the laws. You will still be punished even if you break a law accidentally. When you know the laws, you can work to avoid getting into trouble.

Knowing the Traffic Laws

If you have your driver's license, you should know most of the **traffic** laws. Traffic means the movement of cars and trucks. Some things that are covered by traffic laws include how fast to drive on certain streets and highways, when you can pass another car, and when you should stop. Traffic laws also tell whether you can make a right turn when a traffic light is red and what to do at an intersection that has four stop signs.

If you are unsure of the traffic laws, most states have booklets that explain them. This is the same booklet that you study to get your driver's license. You can get a copy of this booklet at any Bureau of Motor Vehicles.

Skills Practice

With a partner, find out what drivers should do in the following situations:

1. What to do at railroad crossings
2. What to do when an ambulance is coming
3. What to do if a school bus stops in front of you with lights flashing.

You might ask an adult who knows the traffic laws. Or you could check the booklet about traffic laws from the Bureau of Motor Vehicles. Share what you learn with the class.

Traffic Tickets

You can avoid getting a traffic ticket by obeying the law. For example, many tickets are given for speeding. No one is forced to speed. People do it because they want to go faster. People also receive tickets for not stopping at stop signs. Others get tickets for parking in the wrong place.

The front of a traffic ticket explains which law was broken. It will also show your **fine**. A fine is a fee a person must pay for breaking a law. The back of the ticket describes how to pay the fine. Drivers under the age of 18 might have to go to traffic court with a parent to pay the fine. Older drivers might be able to pay their fines through the mail.

If you get a ticket, follow the directions on the back of it. Don't ignore the ticket. Don't throw it away. If you do, you will be in more trouble. You could lose your license and have to pay a bigger fine.

Careful drivers can go through their whole lives without getting a traffic ticket.

Many states give drivers points for breaking the law. For example, drivers might get two points for their first speeding ticket. They might get two to six points for their second speeding ticket in the same year. The faster the drivers are going, the more points they will receive on their driving record. Drivers might receive up to 12 points for their third speeding ticket in the same year. Drivers who receive 12 points within two years often have their licenses taken away for six months or more.

Drivers also receive points for breaking the law in other ways. These include drinking and driving, and leaving the scene of an accident without calling the police.

Accidents

Unfortunately, you cannot avoid all accidents by driving carefully. Sometimes other drivers run into you, no matter what you do. However, there are many things you can do to avoid accidents. You can watch what other drivers are doing. Then you will be ready if another driver does something unexpected, such as suddenly cutting in front of you. You can also take a course in **defensive driving**. Defensive driving means driving carefully in a way that avoids most accidents.

If you have an accident, stop and see if anyone is hurt. If so, get help. Have someone call an ambulance. Try to warn other drivers away from the accident so they will not run into your cars.

Accidents do happen. If ▼ you're in an accident, stay calm and wait for a police officer.

Call the police or highway patrol to report the accident. While you are waiting for the police, exchange information with the other driver. Ask for the driver's name, address, and phone number. It's also important to write down the license plate number, driver's license number, the name of their insurance company, and the name of the car owner. When the police arrive, answer the police officer's questions about the accident.

Don't blame the other driver for the accident. However, don't blame yourself for what happened. The police will usually decide who is to blame.

If anyone was hurt or if the damage was over a certain amount, you may have to fill out an accident report. Ask the police officer if you need to do this. If so, the police officer can tell you where you need to go to get the form. If you don't report an accident, you may lose your license.

If you hit a parked car, call the police and report the accident. You will have to fill out an accident report. If you don't report the accident, you could be charged with hit-and-run. Then you would be in more trouble. Finally, report the accident to your car insurance company as soon as you can.

Knowing the Bicycle Laws

Many young people ride their bikes to get places and just for fun. Below are some basic laws for bike riders. Your state may have other laws. Some states require young bike riders to wear helmets.

- Ride on the right, in the same direction cars travel. Stay on the edge of the road.
- Obey all traffic signs.
- Use hand signals when you stop or turn.
- Never ride your bike on major highways.
- Do not let friends ride on your handlebars.
- If you ride after dark, make sure your bike has a headlight, taillight, and red reflectors.
- Fasten a loud bell or horn to your bike.
- Make sure your brakes work.

Drivers and bike riders share the same roads. Drivers must be careful when passing bike riders.

Knowing the Laws for Pedestrians

A **pedestrian** is someone who is walking, running, or jogging. All of us are pedestrians at one time or

Wearing a helmet ▶ when you ride can save your life.

another. We all need to know the laws. Walking is good for you. However, it should also be safe.

Car drivers and bike riders can get tickets for not obeying the laws, and so can pedestrians. Most communities have a law that you can cross a street only at a corner or crosswalk. If you cross in the wrong place, you are jaywalking, which is against the law.

On the corners of some busy streets you may see a button you can push to change the traffic light. If you want to cross the street, you can push this button to stop traffic. Watch the sign on the other corner. Wait until the sign says "Walk." It may take a moment for the sign to change. Then you can cross the street.

You should walk, run, or jog on the sidewalk. If there is no sidewalk, walk, run, or jog on the side of the road. Stay off major highways except in an emergency. You should never hitchhike.

Skills Practice

With a partner, draw two roads on separate sheets of paper. On each road, draw cars driving in both directions. On one of your drawings, add a bike rider. On the other drawing, add a pedestrian. Both the bike rider and the pedestrian should follow safety laws. Then compare your drawings with others in the class. Do you all agree on where the rider and pedestrian should be on the road?

Other Laws to Know

Your community has other laws that may affect you. Some communities have a **curfew** law. A curfew is the time by which people must be home or off **public property**. Public property includes streets and highways, parks, playgrounds, and buildings that are open to everyone. Some curfew laws may also include public places such as theaters and shopping malls.

For example, anyone under the age of 18 might have an 11:00 P.M. curfew. They would have to be off public property after 11:00 P.M. Those under the age of 14 might have a 9:00 P.M. curfew. They would have to be off public property after 9 P.M. Young people who are with a responsible adult are not bound by these curfews.

Most communities have **littering** laws. Littering means leaving trash or garbage on public property or other people's property. People can get a ticket for throwing trash on the ground.

Remember Jake from the beginning of the chapter? He found out the hard way that his community had a law against littering. Jake had put his garbage in a plastic bag.

Follow the laws to keep your community clean and safe. ▶

In some communities, people can receive fines for not keeping their own property neat.

Yet he still wasn't allowed to put it in the park's trash cans. You can use the park's trash cans after you have a picnic in the park. However, you cannot bring trash from home and throw it in the park's trash cans.

It is also against the law to make a **false alarm**. A false alarm is a warning about a danger that is not real. One example is yelling "Fire!" in a mall or theater when you know there is no fire. Another example is someone pulling the fire alarm at school just to see what happens. People can panic and get hurt in these situations. That's why making a false alarm is against the law.

In many places it is also against the law to make too much noise. People sometimes annoy others with their noise. They can receive a warning or a ticket from the police.

Staying Out of Trouble

Laws were made to help us get along with each other. Laws help thousands of cars use the same highways. Laws help drivers, bike riders, and pedestrians share the streets. Laws also help people live close together peacefully.

It's important to know the laws in your community. However, you don't have to know exactly what the laws say. You just need to know how to obey them.

Decisions, Decisions!

Driving requires wise decision-making skills. Read the paragraphs below and help Tamika make a decision.

On her way home from work, Tamika tried to stop at a red light. The roads were icy, and she slid into the car in front of her. She and the other driver got out. Luckily, neither one was hurt.

Tamika had made a large dent in the other car. However, the other driver knew the roads were slippery. He didn't seem angry. They exchanged names and other information.

After he drove away, Tamika remembered that accidents should be reported to the police. But no one was hurt, and now the other driver was gone.

Tamika couldn't decide whether she should call the police and report the accident. On a separate sheet of paper, follow the steps below. Help Tamika make this decision.

Step 1: Identify the decision Tamika must make.

Step 2: List Tamika's choices.

Step 3: Cross out any choices that are harmful or might be against Tamika's beliefs.

Step 4: Think about the possible results of the remaining choices.

Step 5: Select the best choice.

Step 6: Explain how Tamika would carry out that choice.

Step 7: Describe the possible results of Tamika's choices.

Chapter Review

Chapter Summary

1. It's important to know the traffic laws. The Bureau of Motor Vehicles can give you a booklet that explains the laws.

2. Careful, responsible drivers can avoid getting traffic tickets.

3. If you have a car accident, stop, and get help if anyone is injured. Remember to call the police to report the accident. Exchange information with the other driver. Report the accident to your insurance company right away.

4. Bike riders should ride on the right edge of the road and obey traffic signs. They should also use hand signals, stay off major highways, and not let anyone ride on their handlebars. Bikes should have lights for riding after dark, a bell or horn, and good brakes.

5. Pedestrians should cross streets only at corners and crosswalks. They should follow the traffic signals. Never hitchhike.

6. Many communities have laws about curfews, littering, making false alarms, and other actions.

Chapter Quiz

Answer these questions on a separate sheet of paper.

1. If you're not sure about a traffic law, how could you find out about it?

2. Colleen got a ticket for parking in front of a fire hydrant. She threw the ticket away. What problems could this cause for Colleen?

3. Sam just got his second traffic ticket this year. "So what?" he says. "Getting tickets is part of driving. Everyone gets them." What would you say to Sam?

4. Kurt was on his way to school when he hit a parked car. He broke the car's taillight. However, Kurt was already late for school, so he

decided to keep going. He figured no one saw what happened. Was Kurt's decision wise? Why or why not?

5. When do you have to fill out an accident report?

6. If you have an accident, what kinds of information should you exchange with the other driver?

7. What are some rules of safe bike riding?

8. Let's say you want to cross an intersection that has a traffic light. The light for the cars in the cross street is green. Should you cross the street? Why or why not?

9. Some cities have curfew laws for people under the age of 18. Why do you think these laws were made?

10. Why are laws important?

Putting Skills to Work

Work with a small group to make a plan for teaching safety rules. First, decide whether to teach rules for walking or for riding bikes. Then think of a way to teach the rules you chose.

For example, your group might make up several skits. Or you might make a videotape of what to do. Don't make a video of what not to do.

Share your work with your class. Ask for ways you could improve it. If possible, present your work to someone who needs to learn safety rules.

Skills Issues

Sylvia was angry about her speeding ticket. "I had to hurry to get to my doctor's appointment! I had to drive fast," she told her friends. Do you think it was fair for Sylvia to get a speeding ticket? Why or why not? Discuss this with a small group. Share your group's opinions with the class.

Chapter 22

Finding Help in the Community

Help is there if you know how to find it. Discover the services offered in your community.

Chapter Learning Objectives

- Locate sources of help in the telephone book.
- Explain how to find out which government agency deals with a certain problem.
- Describe a TTY (Text Telephone Yoke).
- Explain bus services.
- Give examples of activities and services offered in the community.

Words to Know

food stamps   slips of paper that can be used to buy food

agency   a department or office that works on certain issues

relay   to pass something along

TTY   Text Telephone Yoke; equipment that helps people with speech or hearing problems use the telephone

recreation   things to do for fun

CD-ROM database   a computer laser disk filled with information

Everyone needs help with something at some time. Read the paragraphs below about Carrie's family to see what kinds of help Carrie's family needs.

Carrie, her brother Mike, and their mother just moved into a small house in a new town. Carrie's mother has to find out how to get the food stamps her family needs. She also needs to know how to contact the gas and electric company to have service turned on at the house. She wants to arrange for phone service, but her daughter has a special need. Carrie has a hearing loss, which makes talking over the phone difficult. Carrie's mother wants to make sure that Carrie can use the phone when she needs to.

Carrie's mother also wants to find out which bus she will need to take to look for a new job. Mike wants to know what there is to do in the area. He doesn't know anyone yet, and he's afraid he will be bored.

Maybe you need help, like Carrie's family. Maybe you just need something to do, like Mike. This chapter can help in both cases. You will learn about the services that are available in many communities.

These are services for people with special needs and for people who are just looking for something to do.

Finding Community Services

You probably already have a list of the services in your community. It's in your telephone book! Look in the front of the white pages. You should find a section with a title such as Easy Reference List or Community Services or Frequently Called Numbers.

In this section, you should find phone numbers to help with a variety of problems. For example, you can find out where to report child abuse. You can also find out how to get help with other kinds of problems in the home.

You can use this section of the phone book to find out how to get help with a drug problem or legal problems. The listings have numbers for places to help you get free or low-cost help if you're sick or are having mental health problems.

If you need to know how to get gas, water, electric, or phone service like Carrie's mother, you can find it in this section. You can also find information about services for senior citizens, voting and elections.

Skills Practice

Look in your phone book for a list of community services. On a separate sheet of paper, write down at least four sources of help in your community. Include the phone numbers to call.

Finding Help from the Government

Carrie's family moved because her mother had lost her job. While Carrie's mother looked for a new job, the family was getting **food stamps**. Food stamps are slips of paper that can be used to buy food.

Suppose you want to know if you can get food stamps. You need to call the right government **agency**. An agency is a department or office that works on certain issues. However, you don't know which agency to call. It might be part of the city, county, state, or federal government.

Your phone book can help. Some phone books have a section called Frequently Requested Government Offices. This is a chart that shows which agency to call for certain information. For example, the chart shows that food stamps are handled by county governments.

Maybe your phone book doesn't have this chart. It probably does have a section for government phone numbers. The pages in this section might be blue or have blue edges. The government offices in this section are usually listed in this order:

- City and town offices

- County or parish offices

- State offices

- Federal (United States) offices

▼ *A phone book is a wonderful source of information.*

▶ **GRANDVIEW, CITY OF**

Police department	555-9887
Emergency: Dial 911	
Public information	555-9886
220 S. Hamilton	
Mayor	555-4568
220 S. Hamilton	
Income tax	555-2353
220 S. Hamilton	
Parks & Recreation	555-0968
100 Grandview	
Recycling	555-0023
220 S. Hamilton	
Senior Center	555-1927
480 Rocky Fork Boulevard	
Water-Sewer-Trash	555-6529
220 S. Hamilton	

▶ **GOVERNMENT OFFICES**

See listing in blue pages under U.S. Governments, State or name of County or Municipality; Libraries-Circulating and Rental; State Police; Etc.

▶ **GRANITE**

Cosmic Granite & Marble	555-4321
171 Granite Avenue	

▶ **GRAPHIC DESIGNERS**

ABAEZ DESIGN Inc.	555-0849
6601 Broadway	
Anon Graphic Design	555-0556
Art & Ideas	555-0617
845 Boulevard East	

You can also check your phone book's Yellow Pages under Government for a listing of phone numbers. When you need some help, look through the government offices that are listed. Start with the kind of government, such as your city or county government, that you think you need. Call any information numbers you find that you think might help. Explain what you need. The person who answers this number may be able to help you.

Finding Help for Special Needs

Think back to Carrie from the beginning of the chapter. She has a hearing problem. Her hearing problem makes talking on the phone difficult. The state where Carrie lives might offer a free **relay** service that would help her. Relay means to pass something along. This relay service passes messages along. The service makes it easier for people with speech or hearing problems to use the telephone.

Carrie needs to get a machine called a **TTY**, which means Text Telephone Yoke. A TTY is also called a TDD, which stands for Telecommunications Device for the Deaf. A TTY is like a typewriter with a small screen for messages. Anyone can order one. You just have to call a number listed in the phone book under Services for Special Needs.

The relay service is easy to use. Carrie types in a phone number on her TTY. An employee at the relay service then reads the phone number. The employee calls the number Carrie typed. Carrie then types a message to her friend. The relay service employee reads the message out loud to Carrie's friend. Then the friend tells the employee a message for Carrie. The employee types the message, and Carrie reads it on her TTY. Carrie can also use this service to order pizza or buy something over the phone. She can do anything with her phone that anyone else can do.

Other special equipment for people with special needs is available. One piece of equipment that is now used is designed for people who cannot use their hands. This machine allows them to blow puffs of air to dial phone numbers.

For more information about what's available, you can call local agencies. You can also look under Services for Special Needs in the phone book.

Skills Practice

Look through the list of community services in your phone book. Check the phone numbers for emergencies, such as calling an ambulance. Find the TTY numbers. Share what you find with a classmate.

Maybe you or someone you know has a physical problem that makes it hard to get around. Many city buses are now equipped with wheelchair lifts. These lifts make it possible to get wheelchairs into and out of the buses.

Many bus companies also have special vans. These vans pick up people at their homes. The vans take them anywhere they need or want to go. The charge for a trip is usually very low. Find out if your community offers this kind of help. Call your city bus company to ask if they offer the service.

Finding Things to Do

Maybe you're just looking for something to do with your free time. Most communities have a **recreation** department or a parks and recreation department. Recreation means activities to do for fun. Your town's recreation department might organize sports teams. It may also offer special courses. You might be able to learn judo or dance or bird-watching. Your recreation department might organize young people on trips to amusement parks and other fun places.

These activities are usually free or nearly free. Call your recreation department and ask about its activities. Or look for an ad at your school or library. Attending courses or going on trips is also a good way to meet new friends.

Using Your Public Library

Libraries aren't just for studying or borrowing books. Libraries can also offer interesting things to do with your time. Many libraries now lend out CDs, audiotapes, and videotapes. Your library might also sponsor speakers and programs for people your age. Ask for a list of the events your library is planning.

Doing research at the library can also be fun. Your library might have computers that let you explore the Internet. You might also be able to use the library's **CD-ROM databases** to get the information you need for school reports. A CD-ROM database is a computer disk filled with an enormous amount of information. Just one CD-ROM can contain articles from hundreds of magazines.

Finding People Who Share Your Interests

Your community newspaper might be able to help you find people in your community interested in the same things as you. Look for a weekly section that lists special interest groups. This section might be called Community Happenings, All Around Town, or something similar. Each group listed will include a phone number. You can call the number to find out more about the group and its meetings.

Look for groups that interest you. Then call the phone number and go to a meeting. You might really enjoy it. You'll also find new friends who share your interests.

Finding What You Need

Everyone needs help sometime, even people who live on their own. Part of taking care of yourself is knowing how and where to find help.

Skills Practice

Do some detective work. Find a group that shares one of your interests. Maybe you like to paint or grow flowers. Use the newspaper or ask people you know about groups that meet to talk about or do something that interests you. Share what you learn with the class. Maybe one of your classmates will go with you to a meeting!

Decisions, Decisions!

Lee's elderly neighbor, Mr. Rothman, lives alone since his wife died. He has always been friendly. Last month, Mr. Rothman had a stroke. Now he uses a wheelchair. Lee never sees him outside anymore.

Lee knows there must be services in the community that could help his neighbor get around. However, he doesn't know if he should suggest them. After all, Mr. Rothman isn't part of his family.

On a separate sheet of paper, follow the steps below to help Lee make a wise decision.

Step 1: Identify the decision Lee must make.

Step 2: List Lee's choices.

Step 3: Cross out any choices that are harmful or might be against Lee's beliefs.

Step 4: Think about the possible results of the remaining choices.

Step 5: Select the best choice.

Step 6: Explain how Lee would carry out that choice.

Step 7: Describe the possible results of Lee's choice.

Chapter Review

Chapter Summary

1. You can use the phone book to find out what services are available in your community. Most phone books list the phone numbers for community services in the front.

2. Phone books also list phone numbers for government agencies. Numbers are listed for city or town, county, state, and federal government offices. Sometimes the phone book has a chart that shows which agencies provide certain services.

3. A free relay service and a machine called a TTY or TDD help people with hearing and speech problems use the telephone. Bus companies have wheelchair lifts and special vans to help people get around.

4. Community recreation departments offer low-cost fun activities, courses, and programs.

5. Public libraries not only lend books, but CDs and videotapes. Many also have computers that anyone can use to explore the Internet and gather information.

6. The newspaper often lists special interest groups. You can attend meetings of these groups and get to know people who share your interests.

Chapter Quiz

Answer these questions on a separate sheet of paper.

1. What are some community services that might be listed in the front of your phone book?

2. The phone book lists federal government agencies. What other types of government agencies does it list?

3. Does it matter which government agency you call? Why or why not?

4. What can you do if you don't know which government agency to call?

5. How does a person with a hearing loss send a message over a TTY?

6. Could you communicate with someone who uses a TTY? If so, how would you do that?

7. Can a person who uses a wheelchair get to work on a city bus? Why or why not?

8. Imagine it's summer and you want to play a team sport. How might you find one?

9. Let's say you want to learn about the Internet, but you don't have a computer. What might you do?

10. Let's say you really like to do needlepoint or build models. How could you find other people who like to do those things?

Putting Skills to Work

Someone your age has just moved into your neighborhood. This person asks, "What is there to do around here?" Work with a small group to list at least 20 things to do in your community. Start with things you and your friends do. Check the newspaper. Also, call your recreation department and public library. Read your list to the class. Your teacher will help the groups make one long list. Write down activities from the list that interest you. Then try them out!

Skills Issues

Does your community offer enough activities for young people? If not, please explain. Share your group's answers with the class. Perhaps many students in your class like a certain activity. Think of ways you could convince the school board, city council, or another group to support that activity. Your class might write letters explaining why that activity should be offered.

Unit Seven Review

Answer these questions on a separate sheet of paper.

1. What are some things that a good citizen does?

2. Someone watches a bridge being built and says, "That's our tax dollars at work." What does this person mean?

3. Jonathan knows he's supposed to pay 15 percent of his income in taxes. He made $12,000 last year. He's going to send the IRS a check for 15 percent of $12,000 without filling out a tax form. Is this a good idea?

4. What does a W-2 form show?

5. Is a jury summons the same as a traffic ticket? Why or why not?

6. Shirley isn't sure what she should do if a school bus stops in front of her car. How could she find out?

7. Let's say you're in a car accident, but it's not your fault. Your car isn't hurt too badly. Is it okay if you just drive away? Why or why not?

8. Which side of the road should a bike rider travel on to stay safe?

9. How can you find out what kinds of help are offered in your community?

10. What other things will you find at your public library besides books?

Glossary

action plan steps for reaching a goal

addiction physical dependence on a drug

advice suggestions as to what should be done

aerobic exercise an activity of 20 minutes or more that makes the heart work harder

agency a department or office that works on certain issues

ambulance a special van driven by people trained to help anyone who is sick or hurt; transports sick or hurt people to hospitals

apply to ask for

appointment a set time to meet someone or do something

ATM an automatic teller machine; machine that allows you to take money out of your checking or savings account using a special card

balance the amount of money in a bank account

balanced diet foods that provide your body with what it needs to stay healthy

bank statement a report that the bank sends you to show how much money is in your checking or savings account; lists any checks you wrote or deposits or withdrawals you made

bill a written request for money for something you bought

blood pressure the push of the blood as it moves through the body

body language showing feelings using your body and your face

budget a plan for spending money

calories units that measure the amount of energy your body gets from food

candidate a person running for an office in an election

car insurance money you pay a company each month so that the company will pay for repairs after an accident

car pools groups of people who share rides in each other's cars

career the type of work a person does throughout his or her life to earn a living

career goal the type of work you would like to be doing several years from now

career plan a step-by-step way to meet a career goal

cash dollar bills and coins

cavity a hole in a tooth caused by decay

CD-ROM database a computer laser disk filled with information

check a written order directing a bank to pay a certain amount of money from the account of the person who signs it to the person named

check register a small chart where you record the checks you have written and deposits you have made

checking account money in a bank that can be taken out using a check or ATM card

citizen someone who lives in a certain city or nation

citizenship membership in a community

classified ads advertisements listed in a special section of the newspaper

communicate to share thoughts, feelings, and ideas with others

concern an interest in other people

conflict strong disagreement caused by a difference in needs or points of view

consumer someone who buys something

cosigner a person who agrees to pay for someone else's credit card bill if that person can't pay it

courage the strength to stand up for what is right

cover letter a letter to introduce you to an employer; sent with a résumé

coworkers people who work for the same company

credit money loaned to you by a bank, store, or credit card company to pay for things you buy

credit bureau a business that puts together credit reports

credit card a card that lets you buy something now but pay for it later

credit report a report of whether you paid your bills or loans on time

curfew a time by which people must be home or off public property

deadline the latest time something can be done

deduction money taken out of a paycheck for taxes, insurance, savings, or other reasons

defensive driving driving carefully to avoid accidents

deposit money put in the bank

deposit slip a slip of paper you fill out that shows how much money you put in the bank

diet everything that a person eats or drinks regularly

doctors people trained and licensed to treat diseases and disorders

down payment the first payment on a large purchase, such as a car or house

due date the date by which a bill should be paid

emergency a situation that needs to be taken care of quickly

emotions feelings

employee handbook a book that describes company rules and job benefits

endorse to write your name on the back of a check

exchange a trade of one item for another

excuse an explanation for poor behavior

exemption a tax deduction for each person in a family

expenses payments you must make, such as rent

express to show or communicate thoughts, feelings, and ideas

false alarm a warning about a danger that is not real

federal national

fee cost

fine a fee paid by someone who breaks a law

fire extinguisher a device used to spray special chemicals on a fire to put it out

fired to be dismissed from a job

flexible able to change

food stamps slips of paper that can be used to buy food

fumes gases given off by chemicals

germs tiny life forms that can cause disease

goal something you want to do

gross pay the total amount of money an employee earns

health mental and physical wellness

health insurance a plan that helps you pay for health costs

honesty the ability to be truthful and fair

hormones chemicals in your body that are produced by glands

housing places where people live

impulse a sudden act done without thinking it through

income the money you earn

income tax money that everyone who works pays to the government

independent able to take care of yourself

informational interview a discussion with someone who has a job that interests you

ingredients the parts of a mixture; what things are in a packaged food

insufficient funds not enough money in a checking account to pay the checks you write

interest (1) something you care about or like to do; (2) money that a bank pays you for keeping your money in a checking or savings account; (3) a fee that you pay when you borrow money

interview a meeting in which one person answers another person's questions

issue a question the community must make a decision on

job application a form you fill out when applying for a job

job benefits insurance, vacation time, and other things you receive in addition to your pay

job review a rating of how well you do your job

jury a group that decides the outcome of a trial

landlord someone who owns a house or an apartment and rents it to others

late fee an extra charge when a bill is not paid on time

layoff a period of time when a company has no work for employees

lease a written agreement between a renter and a landlord; also called a rental agreement

littering leaving trash or garbage on public property or on someone else's property

loan money that is borrowed and must be paid back

long-term goal a goal that can be met in several months or years

maiden name a woman's last name before she is married

mature adult; fully developed physically and emotionally

mechanic a person who works on car engines

medical license a document that gives a person the right to give health care

minimum deposit the lowest amount of money needed in an account

minimum payment the smallest payment that is accepted

mortgage a loan used to buy a place to live

need something you must have

negative harmful, unsafe, against the law

net pay the amount of money an employee receives after deductions are taken out of the gross pay

nutrients what is in food that the body needs to grow and stay healthy

nutrition the process of taking food into your body and using it for energy and growth

obstacle something that stands in the way of reaching a goal

opinion a belief

over-the-counter medicines medicines people can buy without a doctor's order; nonprescription drugs

patient person under the care of a doctor

paycheck a check for the money earned from a job

paycheck stub a piece of paper attached to a paycheck; it lists important information about the paycheck

pedestrian someone who is walking, running, or jogging

peer pressure influence from people your age to do or not do something

personal qualities ways you relate to other people and to the world around you; your personality

pharmacist a person who prepares and gives out medicines according to a doctor's orders

plastic a slang term for a credit card

point of view a way of thinking about something

popular admired or sought after as a friend

positive helpful, healthful

prepared ready

prepared food food that is treated in some way so it will last longer

prescription medicine ordered by a doctor

pressure to encourage strongly or force

priority a level of importance; a goal with a high priority is very important

promotion a new job with more responsibility and more pay

public property streets, highways, parks, playgrounds, and buildings that are open to all people

public transportation buses, trains, and subways that are available to everyone for a fee

realistic within your reach

receipt a slip of paper the bank gives you that shows how much money you put in or took from your bank account

reckless careless and dangerous

recreation things to do for fun

references people who know you well and will tell others you are a good worker

refund a return of your money when you bring back an item to a store

register to sign up to vote

relay to pass something along

rent to pay to live a certain place for a while; also, the money paid to live in a certain place

rental agreement a written agreement between a renter and a landlord; also called a lease

resist to refuse; to say "No"

respect the willingness to consider other people's needs, feelings, and opinions; to show that something has value

responsible dependable; the ability to make wise decisions and accept the results of your actions and decisions

résumé a summary of your education and work experience

retirement the years after a person stops working and earning income

risk a chance that something harmful might happen

route a certain path or direction

savings account money in a bank that gains interest; can be taken out using an ATM card or withdrawal slip

schedule a list of times to do things; or a list of when things happen

security deposit money that renters pay in case they damage an apartment

service to take care of a car's repairs or other needs, such as changing the oil and adjusting the engine

service contract a promise by a store or company to fix a product if it breaks within a certain time

serving the amount of a certain food usually eaten at one time

shift a period of time for work

short-term goal a goal that can be met in a few hours, days, or weeks

signature card a card you sign when you open a bank account

skill something you do well

smoke detector a device that gives off a warning sound when it senses smoke

Social Security a government program that takes money out of each employee's paycheck; after the employee retires, he or she receives money from the government as a monthly Social Security check

Social Security number a number assigned to each person by the government; a form of identification

specialists doctors who treat only certain diseases or disorders

specific clearly explained; detailed

standard deduction an amount of money set by the government; it can be subtracted from your income

stress uncomfortable feelings caused when we have too much to deal with

studio apartment a one-room apartment

summarize to explain briefly what you heard, saw, or read

summons a legal request

symptom a sign of an illness or disorder

tax deduction a cost that can be subtracted from your income when you figure out your taxes

teller a bank employee

temporary learner's permit permission to practice driving with a licensed driver in the car

traffic the movement of cars and trucks

treat to cure or relieve a disease or disorder

TTY Text Telephone Yoke; equipment that helps people with speech or hearing problems use the telephone

unit pricing how much a product costs per unit of weight or volume

vitamins types of nutrients your body needs to stay healthy; examples include Vitamins A, E, and D

want something you would like but can do without

warranty a promise about how long a product will last without breaking

withdraw remove something

withdrawal money taken out of the bank

withdrawal slip a piece of paper used to take money from the bank

withheld held back or taken out

Index

A

Accidents. *See* car accidents
Action plan
    meaning of, 15
    for reaching goals, 18-19
Addiction
    drug/alcohol/cigarettes, 94-96
    meaning of, 87, 94
Ads
    and buying behavior, 226-227
    for housing, 271, 275-276
Advice, meaning of, 41, 43
Aerobic exercise
    benefits of, 94
    meaning of, 87
Agency, government, 315
Alcohol. *See* Drug/alcohol use
Ambulance, and emergencies, 108
Anger
    calming down, 60-61, 62
    making ourselves angry, 61-62
ATM (automatic teller machine), 191, 194, 201
Attacking messages, nature of, 57-58

B

Balance, of checking account, 198-199
Bank statement, meaning of, 191
Banking, 193-202
    bank statement, 191, 202
    cashing paycheck, 211-212
    check register, use of, 198-199
    check writing, 196-197
    checking accounts, 191, 193-194
    choosing bank, 199-200
    deposit slip, filling out, 195-196
    savings accounts, 191, 200-201
Benefits. *See* employee benefits

Bicycle laws, 305
Bill paying, 240-241
    due date on bill, 241
    late fees, 239, 240
    late payments, 241
Blood pressure, meaning of, 103
Body language, 46-47
    feelings expressed through, 46-47
    meaning of, 41, 46
Budget, 207, 212-218
    and future planning, 216-217
    and individual needs, 215-216
    meaning of, 207, 212-213, 217-218
    set up for, 213
    and shopping, 225-226
    staying on, 214, 215

C

Calories, meaning of, 87, 91
Candidate, and voting, 291
Car accidents, 303-305
    actions to take, 304-305
    prevention of, 304
Car buying, 261-265
    car insurance, 255, 264-265
    dealer service, 262
    down payment, 263
    loans, 263-264
    mechanic check, 262
    paying for car, 262-263
    used car, 262
    warranty on car, 261
Car insurance, 255, 264-265
    cost of, 265
    factors affecting cost, 265
Car pools, purpose of, 255, 257

buying with, 242-243
cosigner on, 247
credit reports, 247
fees attached to, 243-245
minimum payment, 239, 242
problems with, 245
protection tips, 248-249
sources for, 241
Credit reports, 247
getting good report, 247
purposes of, 247
Cultural differences, and communication, 47-48
Curfew, meaning of, 301, 307
Curfew laws, 307-308

D

Deadlines
meaning of, 159
at work, 169
Decision making
example of, 7-8
and family, 76-77
about money, 218-219
and qualities of person, 5
and responsibility, 8-9
steps in, 6-8
Deductions
paycheck, 207, 210
taxes, 287, 293
Defensive driving, meaning of, 301, 304
Deposit, bank deposit, 191, 192
Deposit slip, 195-196
filling out, 195-196
meaning of, 191
Diet
balanced diet, 87, 88-89
Food Guide Pyramid, 88-89
meaning of, 87
See also Nutrition

Divorce, 74
Doctors, 104-107
checkups, 105-106
choosing doctor, 104-105
specialists, 104
Down payment
on car, 263
meaning of, 255
Driver's license, 259-260
application for, 259-260
driving test, 260-261
temporary learner's permit, 260
Driving
accidents, 303-305
defensive driving, 301, 304
and drinking, 266
driver's license, 259-260
reckless driving, 265
responsible drivers, 265-266
and traffic laws, 302
traffic tickets, 303
Drug/alcohol use, 94-96
and addiction, 94-95
drunk driving, 266
resisting use, 95-96
Due date, on bill, 239, 240

E

Electrical wiring, safety risks, 117
Emergencies
fire emergencies, 120-121
hospital visits, 108-109
911, 122
Employee benefits, 153-154
Employee handbook, purpose of, 159, 161
Endorsing check, 211
Excuse, meaning of, 9
Exemptions, and taxes, 287, 293-294
Exercise, 93-94
aerobic exercise, 94

F

Falls, in home, 117
False alarm
    as illegal act, 308
    meaning of, 301, 308
Family
    changes in, 73-77
    learning values from, 5-6
Federal, meaning of, 287, 292
Federal assistance
    finding services, 315-316
    food stamps, 313, 315
Feelings
    and body language, 46-47
    and hormones, 71
    and "I messages," 56-57, 58
Fees, for checking accounts, 193-194
Fines, traffic tickets, 303
Fire safety, 115-117, 121-122
    and electrical wiring, 117
    fire extinguishers, 120
    smoke detectors, 115-116
    steps to take during, 120-121
Food Guide Pyramid, 88-89
Food labels, information on, 89-92
Food stamps, meaning of, 313, 315
Friends
    being part of group, 72
    changing friends, 72-73
    and decision making, 29-30
    finding friends, 30, 36-37
    importance of, 71-72
    peer pressure, 31-36
    qualities of good friend, 30-31
Fumes, 117
Furnishing home, 278-279

G

Germs, and disease, 87, 97
Goals
    action plan for reaching of, 18-19

career goals, 175, 176-177, 180-181
    long-term goals, 15, 18
    meaning of, 15
    obstacles to, 16
    and priorities, 15-16
    purpose of, 16-17, 22
    realistic goals, 17-18
    short-term goals, 15, 18
    specific goals, 17
Golden Rule, 49
Grocery store, shopping tips, 229-230
Gross pay, meaning of, 207, 210

H

Health
    addiction, 94-96
    and cleanliness, 97-98
    and doctors, 104-107
    emergencies and hospitals, 108-109
    and exercise, 93-94
    and medicine, 107-108
    and nutrition, 87-92
    safety tips, 97-98
Health insurance, 109-111
    function of, 109
    meaning of, 103
    shopping for, 110-111
    types of policies, 110
Hearing problems
    and relay service, 316
    and TTY (Text Telephone Yoke), 316
Home
    cleaning home, 280-281
    furnishing home, 278-279
Honesty
    meaning of, 5
    and responsibility, 10

Hormones
    and emotions, 71
    meaning of, 69
    functions of, 70
Housing
    buying housing, 273
    meaning of, 271
    renting housing, 272-277
    types of, 272
    See also Home

I

"I messages," to express feelings, 56-57, 58
Impulse, meaning of, 223, 229
Impulse buying, meaning of, 229-230
Income, meaning of, 129, 132
Income tax, 287, 292
Independent, meaning of, 11
Informational interview
    and job search, 136
    meaning of, 129
Insufficient funds, meaning of, 191, 193
Insurance
    car insurance, 255, 264-265
    health insurance, 103, 109-111
Interest
    on checking accounts, 193
    on credit cards, 244-245
    on loans, 241
    meaning of, 191
    on savings accounts, 200-201
Interests, and jobs, 131-132
Issues, voting on, 291

J

Job interview, 150-153
    behavior during interview, 151-152
    post-interview steps, 153
    preparation for, 150-151

Job reviews, 183-184
Job search
    choosing job, 153
    information sources on, 136, 137-138
    and informational interview, 136
    and interests, 131-132
    job application, 148-149
    job interview, 150-153
    and needs of person, 132-133, 135
    and personal qualities, 131
    references for, 147
    résumé, 145-146
    screening tests, 150
    and skills, 131
    want ads, 137
Jobs
    versus career, 135, 175
    communication on job, 163-164
    conflicts on, 165-166
    and coworkers, 160, 161
    deadlines, 169
    employee handbook, 161
    first day at, 160-161
    job benefits, 153-154
    keeping job, 162-163, 171
    losing job, 161, 170
    new skills, learning, 166-167
    promotion, 180-181
    schedule, 167-168
    teams at, 169
    temporary work, 170
    See also Careers
Jury, meaning of, 287, 296
Jury duty, activities in, 296

L

Landlord, role of, 271, 273
Late fees, on bills, 239, 240, 244
Laws
    bicycle laws, 305
    curfew laws, 307-308

T

Teams, team members, 169
Teeth
    care of, 97
    dental care, 103-104
Teller, job of, 211
Temporary learner's permit, 255, 260
Temporary work, 170
Time management
    planning guidelines, 21-22
    versus wasting time, 21-22
Traffic laws, purpose of, 302
Traffic tickets, points, 303
Transportation
    car pools, 257
    cars, 259-266
    public transportation, 255, 256-258
TTY (Text Telephone Yoke)
    function of, 316
    meaning of, 313

U

Unit pricing, meaning of, 223, 230

V

Values, learning from family, 5-6
Vitamins
    functions of, 92
    meaning of, 87
Volunteering, methods of, 296-297
Voting, 290-291
    and candidate, 291
    on issues, 291
    register to vote, 287, 290-291

W

Want, meaning of, 223, 224
Want ads, for jobs, 137-138
Warranty
    on car, 261
    meaning of, 223, 255
    on products, 223, 233-234
Water safety, 119
Weather, safety tips, 118
Withdrawal slip, meaning of, 191
Withholding, taxes, 294-295

Acknowledgments

Photographs

Grateful acknowledgment is made to the following for photographs on the pages indicated:

Cover: Marjory Dressler; **p. 2:** Rhoda Sidney, Photo Edit; **p. 6:** © Steve and Mary Beran Skjold; **p. 14:** David Young-Wolff, Photo Edit; **p. 28:** Penny Tweedie, Tony Stone Images; **p. 32:** David Young-Wolff, Photo Edit; **p. 40:** David Young-Wolff, Tony Stone; **p. 45:** Billy E. Barnes, Photo Edit; **p. 52:** © Steve and Mary Beran Skjold; **p. 59:** Tony Freeman, Photo Edit; **p. 63:** Myrleen Ferguson, Photo Edit; **p. 68:** Uniphoto; **p. 72:** Bob Torrez, Tony Stone; **p. 80:** David Young-Wolff, Photo Edit; **p. 86:** David Young-Wolff, Photo Edit; **p. 93:** Mary Kate Denny, Photo Edit; **p. 102:** Michael Newman, Photo Edit; **p. 109:** Photo Edit; **p. 114:** Tony Freeman, Photo Edit; **p. 118:** © Steve and Mary Beran Skjold; **p. 121:** Michael Newman, Photo Edit; **p. 128:** Henry Kaiser, Uniphoto; **p. 130:** Rhoda Sidney, Stock Boston; **p. 132:** Elena Rooraid, Photo Edit; **p. 134:** © Steve and Mary Beran Skjold; **p. 137:** Scott and Gillian Aldrich; **p. 142:** Jeff Greenberg, Photo Researchers; **p. 152:** Bob Daemmrich, Uniphoto; **p. 158:** Jon Riley, Tony Stone; **p. 166:** © Steve and Mary Beran Skjold; **p. 168:** Christopher S. Johnson, Stock Boston; **p. 174:** Tony Freeman, Photo Edit; **p. 179:** Michael Newman, Jr., Photo Edit; **p. 182:** Photo Edit; **p. 184:** Michael Newman, Jr., Photo Edit; **p. 190:** Tony Freeman, Photo Edit; **p. 206:** Don Smetzer, Tony Stone; **p. 212:** © Steve and Mary Beran Skjold; **p. 215:** Michael Newman Jr., Photo Edit; **p. 222:** Christopher Bissell, Tony Stone; **p. 225:** Tony Stone; **p. 228:** Barbara Rios, Photo Researchers; **p. 231:** Tony Stone; **p. 238:** David Young-Wolff, Tony Stone; **p. 248:** Michael A. Keller, Uniphoto; **p. 254:** Michael A. Dwyer, Stock Boston; **p. 260:** Richard Hutchings, Photo Edit; **p. 270:** Eva Papadopoulus; **p. 279:** Frank Siteman, The Picture Cube; **p. 280:** David Young-Wolff, Photo Edit; **p. 286:** Grant LeDuc, Stock Boston; **p. 300:** John Eastcott, Photo Researchers; **p. 304:** David Young-Wolff, Photo Edit; **p. 306:** Jean-Claude Lejeune, Stock Boston; **p. 307:** Jean-Claude Lejeune, Stock Boston; **p. 312:** Bonnie Kamin, Photo Edit